Commercial Leases 2009

A Surveyor's Guide

CW00551709

Edward Bannister

Field Fisher Waterhouse

RICS
BOOKS

Acknowledgements

Crown Copyright material is reproduced with the permission of the Controller of HMSO and the Queen's Printer for Scotland.

The quote from page 703 of Dilapidations: Modern Law and Practice, by Nicholas Dowding and Kirk Reynolds, published by Sweet & Maxwell in 2004, is reproduced with permission.

Published by the Royal Institution of Chartered Surveyors (RICS)
Surveyor Court
Westwood Business Park
Coventry CV4 8JE
UK
www.ricsbooks.com

ISBN 978 1 84219 432 4

Typeset in Great Britain by Columns Design Ltd, Reading, Berks

Printed in Great Britain by Page Bros, Milecross Lane, Norwich, NR6 6SA

Printed on Magno Silk paper

Contents

Contents

    17.1 Overview   251
    17.2 The green building   252
    17.3 The handbook   255
    17.4 The green lease   256
    17.5 Points to consider   260

18   Miscellaneous   262
    18.1 Rent deposits and bank guarantees   262
    18.2 Indemnities   264
    18.3 The covenant to use reasonable or best   265
          endeavours
    18.4 The landlord's covenant for quiet   266
          enjoyment
    18.5 The landlord's covenant for   267
          non-derogation from grant
    18.6 Land Registry procedures   268
    18.7 Tax   270
    18.8 Further reading and information   271

    Appendices
    A Service Charge Code: drafting suggestions   273
    B List of more common service charge items   285
    C Contamination issues   293
    Bibliography   297

    Index   299

Foreword

I am very pleased to recommend this new edition of Edward Bannister's popular book, *Commercial Leases 2009: A surveyor's guide.*

The demand for the first edition demonstrated an urgent need for a handbook that provided surveyors with a clear and logical approach to modern leases. *Commercial Leases 2008* met this demand, providing a thorough explanation of the complex guidance and practice codes. Some of the testimonials received for the first edition indicate how well the book was received.

The second edition, *Commercial Leases 2009*, will I am sure be an equally important source of advice to surveyors. In particular, this new edition covers the latest developments in Energy Efficiency requirements and Green leases which are essential components in achieving greater sustainability in our commercial property.

As with the first edition, Edward Bannister writes with great clarity, making this subject thoroughly accessible for the surveyor. I am delighted to see that this new edition continues to provide invaluable support for us all.

Peter Goodacre

RICS President 2008–2009

Praise for the Commercial Leases series

'A very user friendly guide and point of reference, written with the surveyor in mind, that will benefit all of us involved with commercial leases.'
Mark Frampton, Director, GVA Grimley Ltd

'Highly recommended for those that wish to be one step ahead in commercial lease negotiations ... I've made it compulsory for every Graduate Surveyor and as a desk top reference for all the property team.'
Jeremy Pilgrim MSc MRICS Head of Property Development and Disposals London Borough of Southwark.

'I am delighted to recommend this guide to surveyors at all levels who are involved with commercial leases. This book should provide invaluable support to you all.'
David Tuffin, Tuffin Ferraby Taylor (TFT), RICS President 2007–8

'Full of practical examples of why clauses are or are not required ... The guide should benefit everyone from graduates to the experienced professional.'
Simon Fowler, Partner, FowlerFortescue LLP

'I found this a very useful and accessible quick reference point in negotiations on new leases.'
Sara Tack, Head of Estates (North), House of Fraser

'Alarmingly useful.'
Steve Faber, Director, UK Offices, RREEF Real Estate

'Essential reading and reference for commercial surveyors – keep it on your desk next to the RICS Red Book.'
Robert Bryant-Pearson FRICS Chief Executive, Allied Surveyors plc.

'As with the first edition, Edward Bannister writes with great clarity, making this subject thoroughly accessible for the surveyor. I am delighted to see that this new edition continues to provide invaluable support for us all.'
Peter Goodacre, RICS President 2008–9

Preface to the second edition

There have been some statutory changes and case law developments since the first edition of this book was published, which are reflected in updated and revised text across the relevant sections.

Climate change and 'green' issues continue to make the news and 2008 has seen the phased introduction of new requirements for the production of energy performance certificates (EPCs) upon the construction, sale or letting of (and the carrying out of certain works to) most types of commercial buildings. A new chapter focusing on the principal issues for landlords and tenants surrounding EPCs has therefore been added in this edition.

In addition, there has been much discussion in the market about the coming of 'green leases', which aim to incorporate new provisions and obligations reflecting an increasing concern about the effects of climate change. Given that we remain very much at the early stages of the evolution of the 'green lease', a further new chapter added on this subject presents only an overview of the general principles, which may then be applied in different ways, depending upon the approach to be taken.

I would like to express my thanks to all those within the Real Estate and Tax Departments at Field Fisher Waterhouse for their invaluable contributions, comments and suggestions in the production of this second edition.

As ever, any errors or omissions are mine.

Edward Bannister

Partner for Field Fisher Waterhouse LLP

About the author

Edward Bannister is a solicitor and partner at Field Fisher Waterhouse LLP. He has over 20 years' experience acting for leading UK retail chains and stores, retail and leisure developers, and investors. He is a member of the City of London Law Society Land Law Committee and is on the contributory board for *Property Law Journal*

List of Acts, Statutory Instruments and abbreviations

The following Acts and Statutory Instruments are referenced in this publication. Where an Act or Statutory Instrument is mentioned frequently, it is referred to by the abbreviation in brackets that follows.

Arbitration Act 1996

Building Regulations 2000

Building and Approved Inspectors (Amendment) Regulations 2006

Capital Allowances Act 2001

Companies Act 2006

Control of Asbestos Regulations 2006

Construction (Design and Management) Regulations 2007 (CDM)

Defective Premises Act 1972

Disability Discrimination Act 1995

Disability Discrimination Act 2005 (DDA)

Energy Performance of Buildings (Certificates and Inspections) (England and Wales) Regulations 2007

Environmental Protection Act 1990

Finance Act 2008

Fire Precautions Act 1971

Freedom of Information Act 2000

Health Act 2006

Income and Corporation Taxes Act 1988

Insolvency Act 1986

Land Registration Act 2002 (LRA 2002)

Landlord and Tenant Act 1927 (The 1927 Act)

Landlord and Tenant Act 1954

Landlord and Tenant Act 1988

Landlord and Tenant (Covenants) Act 1995

Law of Distress Amendment Act 1908

Law of Property Act 1925

Leasehold Property (Repairs) Act 1938

Occupiers Liability Act 1957

Planning (Listed Buildings and Conservation Areas) Act 1990

Regulatory Reform (Fire Safety) Order 2005

Reinsurance (Acts of Terrorism) Act 1993

Telecommunications Act 1984

Terrorism Act 2000

Town and Country Planning Act 1990

Town and Country Planning (General Permitted Development) Order 1995

Town and Country Planning (Use Classes) Order 1987 (The Use Classes Order)

Tribunals, Courts and Enforcement Act 2007

Value Added Tax Act 1994 (The VAT Act 1994)

Table of cases

Introduction

This guide is intended as a general summary of some of the principal points which arise or which need to be considered when reviewing an existing or new lease of commercial premises in England and Wales and any associated heads of terms.

It does not cover every potential area of concern and is not intended to be a comprehensive review. Certain types of use and property will require some 'bespoke' clauses – for instance, a nightclub built on remediated land will have a raft of clauses which one would not expect to find in the lease of a city office. However, this guide does try to cover the general issues which find their way into negotiations over heads of terms and leases.

1.1 Drafting and interpreting a lease

A question often asked of lawyers is: 'Why is a lease so long?'. In the last 20 years the average length of a lease, with a service charge and rent review clause, has gone from around 20 pages to around 80 pages in length with some 'standard' leases now achieving over 100 pages.

There is no easy answer to this question; undoubtedly, life has become more regulated: we have far more health and safety legislation in place and more complicated buildings, plant and equipment. Professionals and clients have become more focused and sophisticated; landlords

1

require more control over their valuable investments and tenants seek more flexibility for their money. All of these are good reasons; the bad one is that some lawyers fear change and draft long clauses as 'protection' against everything.

The promotion of codes of conduct and government threats are making people look again at leases and how they should be drafted; whether this actually results in shorter leases remains to be seen.

A final point on this (but by no means to be taken as a justification for long leases) is that if a lease is silent on a point then, generally, the tenant can do what it likes – subject to compliance with statute. Landlords, therefore, are always keen to ensure that there are adequate controls in place; if the tenant seeks flexibility, the landlord will need to circumscribe that flexibility with restrictions and qualifications.

1.2 What is an 'institutional lease'?

In drafting a lease, the landlord tries to obtain as much protection as possible so as to ensure that the property is properly maintained and that, so far as is possible, the landlord does not incur any (unforeseen) costs, which cannot be charged on to the tenant. This is because the English property market is treated by landlords as an important form of investment and leases have gradually evolved so that landlords can expect to receive rent without any deductions and with all occupation costs, such as repair, insurance, rates etc. passed on to the tenant; this is known as an 'FRI' lease, one on full repairing and insuring terms, i.e. the tenant, either directly or indirectly, pays for everything. For this reason, most leases work in favour of the landlord and impose often onerous obligations on the tenant. It is these obligations which we have summarised in this guide.

No two leases are ever the same, but this guide is based upon clauses which an 'institutional' landlord would expect to see in a modern lease.

The phrase 'institutional lease' is one which is used frequently in negotiations but has no precise definition other than being one which is in a form which is acceptable to an institution, such as a pension fund, as an investment; until recently, this has been taken as being one with upwards only rent reviews, on FRI terms. Institutions have become a little more flexible, as the following points (which the author has come across in 'institutional leases') indicate.

- Leases are now, more often than not, for terms of between 10 and 15 years – rather than 20 or 25 years – some also containing break clauses.

- Repairing covenants sometimes carve out certain specific liabilities and can be governed by a schedule of condition.

- Some service charges contain caps or other limitations on liability.

- Internal alterations can sometimes be carried out without reference to the landlord's consent.

- Insurance clauses sometimes allow the tenant to break where there has been damage by an uninsured risk and the landlord decides not to reinstate. Even if they decide to reinstate after damage by an uninsured risk, often the landlord will not be able to claim any rent from the tenant, in the meantime.

- Upward only rent reviews have been under a sustained attack from occupiers for some time – this has not resulted in their demise, they are very much still a feature of many leases, but, as a result, there are various other options, such as stepped increases, or increases linked to an index, coupled with shorter leases.

The *Code for Leasing Business Premises* and the *Service Charge Code*, which are both promoted by some leading institutions, also chip away at the concept of an FRI lease, the landlord not necessarily being able to recover absolutely everything from the tenant.

An institutional lease still has to be acceptable to an institution, but now there is a wider, and more flexible, definition of what is 'acceptable'.

1.3   The Code for Leasing Business Premises in England and Wales 2007

The second edition of *A code of practice for commercial leases in England and Wales* (2002), prepared by parties representing both landlords and tenants, was designed to reflect 'best practice' to be adopted by landlords' and tenants' advisers when negotiating commercial leases. However, there continued to be much debate over the effectiveness (or otherwise) of the 2002 Code in influencing the negotiation of lease terms; indeed, the general perception that the 2002 Code was often ignored by landlords and was having little impact in bringing about change led the government to raise the possibility of legislative intervention to regulate particular areas of concern (originally, upwards only rent reviews, and more recently, assignment and underletting).

Against this background, the 2002 Code was reviewed further, resulting in its replacement, with effect from 28 March 2007, by a revised code: *The Code for Leasing Business Premises in England and Wales 2007*, again endorsed by cross-industry groups representing both landlord and tenant interests and also by government.

We comment on the 2007 code (referred to in this guide as 'the Lease Code') where recommendations are made which should (applying best practice) be carried through into the lease.

The Lease Code's stated aims are to 'create a document which is clear, concise and authoritative ... to be used as a checklist for negotiations before the grant of a lease and lease renewals'. Landlords are exhorted to be 'transparent about any departures from the code in a particular case and the reasons for them.'

The Lease Code has a clear political agenda, showing that landlord and tenant (and government) bodies can work together to promote a fair form of lease. At the same time, the Lease Code is targeted at small businesses with limited access to professional advice. The Lease Code contains a lot of sensible suggestions (including a model 'heads of terms') and will go some way towards establishing what the industry would generally consider to be market practice and reasonable.

This guide has a similar purpose to the Lease Code: if the professionals involved in lease negotiations have a detailed grasp of the implications behind certain clauses, coupled with an understanding of what the market would consider 'appropriate', lease clauses may become less contentious, giving the parties more time to focus on issues which are key to them and the main commercial terms.

However, ultimately, the terms of any new lease will reflect the nature and value of the property, the negotiating strength of the parties, how hard the tenant wants to push, how much the tenant wants to pay for flexibility and the market conditions at the time.

We would adopt the wording at the end of the introduction of the Lease Code and conclude with the hope that this guide 'will help the industry in its quest to promote efficiency and fairness in landlord and tenant relationships'.

The property

2.1 Overview

The lease will specify the area which the tenant is
entitled to occupy (the 'demise') and will also set out
various rights granted to the tenant and rights reserved
to the landlord and other occupiers. (Usually the rights
granted to the tenant are similar to those rights reserved
to the landlord and other occupiers, although the
landlord will often seek to reserve to itself wider rights,
particularly to enable works to be carried out to other
parts of the building and/or other adjoining or adjacent
property of the landlord.)

The general principle is that if a building is demised to a
tenant, without any specific exclusions or qualifications,
then it is implied that the demise includes the airspace
above and the subsoil below; if this is what is being
demised, the landlord will need to ensure that it reserves
rights in respect of services under the building and
possibly (for example) the right for crane oversail and/or
overhead cables – especially where the landlord retains
an interest in adjacent premises.

(A refinement of this last point is that the landlord may
expressly exclude the airspace from the demise of a
building, but provide the tenant with all necessary rights
of entry into the airspace in order to repair the roof and
install and maintain aerials, satellite dishes, cabling, etc.)

In the absence of precise and clearly drafted lease
provisions, it may not always be obvious what

constitutes a 'building': see *Pattrick and another v Marley Estates Management* [2007] EWCA Civ 1176. In that case, the court construed lease provisions to mean that former chapel cloisters which had a roof, floor, three walls and a colonnade on the fourth side (and notwithstanding that the colonnade was open to the elements) were a 'building' within the meaning of the landlord's covenant to repair. By contrast, while windows forming part of the demised premises were held not to form part of the 'main structure' of the building (which the landlord was responsible to repair), the landlord was nevertheless liable under its external decoration covenant to decorate the external parts of such windows as they did form part of the 'exterior' of the building.

The grant of a lease (unless expressly stated to the contrary) is also deemed to include (by virtue of section 62 of the *Law of Property Act* 1925) all rights and easements which the premises demised enjoy at the time of the grant, as well as all fixtures attached to the premises at that time.

Given the general principles outlined above, it is important to ensure that the description of what is being demised is accurate and that there is no conflict between the wording used in, and the plans attached to, the lease.

Having established exactly what is being demised, surveyors and lawyers should check not only that the landlord owns the full extent of the premises but also that the landlord has full title to grant the necessary rights, especially where those rights extend beyond land in the direct ownership of the landlord.

2.2 The description

An example of a definition of the demise of a lease of part (taken from a lease of a shop) could be:

'the premises (including any part or parts of it) known as Unit [ ] comprising [ ] square feet net internal area, the floor plan of which is shown edged red on the plan annexed, including (but not by way of limitation):

- all the landlord's fixtures and fittings and fixtures which shall from time to time be in or upon the Property (whether originally fixed or fastened to or upon the Property or otherwise) except any such fixtures installed by the Tenant that can be removed from the Property without defacing it;

- Service Media within and exclusively serving the Property;

- all additions and improvements to the Property;

- all the shop front and fascia and plate glass;

- the internal plaster surfaces and finishes of all structural or load bearing walls and columns but not any other part of such walls and columns;

- the inner half severed medially of any internal non-structural non-load bearing walls (if any) that divide the Property from other parts of the Building;

- all other non-structural or non-load bearing walls and columns;

- the screed and floor finishes and all other floor coverings down to the joists or other structural parts;

- the plaster or other surfaces of the ceilings and suspended ceilings within the Property and the voids between the ceilings and suspended ceilings;

- window frames and window furniture and sash cords and all glass in the windows and all doors, door furniture and door frames (both internal and external);

but excluding the roof foundations and all structural parts of the Property.'

It is clearly important for the description to be correct and for the lease plans to tie in with the description used. If the lease is of an entire building and external areas, a simple address and plan will usually suffice.

Problems generally occur where there is a lease of part – what is to be included must be carefully and clearly described, bearing in mind that the description used will govern those areas which are to be the responsibility of the tenant (if included in the demise), who will be liable for their repair and maintenance and who may or may not be able to alter the relevant area.

2.3 Measurements

Some leases have reference to the floor area of the demise (as in the example above): this will be used to confirm the floor area leased to the tenant and will then be carried through into the rent review clause and used as the multiple for calculating the new rent; it may also form the basis for calculating the service charge, if applicable.

The RICS *Code of Measuring Practice* (6th edition, 2007) sets out the standard practices for measuring floor area which will usually be based on a net internal area (NIA) or gross internal area (GIA), depending on the type of property being measured and the purpose of the measurement: summarising the Code produces very basic guidelines which follow in the table.

	Net internal area	Gross internal area
Applicability	Offices and shops. In certain circumstances it may also be used for warehouses and industrial.	Retail warehouses, department stores, food superstores, variety stores, industrial and retail warehouses – which do not contain much office space. (If there is a lot of office space then NIA may be used instead.) GIA should also be used for calculating build costs and insurance reinstatement values. The Code adopts GIA for leisure, but with certain areas (such as public seating and kitchens in restaurants) being stated separately.
Excludes	Common reception areas, atria and similar; areas continuously occupied by plant and equipment, WC areas, plant room, meter cupboards and stairwells, structural walls and columns, communal passages and fire escapes.	The thickness of the perimeter wall and external projections.
Includes	Kitchen areas, cupboards accessed from useable space notional lift lobbies where the lift adjoins the office space (rather than a lift lobby) and notional fire corridors; internal non-structural walls within the premises.	Just about anything within the perimeter structural walls, including any mezzanine.

2.4 Additional rights

It is one thing to have the correct description of the
demise; it is also very important to describe correctly any
areas outside the demise but which are used by the
tenant and, where this is the case, for the lease to grant
the necessary express rights to, and over, those areas.
Some common examples would be:

- visitor/staff car parking spaces;
- loading areas;
- refuse collection areas;
- waste compactors;
- recycling facilities;
- fire escapes;
- locations for air conditioning plant and equipment;
- locations for occupier signage;
- positions for CCTV and other security facilities and associated cabling;
- passenger and goods lifts;
- washroom facilities; and
- reception areas.

2.5 Capital allowances

What is or is not included in the demise may well have a
bearing on who can claim what by way of capital
allowances.

The *Capital Allowances Act* 2001 provides a business
with the right to claim capital allowances (a limited form
of tax relief for qualifying capital expenditure – the
allowances being offset against income) for moveable
plant and equipment – 'chattels' – as well as items fixed

to the building – 'fixtures'; these are items which form part of the property such as heating, air conditioning and ventilation systems, hot water systems, lifts, security systems and sanitary fittings. The basic system of capital allowances is that the person entitled to them is the person who owns the items. Nevertheless, in the case of fixtures a person who has incurred capital expenditure and who owns an interest in the relevant land (such as a tenant) is treated as owning the fixtures for the purpose of the capital allowances even though true ownership may have passed to the landlord as a matter of land law.

The *Finance Act* 2008 provides for a reduction in the allowances claimable from 1 April 2008, from 25 to 20 per cent for the writing down allowance for plant and machinery. More particularly, in the case of a building, it provides for a reduction in the rate of writing down allowances for 'integral fixtures' of a building from 25 to 10 per cent. 'Integral features' does, however, include general electrical and lighting, and cold water systems – these previously did not qualify for capital allowances at all. In addition, the *Finance Act* 2008 provides for capital allowances at the rate of 100 per cent for the first £50,000 of annual expenditure, even if this is on integral features of a building (the so-called 'annual investment allowance'). Certain items of 'green' technology also qualify for capital allowances at the rate of 100 per cent.

2.6 Points to consider

- The description of the property should be clear and supported by reference to a scaled plan. For leases with a term of more than seven years, this plan must also show a north point and otherwise comply with Land Registry requirements: for instance, the plans must be drawn to an approved (metric) scale such as 1:1250 or 1:500.

12

- Which 'fixtures and fittings' should be included in the definition, bearing in mind the fact that the landlord will be usually be responsible for the insurance of the 'property' and the tenant for its repair? Many leases distinguish between landlord's fixtures and fittings (which are included in the demise) and tenant's trade fixtures and fittings (which are sometimes included in the demise and sometimes not). There may also be a capital allowances point to consider.

- Is the shop front/fascia included?

- If there is any doubt, agree (and, perhaps, include in the description) the extent of the floor area – as this may have an impact on rent review.

- Check that all necessary rights are available in order to make full use of the property, including rights for the passage of all services, car parking, signage, use of communal services (such as compactors and dustbin areas), installation of plant and equipment (such as air conditioning condensers and satellite dishes) and rights of escape (see also Chapter 9 – Alterations).

- Where taking a lease of part of a building, the main structure of the building should be excluded, as the tenant's repairing liability will specifically refer to the tenant being responsible for all the area leased to the tenant and clearly, in these circumstances, any structural elements should be specifically excluded.

- As buildings become increasingly complex, problems can arise in relation to responsibility for items such as plant and machinery. For example, air conditioning exclusively serving the demised premises is often referred to as being part of the tenant's responsibility; however, this could create problems where air conditioning is part of the landlord's main system, those problems relating not only to questions of breach of repair covenant, but also breach of warranties. In such circumstances, it would probably be better for the landlord to assume responsibility, charging the cost back through the service charge.

- Where the lease includes the ground, consider whether the ground could have been contaminated and (when acting for a tenant) whether the ground should be excluded from the demise to avoid this potential liability; if this is the chosen course, then further rights may be needed in respect of the subsoil – see Chapter 12 for further commentary.

Lease term

3

3.1 Overview

Until fairly recently, commercial leases were usually granted for a lease term of 20 or 25 years, with rent reviews once in every fifth year of the lease term and with no right to terminate the lease before the expiry of the lease term.

The British Property Federation (BPF) IPD Annual Lease Review for 2007 has produced the following 'headlines' when looking at what is the 'average' lease term in the current market (and the trend is generally downwards).

Taking breaks into account and weighted by rent passing:

- the average length of all recent leases fell to 9.8 years in 2006 – from 14.3 in 1999;

- retail lease terms dropped from 12.5 years in 2005 to 11.1 in 2006;

- office leases were at around 8.4 years for 2006 – down from 9.9 in 2005.

Generally:

- less than 4 per cent of the leases completed recently were for more than 15 years, although these leases accounted for 14.5 per cent of passing rent;

- 17.5 per cent of leases in 2006–07 for 5 years or less had break clauses.

A full copy of this report is available from the BPF website: www.bpf.org.uk

The introduction of Stamp Duty Land Tax (SDLT) in December 2003 has introduced another influence (other than general market requirements) on lease terms, namely that the longer the lease, the higher the tax. It is now the case that a short lease with an option to renew is better (from a tax position) than a long lease with a break clause.

In the current market, leases are now usually granted with lease terms of no more than 10 or 15 years and sometimes include a tenant's right to terminate the lease before the expiry of the lease term. (Leases of more than seven years now need to be registered at Land Registry – so that plans used must be Land Registry compliant – see Chapter 2).

The shorter the lease term, the more likely it is that the lease will be excluded from the security of tenure provisions which are automatically incorporated, unless excluded (see also Chapter 13 – Security of tenure).

Furthermore, with short term leases (around five years or less), tenants are more likely to be able to agree some form of cap on service charges and, possibly, some limitation on their repairing liability – for instance, by reference to a schedule of condition.

3.2 The effect of SDLT

The simplest way of explaining the impact of this tax on the length of a lease term is by way of example.

A lease for a term of 10 years at a rent of £100,000 (plus VAT) attracts SDLT of: £8,272 – if it has an option to renew for a further period of 10 years then the SDLT is only paid if the option is taken up and a new lease granted.

A lease for a term of 20 years at the same rent attracts SDLT of £15,199 – the tax remains the same whether it has a break clause in year 10 or not.

3.3 Break clauses

3.3.1 An example of a basic break clause

Each law firm has its own way of drafting these clauses; set out below is one which is designed to cover the basic points, without imposing any material preconditions and, as such, is Lease Code compliant.

The timing of the notices will always be open to debate, but here we have tried to create a balance between landlord and tenant and have avoided being too prescriptive as to the exact timing and date of the notice.

'A The Tenant may terminate the lease on [ ] 20[ ] [*for the sake of clarity a specific date is better than a reference to e.g. "upon expiry of the fifth year of the term"*] ("break date"), subject to having first: (i) served the notice in accordance with clause B and (ii) paid the rent(s) in accordance with clause C; (failure to comply with clauses B and C shall prevent the Tenant from being able to terminate this lease on the break date).

B The Tenant must serve on the Landlord at least [3] months prior written notice terminating this lease, such notice to expire on the break date.

C The Tenant must have paid the principal rent [*i.e. the annual rent reserved*] in accordance with clause [ ] in full prior to the break date, (and there shall be no arrears of that principal rent in respect of any earlier Quarter Days as at the break date), in which case the Landlord shall refund such proportion of the principal rent (but not any VAT thereon) which relates to the period from (but not including) the break date to the next Quarter Day, that apportionment being calculated pro rata on a daily basis on the basis of 365 days, that refund being made within 10 working days after the break date.'

3.4 General points and preconditions and material compliance

If the lease contains a break clause in favour of the tenant, it is important to ensure that the terms of the break clause are complied with and that there are no preconditions which make it difficult for the tenant to exercise the break clause. The courts take a very strict view of contractual conditions and even a very minor breach of the break clause preconditions could prevent the tenant from being able to terminate the lease.

In one reported case, the tenant had the benefit of a break clause but the break clause was conditional upon the tenant painting the demise with two coats of paint. Paint technology having moved on since the grant of the lease, the tenant used one coat of paint. The court held that the tenant's break notice was invalid, as it had not complied with the terms of the lease.

A further example of the need for literally full compliance is a condition to pay rent reserved by the lease quarterly in advance. The effect of this is that if it is paid pro rata up to the break date, that will not amount to compliance – the full quarter's rent has to have been paid. From the tenant's point of view, the lease should also expressly require a pro rata refund once the break has been effected, since the rent paid in advance of the break date which relates to that part of the rental period falling after that date will be otherwise irrecoverable.

A further problem with this type of break clause (preconditions that have to be complied with) is what is meant by 'rent', as this is often defined in the lease as extending to such other items as insurance premiums, service charge and even penalty interest – and some of those items may be uncertain and/or in dispute. The Lease Code's advice to tenants is:

> 'Be careful that it is only the principal rent and not any other sums (such as service charges) that must be paid in cleared funds before the break date'.

There are also substantial potential dangers with a break clause which is conditional upon 'material compliance': this does dilute what would otherwise be an absolute requirement, but it is still an objective test which does not allow the court to import equitable concepts of fairness – the tenant has to comply in every other respect with the covenant. [*Fitzroy House Epworth Street (No 1) Ltd v The Financial Times Ltd* [2006] 1 WLR 2207]

Furthermore, what does 'material' mean; does a series of minor breaches amount to a material breach; if there has been a material breach in the past but it has been rectified by the time the break clause has been exercised, has the tenant 'materially' complied? In the *Fitzroy House* ruling it was held that 'materially' had to be assessed by reference to the ability of the landlord to re-let or sell the property without delay or additional expenditure. Although the courts are likely to be sympathetic to the tenant's position, the best approach is to avoid any reference to 'material'; the landlord will still normally have a right of action against the tenant for the breach, even though the lease has been terminated.

Some break clauses require the tenant to return the property 'with vacant possession free of any rights of occupation' – or similar wording. This type of wording can cause all sorts of problems: 'vacant possession' is more stringent than it looks – all rubbish would need to be removed in order for this to be complied with and 'vacant possession' and 'rights of occupation' would mean that any subtenancy would have to have been lawfully and fully terminated.

The Lease Code addresses this point with the following advice to a tenant:

> 'When granting any subleases or in sharing possession with any suppliers or business partners, always make sure your agreement with them expires on a date before your right to break, AND that you have not given them any rights to stay in the property beyond the term of your agreement with them'.

Where faced with advising a client who has a conditional break clause, you should ensure that the client is advised to take action well before activating the break clause and ensure full compliance. In certain circumstances, the only option may be to move out of the property and 'mothball' it!

3.5 Landlord's break right and the *Landlord and Tenant Act 1954*

Although the landlord may have a contractual break right, if the lease has not been excluded from the renewal rights under the 1954 Act, the landlord still has to follow the statutory termination provisions, serving the relevant notices, in addition to any contractual procedure. These are discussed in Chapter 13.

3.6 The Lease Code

The Lease Code urges landlords to be more flexible in the terms they offer tenants:

> 'The only preconditions to tenants exercising any break clauses should be that they are up to date with the main rent, give up occupation and leave behind no continuing subleases. Disputes about the state of the premises, or of what has been left behind or removed, should be settled later (like with normal lease expiry).'

3.7 Points to consider

- Break clauses with any conditions are fraught with difficulties and, as a result, they may not be operable – legal and detailed surveying advice should be taken well in advance of any break date.
- Where a lease has a break clause, ensure that any sublease can be terminated in time to comply with that break clause and that it excludes any statutory renewal rights.
- A longer term provides security but will have an impact on the SDLT payable at the outset of the lease.
- A longer lease will almost invariably have a greater repair/dilapidations liability – see Chapter 8.
- The length of the lease may have a bearing on rent review – this will depend on the nature of the building and use and the market at the time of the review, as well as other factors, but the potential effect should be considered at the outset.
- The longer the lease, the more flexibility the tenant should require on user, alterations and dealings – what may be 'standard' now may not be in 15 years time.
- The above factors (and others) will have a bearing on how easy it will be to assign the lease.

Rent, outgoings and other payments

4.1 Overview

A tenant will usually be responsible for the payment of rent and all of the business rates, service charges (where appropriate), insurance and any other outgoings in relation to the property.

4.2 Rent and VAT

The rent will normally be expressed as being payable in advance and, if the landlord has exercised its option to tax in respect of the property, will attract VAT. The tenant will be able to recover the VAT paid under the lease in accordance with its usual VAT status.

The lease will usually specify that the rent is payable on 'the usual quarter days' which are 25 December, 25 March, 24 June and 29 September in any one year, although it is becoming more common that the quarter days are 1 January, 1 March, 1 June and 1 September – usually referred to as the 'modern quarter days'.

There is also building pressure from retailers for rent to be payable monthly, in advance, instead of quarterly: the advantage to tenants being that it would help them to be able to manage cash flow and bring rental payments into line with other outgoings; landlords would lose out on the interest they earn on quarterly payments. Evidence of this pressure is exemplified by the British Retail

Consortium's campaign – the 'Flexible Landlord Standard' which is supported by 80,000 small businesses and a string of major chains – see www.brc.org.uk/rentmonthly/index.asp

Frequently, the service charge (estimated) will be payable at the same time, with adjustments once the accounts have been finalised.

Insurance premiums are generally collected annually in advance.

4.3 Set off

The lease will usually contain an express statement to the effect that 'no deduction or set off' can be made from the rent.

If properly drafted, this should prevent the tenant, say in a service charge dispute, from deducting the disputed service charge payment from the rental payment. If the clause just refers to 'no deduction or abatement' then this will not be enough to prevent set off – there must be a specific mention and exclusion of 'set off' [*Connaught Restaurants Ltd v Indoor Leisure Ltd* [1993] 2 EGLR 108, CA, as confirmed in *Altonwood Ltd v Crystal Palace FC (2000) Ltd* [2005] EWHC 292 (Ch); *Edlington Properties Ltd v JH Fenner & Co Ltd* [2006] EWCA Civ 403].

Some leases do specifically allow the tenant (as an exception to the 'no deduction or set off' principle stated above) to deduct tax, if required – usually by adding the words 'save to the extent required by statute/law'.

This is an important point, as noted below, where dealing with 'foreign' landlords; although, if the wording is not in the lease, it is difficult to see how a landlord could legitimately argue that the tenant should pay in full, where the law requires otherwise.

4.4   Tax deduction

If the landlord's usual place of abode is outside the
United Kingdom, the tenant or letting agent should
ensure that the landlord obtains approval from HM
Revenue & Customs (HMRC) for the landlord to receive
rents gross, with no tax deducted. This is known as 'The
Non-Resident Landlords Scheme'. The scheme requires
letting agents (who need to be registered under the
scheme) to deduct basic rate tax from any rent collected
on behalf of non-resident landlords and pay the tax
deducted to HMRC quarterly. ('Letting agents' do not
include banks who are just operating a rental income
account or solicitors who have just received apportioned
rental income as part of a completion.)

If the non-resident landlord does not have an agent, then
the tenant itself has to make the deduction and payment
to HMRC.

These deductions do not need to be made if the landlord
has obtained approval from HMRC; where approval is
given, notice of the approval will be sent to the landlord
and any named tenant/agent and the approval is
normally backdated to the start of the quarter in which
the application was received – note that the quarter dates
used by HMRC are 1 July, 1 October, 1 January and 1
April. The application needs to be made on form NRL (2
for companies and 3 for trustees including corporate
trustees); the approval does not mean that the rental
income is exempt from UK tax, just that the rent can be
paid gross to the non-resident landlord.

If the landlord changes its letting agent or the tenant
changes, then the landlord needs to send in the details
and HMRC will issue a new notice – in the meantime
tax must be deducted, pending receipt of the new notice.

Further information on this can be obtained from:
www.hmrc.gov.uk/cnr/nr_landlords.htm#2

4.5 Penalty interest

If the tenant is late in paying any sums due under the lease, the landlord is usually entitled to charge interest at a specified rate of around (usually) 4 per cent above bank base lending rate from the due date until the date of payment.

4.6 Rates

Business rates will often be a considerable expense to the tenant and these are paid to the local rating authority and not to the landlord. In certain circumstances, the rating liability can be reduced or relief claimed.

4.7 Empty rating relief

On 1 April 2008, the levels of rating relief were reduced to six months for empty industrial property and to three months for empty office and retail property. There are a few cases where the relief level is more generous, most notably when the tenant is subject to certain insolvency proceedings.

In some leases there will be a clause to the effect that the tenant has to indemnify the landlord for any empty rates relief the tenant may have claimed before the expiry of the lease – because, in doing so, the tenant will prevent the landlord from being able to claim or the effect will be to reduce the landlord's claim.

Where a tenant is under a positive obligation to keep a shop open, then the landlord's position is not unreasonable; however, the argument is not so strong where the tenant is free to use the property or not, as it chooses; most tenants resist such a clause but the new position will bring the clause back into prominence.

4.8 Dilapidations

If the landlord serves a schedule of dilapidations or takes proceedings to terminate the lease or enforce the lease terms, the costs incurred in doing so can usually be recovered from the tenant – see Chapter 8.

4.9 Costs

The lease will also have various provisions whereby the landlord's consent is required before certain action can be taken and the landlord is entitled to charge the tenant for any costs incurred in relation to considering any application and these charges can extend to lawyers', accountants' and surveyors' fees, depending upon the nature of the application.

4.10 Points to consider

- Where possible costs should be qualified by being 'reasonable', albeit where the tenant is in default it is a little more difficult to argue the point.

- Many tenants seek 'days of grace' (e.g. 7 or 14 days to pay) to avoid paying interest just because they miss a payment date – the point is well made where the payment is not known in advance – such as insurance – it is less justified where the payment is known, such as the annual rent; ultimately this point is down to negotiation.

- Many tenants require a VAT invoice before being liable to pay, although a landlord is under a statutory duty to provide a VAT invoice within 30 days of the tax point anyway (regulation 13 *Value Added Tax Regulations* 1995 (SI 1995/2518) pursuant to the *VAT Act* 1994).

- Where the landlord may owe the tenant money, it may be appropriate to allow for set off in relation to that specific matter.

Rent review

5.1 Overview

Most leases enable the landlord to increase the rent at specified intervals, usually once every five years. It is through the rent review clause that the landlord seeks to protect its investment.

> 'The purpose is to reflect the changes in the value of money and real increases in the value of the property during a long term ... to provide the landlord with some means of relief where, through increases in property values or falls in the value of money, in an inflationary period, a fixed rent has become out of date and unduly favourable to the tenant ... Without such a clause the tenant would never get the length of lease and the security which he requires ... ' [*Case in Point – Rent Review* by John Male QC and Thomas Jefferies (RICS Books, 2005)]

At each rent review, the rent payable under the lease is reconsidered in the light of rents payable at that time for similar nearby premises. If there has been an increase in the rents payable in the area since the start of the lease, or the last rent review date, then the landlord will be entitled to increase the rent to reflect that increase.

Most leases specifically prohibit any rent review resulting in a decrease in the rent, in other words, the rent will never go down, whatever the market conditions at the time – i.e. it is 'upwards only'. The potential problem (of subsequently finding that the rent paid exceeds the market rent) can sometimes be mitigated during negotiations, for instance, by agreeing to a tenant's break clause to link in with the rent review date(s), or taking a relatively short term lease.

If the landlord and tenant are unable to agree a revised rent, then the matter is usually referred to an (agreed) third party and if they are unable to agree on the appointment, the appointment will be made on the application of either party by, usually, the President of RICS. That independent third party surveyor will either act as an 'expert' or an 'arbitrator', depending upon the specific lease terms.

Arbitration is a more formal procedure, where the parties can each put forward their arguments to the arbitrator, who makes a decision based on the evidence presented; proceedings with an expert are less formal and the expert will make a decision based upon its own views. It is possible to appeal against an arbitrator's decision in certain circumstances, but very rarely can one appeal against the decision of an expert.

It follows that, if the rent review is referred to that independent third party surveyor, their decision will normally have to be accepted as final.

Whilst the rent review procedure is being followed, the rent continues to be paid at the old rate. Once the rent review has been finally determined, the rent is adjusted accordingly and any shortfall (between the old and the new rent) is payable, together with interest on that shortfall, usually at a rate of interest fixed at the base bank lending rate at the time.

Rent review clauses can have material financial implications for both the landlord and the tenant. It is important to ensure that the rent review clause is considered both from a legal and valuation perspective. In practice, rent review clauses are often drafted by lawyers 'in a vacuum', without detailed consideration of the practical effect of the drafting on a particular building and the market for that building.

The rest of this chapter primarily reviews in more detail a standard (open market) rent review, but there are alternatives, or a combination of alternatives, which may be encountered.

- **Fixed increases:** these will be on stated dates; some leases have fixed increases for the first review date(s) and then revert to open market reviews.

- **Turnover rents:** the rent being an agreed percentage of the tenant's profits, subject to a minimum base rent, often set at around 80–90 per cent of the open market rent. A review of some of the issues arising in turnover leases is set out below.

- **Indexed rents:** the rent increases at set intervals, in line with increases in a stated index. A summary of a Retail Price Index (RPI) rent review is set out at the end of this chapter.

- **Geared rent:** the tenant pays a stated percentage of the rents received by it, or the rents receivable by it; needless to say, there can be a substantial difference between the two!

- **Ground rent:** a ground rent is usually a relatively small sum of money – historically the rental value of the land, with no buildings.

- **A mixture:** the revised rent is the higher of the open market rent, the rent then payable and the rent increased by a factor of [ ] per cent and/or linked to an index – usually compounded – the 'mixture' approach is usually taken where there are few comparables at the time of the letting.

5.2 The rent review mechanism

Most rent reviews follow a fairly standard pattern; many of the disputes over rent reviews occur when that pattern is changed, often in a very subtle way. Accordingly, a good point to start from is to understand how a 'normal' rent review clause works and then look at some of the issues which arise when rent review clauses move away from that 'norm'.

5.3 A 'standard' rent review clause

A 'standard' rent review clause is based on a hypothetical lease, which will normally be based on the actual terms of the lease, but will incorporate certain standard assumptions (e.g. the term of the hypothetical lease), specific assumptions (e.g. the hypothetical tenant has had the benefit of any rent-free period) and matters to be disregarded (e.g. the hypothetical tenant's occupation). The assumptions and disregards may have a significant effect on a rent review and these will be reviewed in more detail below.

When trying to interpret a rent review, it is important to analyse the language with reference to what it meant to the parties at the date of the lease and not what it may mean now. For instance, in 1986 the term 'warehouse' did not include or mean retail warehouse; at that time, it only related to storage: *McDonald's Real Estate LLP v Arundel Corporation* [2008] EWHC 377 (Ch).

The following clause sets out the basic mechanism of a rent review clause – it does not go on to cover dispute resolution (as each lawyer, surveyor and client has their own way of dealing with this aspect of the rent review and it is relatively non-contentious).

'A Rent review

On the [ ] in the years 200[ ] and 20[ ] (each of which dates is referred to as **'the review date'** and **'relevant review date'** shall be construed accordingly) the Yearly Rent shall be reviewed (such reviewed rent shall be known as **'the revised rent'**) and with effect from the relevant review date shall be the greatest of: (a) the yearly amount of the first rent payable by the Tenant to the Landlord immediately before such date of review (or which would have been payable but for a suspension of rent pursuant to the [rent suspension clause where damage has occurred as a result of an insured risk]) and (b) an amount which shall represent the open market rental value of the Property at the date of review assessed in accordance with the following provisions of this clause.

B Open Market Rental Value

The open market rental value of the Property shall be the yearly rent exclusive of Value Added Tax (as may be agreed between the Landlord and Tenant or determined in accordance with subclause [ ]) that might reasonably be expected to be payable in respect of the Property as a whole in the open market by a willing landlord to a willing tenant with vacant possession without taking a fine or premium for a term of [ ] years commencing on the relevant review date and otherwise on the same terms and conditions of this Lease (except the amount of the Yearly Rent but including the provisions for the review of rent) ['the background assumptions'] and assuming (if not the fact) those matters set out in subclause C but disregarding those matters set out in subclause D.

C Assumptions

The matters to be assumed pursuant to subclause B are that:

- the Property is fit for immediate occupation and use by a willing tenant and that no work has been carried out that has diminished the rental value of the Property
- the Tenant has complied with all the obligations on the part of the Tenant imposed by this Lease (but without prejudice to any rights of the Landlord)
- the Property has not been damaged or destroyed
- the willing tenant has received the benefit of any rent free or reduced rent or other inducement for the purposes of its fitting out only.

D Disregards

The matters to be disregarded pursuant to subclause B are:

- any goodwill attributable to the Property by reason of any trade or business carried on in the Property by the Tenant or any underlessee or other permitted occupier
- any effect on rent of the fact that the Tenant or any underlessee or other permitted occupier has been in occupation of the Property

> • any effect on rent of any alterations or improvement to the Property or any part thereof carried out during or prior to the commencement of the Term by the Tenant or any underlessee with the prior consent in writing of the Landlord (or without prior consent where the Landlord has been held by the Court to have unlawfully withheld its consent) other than an improvement effected at the expense of the Landlord or in pursuance of an obligation to the Landlord (other than any obligation to comply with statutory requirements) whether under this Lease or otherwise.'

5.4 Standard assumptions

The standard assumptions provide that the hypothetical lease will be similar to the existing lease. Clause B in the 'standard' review clause contains standard assumptions, which, over time, have been the subject of many court cases and which in a number of instances have now established, with a fair degree of certainty, the meanings of the words used.

5.5 Assumptions and disregards

What are 'usual assumptions and disregards'? The draft rent review clause above has some standard provisions, which we would consider the 'norm'.

Often leases have further clauses; the more assumptions and disregards used, the more likely (as a general rule) it is that there will be problems. The problems will come in various guises, for instance:

• Interpretation: the 'standard' assumptions and disregards are understood; however, the third party may not be able to work out how to apply a new assumption or disregard.

- Lack of comparables: linked with the first point, are there other leases with similar provisions and, if not, what effect should they have on the rent?

- Discount: if the assumptions or disregards are unusual and/or onerous should there be a discount applied to the revised rent on rent review; if so, how much? (This is considered in more detail, below.)

The assumptions attempt to anticipate issues which may have arisen since the grant of the original lease or which should be applied at the time of review.

The disregards are usually there to protect the tenant from the potentially adverse impact of its occupancy on the rent review which would otherwise arise, as the hypothetical tenant might be prepared to pay more for an existing business which is fully fitted out and trading well, than for an empty unit.

So, the 'standard assumptions and disregards' can briefly be described as being the **assumptions** that:

(i)   any rent free period that would be granted in the open market for fitting out has expired;

(ii)   the property is there, ready for the tenant's use; and

(iii)   the tenant's covenants have been complied with (along with the standard assumptions noted above);

and that there is **disregarded** the effect on rent of:

(i)   any occupation and goodwill of the tenant or subtenants; and

(ii)   improvements to the property which the landlord has not paid for.

As noted above, lawyers frequently add other assumptions and disregards which sometimes do not have the intended effect. Still, many properties and leases are very different from the norm and circumstances also may dictate further drafting, such as:

- a disregard of the fact that the tenant also occupies adjacent property – this may be inferred from an assumption that the hypothetical lease is being marketed on the 'open market' and is to be at the open market rent reasonably obtainable – i.e. not taking into account a 'special tenant' – but this drafting should try to take the point beyond doubt;

- disregards tenants should ensure that extend to the presence and activities of subtenants;

- where works have been carried out (by the tenant or at the tenant's cost), before the start of the lease then the tenant would want to make sure they too are disregarded, as the disregards tend to apply only to those matters arising during the term of the lease – the draft above does this – however, where the tenant has 'bespoke' fitting out requirements, the parties may well need to make it clear that they are disregarded and that where the landlord has contributed to the cost of those works they are still disregarded – as they may well have diminished the marketability of the property in the open market;

- the landlord may want certain sublettings to be taken into account – although the usual assumption is that the property is vacant;

- where the lease contains unusual terms it may be appropriate to exclude those terms from the hypothetical lease – especially where they could distort the rent – by way of an express disregard.

5.6 Disregards by reference to section 34 of the *Landlord and Tenant Act* 1954

Some (usually older) leases disregard matters by reference to those matters set out in section 34 of the *Landlord and Tenant Act* 1954; there are sometimes technical drafting issues with this way of dealing with disregards and it is better to set out exactly what is disregarded in the lease.

5.7   Discounts

We have mentioned that onerous restrictions or provisions in the lease could have an impact on rent review, prompting the third party to provide a discount from the market rent which would otherwise be payable on review. We set out some basic ranges for discounts, taken from decided cases. These are only illustrations; each property and each rent review clause has to be considered on an individual basis:

● keep open covenant: up to 15 per cent;

● restrictive user clause: up to 10 per cent;

● onerous repairing clause: up to 28 per cent;

● a break clause (with onerous conditions): up to 10 per cent;

● hypothetical term: +/– 10 per cent;

● restrictive alterations clause: up to 5 per cent.

5.8   Rent review pattern

The rent review will be at set dates during the lease term; sometimes the lease will give the actual dates; alternatively, the lease will use wording such as 'once in every five years of the term', without giving a date. There used to be a concern that, in some cases, the effect of the wording was such that it resulted in there being a review in the penultimate day of the term. This concern is largely irrelevant now as for leases protected by the *Landlord and Tenant Act* 1954 either party can now apply for an interim rent at the end of a lease (previously it was just the landlord) and that rent is now generally meant to be the market rent (rather than a discounted rent, as was the case previously).

Most leases now work on a five-year review pattern, some have three-year reviews and some of the older leases have seven years, or longer. The point to consider here is whether the review pattern is normal for the market (of that property in that location) at the time of the review, and, if it is not, what effect will that have on the rent review. At the moment most office and retail tenants will pay more for relatively short term or longer leases with tenant break clauses; they will pay less for long leases or leases which assume a long term lease at rent review. However, certain particular tenants with high fit out costs and where location is important may well want longer terms.

5.9 Referral to third party

The rent review will usually state that if the rent has not been agreed by the review date, or within a short time before the review date, then either party can refer the matter to a third party.

Problems occur when it is only the landlord who can implement the review process and/or when the landlord can implement the review process by serving a notice to the effect that £X is the rent, unless the tenant serves a counter notice (or takes some other stated action) within a stated time frame (usually referred to as a 'trigger notice'). Issues on trigger notices also tend to involve the question of whether 'time was of the essence', a point which we will cover in more detail later.

Once the matter is referred to a third party, if an arbitrator, it will be governed by the *Arbitration Act* 1996 and if the third party is to act as an expert, the lease will often state the actions and steps which need to be taken and how that expert will act; if and to the extent that the lease is silent, the expert will act as he thinks fit.

Some leases allow the landlord to choose which form of third party review process to use; this 'flexibility' gives the landlord a degree of control which tenants should resist: the choice should be made as part of the lease negotiations. Landlords may argue that they need the control, as they own (or may subsequently own) other nearby properties and want to ensure consistency.

5.10 Arbitrator or expert?

This is an area which is open to debate. A lot will depend on the amount of rent involved, whether the rent review is 'standard', whether the building has a lot of comparables (making it more likely to be a straightforward rent review) and whether there may be complex or 'high value' issues to be determined. The basic points to consider are as follows:

- Arbitration tends to be more formal and is quasi-judicial in its approach; reference to an expert is (subject to the lease) relatively less formal.

- An arbitration award can be enforced as a court judgment; an expert's award can only be enforced under contract.

- The arbitrator can only come to a decision based on the facts/evidence presented to him – although the arbitrator does have powers (unless excluded in the lease) to investigate – which includes the power to order documents to be disclosed, the power to compel the attendance of witnesses and the power to cross-examine at an oral hearing any witnesses.

- The expert uses his own knowledge to come to his decision, and he can ignore the parties' own submissions and, subject to the lease, cannot compel disclosure of documents or information.

- Subject to the requirements of the lease, the expert can usually act more quickly and costs can be lower with an expert – although that should not always be assumed (especially where the lease terms set out a specific and detailed procedure for the expert to follow in assessing the rent review) – and the expert has full control over how to conduct the rent review (subject to the terms of the lease).

- There is little room to challenge an expert's decision (unless he has decided the wrong issue or acted outside his terms of reference, as set out in the lease, or in bad faith) and although the expert could be sued in negligence, this rarely occurs in practice.

- An arbitrator has an express immunity from any decision – unless it is in bad faith – the expert has no such protection but, as noted above, it is very difficult to pursue an expert in negligence: it is not enough to establish that another expert would have come to a different decision.

- An arbitrator has to give a reasoned written award; unless the lease states otherwise (and sometimes they do); the expert does not have to give a reasoned decision, unless the lease requires otherwise.

- The expert has no jurisdiction to award costs, unless covered in the lease; his fees are a matter for the parties; whereas the arbitrator can award costs (subject to the lease) and the court can regulate his fees.

- There is also the point that an 'expert' should be just that, whilst an arbitrator is drawn from a list and might not have the required competence (in relation to a particular review/property) – the merit of this point we leave for others to debate. The President of

RICS has a section devoted to trying to marry up expertise and the nature of the particular review.

As a very general principle, the higher the rent and the more complex the issues, the more likely it is that arbitration is more appropriate; however, in certain specialised rent reviews or where the property is unusual it may be better to have an expert. No doubt, which is more appropriate will continue to be debated, as long as there are open market rent reviews.

5.11 The decision

The third party will be appointed to determine the revised rent. In order to do this they will have to consider what rent a hypothetical lease of the premises, being offered on the market at that review date, would command on certain stated assumptions and disregards. In other words, the third party is considering a fictitious transaction. The problems occur when that fictitious transaction is so far removed from the reality – i.e. the actual property and lease themselves – that the rent is distorted; sometimes that distortion can favour the landlord and at other times the tenant. An extreme (but sometimes encountered) example of this is where the hypothetical lease is to be in the form of a draft lease attached to the lease and is very different from the actual lease.

5.12 Rental discounts and additional rent

Rent reviews usually direct that the hypothetical lease rent review is the same as the one in the actual lease. This can give rise to issues where the rent review either has a provision for an additional rent to be paid over and above the market rent, or provides for a discount (from the market rent on review). If it provides for a discount, the hypothetical tenant will arguably pay more and if it provides for uplift, the hypothetical tenant will arguably pay less. The courts are not consistent in their treatment of these discounts/additions in the hypothetical lease (as much will depend on the interpretation of the actual wording of the lease in question).

One approach taken is the 'commercial approach' – as opposed to literal interpretation: the court may be slow to accept that a rent review should assume that the additional rent should be taken into account to come to the market rent – logically it should be ignored, as otherwise, the review would take away on one hand what it awarded on the other; in one case, the reason for the additional rent was to rentalise the cost of improvements required by the original tenant – the court held that in order to protect the commercial purpose, the wording would have to be ignored [*Lister Locks Ltd v TEI Pension Trust Ltd* [1982] 2 EGLR 124; see also *Watergate Properties (Ellesmere) Ltd v Securicor Cash Services Ltd* [2005] PLSCS 199].

The literal approach has also been applied by the courts, notwithstanding the fact that the decisions have a distinct tendency to appear illogical; usually the literal approach has been followed where the lease has been clearly (if illogically) drafted – so as to deny the application of the 'presumption of reality'.

The simple way of avoiding these issues is to make it clear that the discount, or additional rent provisions (in the actual lease), are to be ignored in assessing the open market rent under the hypothetical lease.

5.13 What is being reviewed: the hypothetical lease term?

The exercise at each review is to consider what rent a new tenant taking a lease at the rent review date would pay, on the basis that the terms would be the same as the current lease – at least that is the starting point. The rent review surveyor has to consider how far that principle is applied by the actual terms of the lease.

One of the more contentious areas in respect of rent reviews, at the moment, is the length of the lease term to be assumed at rent review. The average term of a new commercial lease in the UK is around seven years; longer term leases (of 20–25 years) are no longer common, except in certain sectors – such as leisure and department stores, which have high up-front fitting-out costs which need to be amortised over the lease term. However, there are still a lot of older leases around and these leases could be 'attracting' a discount of 10–20 per cent on review, simply because the hypothetical tenant would not want to pay a 'full' rent for a long lease term; (for example, in *Canary Wharf Investments (Three) v Telegraph Group Ltd* (2003) 46 EG 132, an assumed 25 year term attracted a discount of 10 per cent).

Many modern leases now opt for something along the lines of an assumption that the new lease will be granted for 'a term (commencing at the relevant review date) equivalent to the unexpired residue of the term of the lease or 10 years, whichever is the longer'.

This may have unforeseen effects on the rent review which will only be determined by the actual market at the time; one drafting solution is to use words along the lines of: 'a letting for a term of a length which produces the best rent reasonably obtainable in the open market at the review date'. This would avoid the problem exemplified by the *Canary Wharf Investments* case referred to above: what may be a standard (and desired) length of lease term ten years ago may be very rare today.

However, there is still the potential for there to be an argument over double discounting: for example, a tenant granted a long rent-free period initially, may argue at review that there should be a discount to reflect the absence of a rent-free period at review by way of an incentive. (Note that this is not the same point as the disregard of rent-free periods linked to fitting out works.) This type of argument does not now appear to find much support in arbitrations and has been held by the courts to require exceptionally clear drafting.

5.14 Challenging the third party's decision

5.14.1 *The expert's decision*

There are very limited grounds upon which to appeal against an expert's decision – principally, where the expert has stepped outside what he was asked to decide by the lease.

The basic recourse against an expert's decision is on the grounds of negligence and this has been very difficult to establish. This has prompted some leases to set out a series of requirements that the expert has to follow, such as allowing submissions and counter submissions, holding a formal hearing and giving a written decision. If a lease does have a list of requirements which the expert must follow, this does introduce a marginally greater chance of a successful appeal being lodged – in any event, it increases the likelihood of a challenge. This seems to run counter to some of the main benefits of using an expert – simplicity and certainty.

In other words, setting out a list of requirements for the expert makes the process similar to arbitration; possibly, if there is a concern on the point, the lease should provide for arbitration?

The extent to which a challenge may be lodged will be determined, to a great extent, by the wording in the lease – the simple statement that the 'expert's decision is final and binding on the parties' may well be enough to preclude the court from interfering with that decision. This wording is sometimes qualified by the wording 'save on a point of law' or 'save in the case of manifest or material error' – which may give an aggrieved party the opportunity of challenging the expert's decision, if that decision was based upon an (incorrect) point of law or a material error, as the case may be (consider *Postel Properties Ltd v Greenwell* (1992) 47 EG 106).

5.14.2 *The arbitrator's decision*

There is slightly more room with regard to an arbitration as a result of section 68 of the *Arbitration Act* 1996 which entitles an aggrieved party to apply to set aside an award on the grounds of 'serious irregularity', as well as section 69, which allows an appeal on a point of law with the leave of the court.

5.14.3 *Serious irregularity*

Serious irregularity means an irregularity of one or more of the following kinds and which the court considers has caused or will cause substantial injustice to the applicant:

- failure by the arbitrator to comply with their general (statutory) duties;
- the arbitrator exceeding their powers;
- failure to conduct the proceedings in accordance with the procedure agreed by the parties;
- failure to deal with all the issues that were put to the arbitrator;
- uncertainty or ambiguity as to the effect of the award;
- the award being obtained by fraud or the way in which it was procured being contrary to public policy;

- failure to comply with the requirements as to the form of the award;

- any irregularity in the conduct of the proceedings or in the award which is admitted by the arbitrator.

5.14.4 Appeal on point of law

This requires leave of the court. The conditions for leave are:

- that the determination of the question will substantially affect a party's rights;

- that the question was one which the arbitrator was asked to decide – and did not;

- the decision was obviously wrong, or the question is one of general public importance – which will seldom apply to a rent review; or

- it is just and proper.

Only if leave is granted will the court decide whether or not the arbitrator did get the law wrong. Section 68 has been considered in recent cases [for example: *Checkpoint Ltd v Strathclyde Pension Fund* [2003] EWCA Civ 84; 1 EGLR 1, CA and *Warborough Investments Ltd v S Robinson & Sons (Holdings) Ltd* [2003] EWCA Civ 751; 2 EGLR 149] and the general points covered in those cases were drawn together in *St. George's Investment Co v Gemini Consulting Ltd* (2004) ChD 8/10/04; (2005) 01 EG 96, and can be summarised as follows:

- The sole issue for the court to consider is whether an arbitrator has committed a serious irregularity in making his award, not whether his award is correct.

- In deciding whether a serious irregularity has caused substantial injustice, the court should not decide what rent the arbitrator might have fixed if he had dealt with the case differently; rather it should try to assess how the aggrieved party would have conducted its case but for the irregularity. Only if there has been a substantial injustice because that party was unable to obtain a fair hearing will the irregularity be treated as one which would result in the award being set aside.

- An arbitrator may use his expert knowledge to arrive at the award, provided it is knowledge that one would reasonably expect the arbitrator to have and that he uses it to evaluate the evidence called and not to introduce new evidence.

- If the parties' valuers introduce evidence which the other is able to comment on, an arbitrator is entitled to arrive at his award by using that evidence in a totally different way.

- An arbitrator must not make an award based upon matters which were not presented to him or on which the parties were not given an opportunity to comment.

However, the general principles behind arbitration – in particular that there is a general aim for it to be 'final', wherever possible – dictate that the courts are slow to interfere with an arbitrator's award. The courts will only set aside an award in an extreme case – in laymen's terms, where 'justice' calls out for the award to be corrected – not, for instance, because of a minor technical or procedural irregularity.

5.15 Balancing payments

Whilst the review is being determined, the tenant continues to pay rent at the previous rate. Once the rent review has been decided, assuming this is after the rent review date, the tenant will need to pay (if there has been an increase) the shortfall between the old rent and the new rent, together with interest on that shortfall, usually at a rate of interest at around base rate. If drafted neutrally, the interest should be calculated from the quarter day upon which that part of the shortfall would have been paid if the review had been determined by the review date. Some leases provide for interest to be payable on the whole of the shortfall from the rent review date – where the increase is substantial this will result in the landlord receiving a material windfall.

This balancing payment is normally due within a stated period after the review has been decided and, at the latest, on the following quarter day.

5.16 Time of the essence

The rent review clause can contain traps, for both landlords and tenants and their advisors, where notices have to be served within certain stated times and the lease is drafted in such a way so as to make time of the essence.

Each case has to be considered on its drafting but there are some general principles which may help in trying to establish whether 'time is of the essence'; if it is 'of the essence' and the action does not take place within that time then, for instance, the landlord's ability to commence a review or the tenant's ability to reject the landlord's proposed rent will be lost: no review or a very high rent, the result! The general principles are:

- The general presumption is that there should be no implication that time is of the essence. A clause may state that a notice has to be served by a certain date; if that date is missed, that, of itself, does not mean that the notice cannot be sent later.

- This principle (that time is not of the essence) can be rebutted by express wording in the lease stating that 'time is of the essence', or by wording which may not go quite that far but which makes it clear what will happen if, for example, a notice is not served by a certain date – the rent will increase by the amount stated in the landlord's notice. These provisions make time of the essence by implication.

- Where the position is not clear, the courts will be slow to infer time being of the essence – because of the general presumption.

- Even if time is not of the essence, a party may make time of the essence by serving notice that for example, the date has passed by which x should have been done and if x is not done within a reasonable time then x can no longer be done and time is of the essence. If the recipient fails to respond then, provided that reasonable notice had been given, the recipient is likely to have lost the opportunity to do x.

These general principles frequently find their way into the courts and there is no substitute for promptly responding to any notices (having checked the lease) and checking the lease for any crucial dates and diarising them. However, the general drafting trend has been to move away from making time of the essence in rent review clauses.

5.17 The break clause and time of the essence

One way that the principle that time is not of the essence can be displaced is by the interrelationship of the rent review clause with other clauses (e.g. the tenant's ability to terminate is linked to review).

What emerges from the case law is that where a tenant's break right is very closely linked in time to a rent review process, which can only be initiated by the landlord, and where the decision by the tenant, whether or not to exercise the break, depends on the outcome of the review process, the courts are likely to find that time will be of the essence in respect of the relevant steps in the rent review process, notwithstanding the absence of express wording in the lease to this effect.

However, where the timing of the rent review is outside the landlord's control or where the tenant can initiate the review process, the court will be reluctant to use the presence of a tenant's break clause (even one closely linked in time to the rent review) to imply time of the essence into the rent review process.

5.18 The Lease Code

The Lease Code recommends that landlords offer alternatives to an upwards only rent review, such as index linked rents and upwards/downwards reviews, which the landlord would 'price' accordingly; crudely, the more favourable that the rent review structure is to the tenant, the higher the starting rent will be. (Landlords' failure to promote earlier versions of the Lease Code in the area of upwards only rent reviews has been under government scrutiny but, for the time being, the government has decided not to legislate against upward only reviews.)

The Lease Code's promotion, amongst other things, of upwards/downwards rent reviews, albeit tempered with the possibility of ensuring that the rent never drops below the initial rent, is unlikely to be widely adopted in the current investment market, especially for substantial office and retail/leisure units. Despite its promotion in the Code, many landlords still feel that the amount of money they have locked up in their buildings should be protected. The Code may have the effect, however, of increasing the number of leases with fixed uplifts, instead of rent reviews, which at least will provide for certainty, as well as variety.

Other rent review related matters promoted by the Lease Code include the following:

- either party should be entitled to implement a rent review;

- avoid clauses which make time of the essence at review;

- interest on the shortfall between the new and old rent should be at no more than the base lending rate;

these three points could be considered 'standard' nowadays; the following one is not:

- try to introduce a provision whereby the landlord forfeits interest on the shortfall if the landlord does not initiate the rent review process prior to the review date.

If either party can implement a review, so a landlord would argue, why should the landlord be penalised if it fails to trigger the review process?

5.19 Indexed rent reviews

Indexed rent reviews are commonly based on the Retail Price Index (RPI), although the Consumer Price Index (CPI) is becoming more common. The mechanism can be based on:

- the index figure for the month preceding the grant of the lease;

- a review period (annual); and

- the index figure for the month preceding the relevant review date.

The reviewed rent is then determined by multiplying the current rent by the index figure for the month preceding the review date and then dividing it by the index figure for the month preceding the grant of the lease.

RPI and CPI are indices used by the government to calculate the inflation rate. RPI takes an 'average shopping basket' based on household spending on most types of goods and services. In contrast, while using the same basic data, CPI excludes some RPI goods and services and includes others not covered by RPI. CPI also uses a different method of mathematical calculation and classifies goods and services differently, resulting in a lower inflation rate than RPI. Further details are set out in the Office of National Statistics' publication: *Consumer Price Indices – A brief guide* (2004), which is accessible on the National Statistics website at www.statistics.gov.uk.

Indexed review clauses should always provide for an 'upwards only' review.

Further, an indexed rent review clause should also cater for a change in the nature of the relevant index or if the particular index ceases to exist. In addition, the clause should also contain arbitration provisions to deal with any disputes that may arise during the term of the lease.

See also section 5.21 for the SDLT implications when dealing with an indexed rent lease.

5.20 Turnover rent reviews

Turnover rent reviews have been around for some 40 years, but in the current economic climate may well become more common, as the possible adverse effect of an 'upwards only' rent review is put under the spotlight. They can work well in shopping centres and parades as well as airports and railway stations. The Lease Code's encouragement of more flexible leases may also promote their increased usage.

Turnover rent reviews will normally be based upon one of the following variations:

- the tenant pays the higher of a basic rent (normally between 70 and 80 per cent of the market rent) and a turnover rent (typically set between 6 and 15 per cent of 'gross turnover' from the property). The base rent is payable quarterly in advance with the turnover rent paid if the trigger point is achieved;

- the tenant pays both a (lower) base rent and a percentage of the tenant's turnover.

By setting up a turnover rent structure the landlord has much more trading information available and can use that information to improve the footfall (and turnover) of the scheme; the landlord shares in the upside and the tenant is not caught having to pay a high rent in an economic downturn.

The drafting of a turnover lease can be very complex and is not for this book, but we set out some points which need to be considered when agreeing a turnover rent in the heads of terms and when reviewing one in a lease.

- Should the base rent be re-based in line with a normal rent review or should the turnover rent fall away after the first few years of the term?

- If the best rent is to be reviewed to a percentage of market rent, the lease will have a standard review clause to establish the new base, but the review clause should disregard the turnover rent review provisions and other related clauses in the lease.

- Should the turnover rent remain in place upon assignment? (Usually the per cent figures for base rent and turnover will be specific to the tenant.)

- On the basis that the turnover is very specific to the named tenant, what further restrictions should there be on assignment (and there should normally be an absolute prohibition against subletting while the turnover provisions are in effect)?

- There should be a positive obligation to trade actively from the property, but what happens if the tenant does not – some leases apply a notional turnover in these circumstances or the lease reverts to market rent?

- What other clauses are needed to require 'active trading': keep shop front well lit; tenant to make sure that window displays are visually stimulating; restrictions on use or goods sold?

- Should the turnover rent be reinstated in any lease renewal – if not, it should be specifically excluded?

- What should be included: telesales and internet sales, for instance?

- What should be excluded: credit card charges and refunds (once made), for instance?

- When should it be paid? Usually this will be based on best estimates/previous figures with readjustments at the end of the financial year.

- What information should be provided by the tenant, when and in what format? (Many shopping centres have complex systems which provide direct electronic access to the tenant's tills.)

- From the tenant's perspective, should the tenant seek greater involvement from the landlord, such as a contribution towards promotion of the centre or not to have certain (competing) uses in the centre and exclude certain activities/sales from turnover?

5.21 Stamp Duty Land Tax

Rent reviews may have Stamp Duty Land Tax (SDLT) implications. Under a SDLT calculation, the highest annual rent payable for any of the first five years of the lease term is taken to be the annual rent figure for the rest of the term. Therefore, where the rent is reviewed on or after the fifth year, there is no SDLT implication because the SDLT due on the lease rent after the fifth year of the term is based on the highest rent reserved in the first five years of the lease term – which would simply be the initial rent reserved under the lease. However, where there is a rent review within the first five years, the SDLT due on the fifth year and onward rent would be based on the rental figure that would be achieved at the rent review.

Where there is a rent review, the SDLT calculation still has to be calculated for the whole term. Given that the reviewed rent is unknown at the time of calculating and paying the SDLT due, a reasonable estimate must be made. The estimate allows the SDLT return to be completed in respect of the grant of the lease.

Once the rent review has been determined (and therefore the rent for the SDLT calculation becomes certain), the SDLT should be recalculated using the actual rent figures. Again, the rent payable in respect of the period after the end of the fifth year of the term of the lease is assumed to be the highest amount of rent payable in respect of any consecutive twelve month period in the first five years of the term.

Once the recalculation is made, the following could occur:

- the transaction now becomes notifiable and a SDLT return needs to be made for the first time;
- a further SDLT return needs to be made and additional tax is now due plus interest;
- if the estimate previously given proved too generous, a refund of the surplus tax (plus interest) should be reclaimed from HMRC.

These SDLT rules apply to most types of rent review.

The main issues arising for a tenant, where a rent review occurs within the first five years, is the administrative burden of making additional SDLT returns once the rent review has been determined and the prospect of paying too much SDLT at the outset or paying too little – which, in the case of the latter, the additional tax would be due at a later stage with interest. This could be a significant sum, where the rent is high.

There would be an increased administrative burden where rent reviews fall due each year based on an increase in RPI + 2 per cent, for example. Here, the tenant would be required to make estimates for each yearly review and could be required to file a SDLT return each year until the fifth review has been determined.

Whilst it is not usual to have rent reviews falling within the first five years, tenants should bear the above in mind when agreeing heads of terms.

5.22 Points to consider

- Does the rent review clause reflect the terms of the lease? If it introduces unusual artificial assumptions and disregards (which are normally there to increase the rent payable (e.g. disregarding a restrictive use or a restrictive assignment clause contained in the lease) are they clear – do they have, in fact, a negative impact on review because they make the review clause onerous?

- Does the clause have the usual disregards: (a) tenant's (and subtenant's) alterations and improvements to the property, (b) the tenant's (and any subtenant's) occupation and (c) goodwill (these three matters are usually referred to as 'the usual disregards')? If not, the landlord could argue that an occupying tenant would pay more rent for the lease than an incoming tenant.

- Does the clause enable the tenant to push for settlement of a rent review (and not allow a landlord to prevent or delay its implementation)?

- Does the clause make 'time of the essence'? If it does, the tenant could find itself trapped into accepting the landlord's opening rental offer by default, without having any ability to object.

- Does the clause disregard any uplift in rent as a result of works carried out pursuant to statute (e.g. the DDA)?

- There is usually little room for negotiation on the terms of a rent review clause; however, if the tenant feels that the clause is oppressive, it might still be worth trying to negotiate a break clause which can be exercised at the same time as the rent review is determined or agree a cap on the amount by which the rent can be increased.

- Depending upon the type of property and the landlord's requirements, it might be worth agreeing a turnover rent, which will normally provide for a fixed rent at a percentage of the market rent and an additional rent linked to a percentage of the profit received by the tenant.

- Where the lease contains a 'tough' rent review clause (or other restrictive clauses in favour of the landlord) the tenant may be able to argue that the tenant should get a discount on rent review to reflect the onerous nature of the lease.

- Where the lease concerned is a long (for example, 25 years) lease at a market rent, the tenant may be able to argue that, on review, there should be a discount to reflect the fact that there will be a (notional) substantial SDLT payment to be made by the hypothetical tenant.

Service charges

6

6.1 Overview

Where there are several units within a building or an estate, the tenant will be responsible for an appropriate proportion of the service charge costs incurred by the landlord in providing general services to the tenants.

Service charges tend, by their nature, to be confrontational and as a result an industry working party was established which resulted in the publication in 1996 of *Service Charges in Commercial Property: A Guide to Good Practice*. However, while that guide aimed to set out some general principles reflecting 'good practice', and although it had the support of cross-industry bodies, adherence to it was voluntary.

Particularly given the fact that service charge provisions have continued to be an area of common disagreement and dispute, the guide (then in its second edition) was replaced with effect from 1 April 2007 by a new Code, the *Service Charges in Commercial Property: RICS Code of Practice* ('the Service Charge Code'). Although not compulsory, its designation as an official RICS guidance note means that surveyors cannot afford to ignore it.

We will come back to the Service Charge Code and its impact at various points in this chapter.

6.2 General drafting principles

The general intention of a service charge clause is to ensure that all costs and expenses incurred by the landlord in maintaining the estate/building are recovered from the tenants. This will usually extend to all major items of structural repair, including the replacement of roofs, lifts, air conditioning/heating equipment, management charges, insurance costs, the correction of any inherent defects and any other liabilities which the landlord may incur in relation to the estate/building.

Although that is the general intention, a recent run of court cases has made it clear that the courts will take a robust (and anti-landlord) line where a landlord is seeking to recover substantial service charges in 'inappropriate' circumstances – for instance, major structural repairs in a short-term lease – despite wording in the service charge clause which indicates that the landlord should be able to recover.

Furthermore, there is no implied presumption that the service charge clause should cover all expenses; well-drafted clauses often put in an express statement to that effect.

Service charges are usually payable quarterly in advance, (based upon estimates previously provided by the landlord's managing agents), and at the end of each service charge year the managing agents prepare a final service charge statement detailing the amounts actually incurred.

Where the service charge is substantial, the service charge accounts will usually be audited by a firm of accountants. Often leases will allow the landlord to raise an interim charge – where an unforeseen cost has arisen during the course of the service charge year.

If (which is rare) the lease does not specify how and when the service charge is to be collected, a landlord will probably only be able to recoup that charge after having paid for the particular service itself.

The final accounts will be drawn up after the end of each service charge year and many leases will state that the landlord's surveyor will issue a certificate confirming the amounts incurred and any final sums due – that certificate being 'final and binding'. Although the court decisions are not 100 per cent clear, since the managing agent will be appointed by the landlord the courts will be slow to hold that any such certificate (despite the wording in the lease) is to be treated as final – where there is a dispute. However, if the certificate is confirmed by an independent party – such as an accountant or a third party surveyor – the courts will probably accept that the certificate is final – if that is what the lease states.

The lease will often specify that the final accounts are prepared within a set period of time – usually either within three or six months after the end of the service charge year. The Service Charge Code (paragraph 49) states that:

> 'The owner will submit certified accounts to the occupiers in a timely manner and in any event within four months of the end of the service charge year.'

Clearly where the lease is within a shopping centre the four month period may be more appropriate than where the lease is within, say, a business park and the services provided are minimal. The Service Charge Code (paragraph 52) also suggests that the tenant should be provided with the opportunity of inspecting supporting documents in relation to the service charge accounts.

If the tenant has made an overpayment during the course of that service charge year, that overpayment is usually credited against the next service charge year; if there has been an underpayment then the tenant will be obliged to settle that underpayment, usually within 7 to 14 days of demand.

Although the landlord will usually covenant to provide the services, that obligation will often be qualified, for instance, by it being stated that there is no liability on the part of the landlord unless the landlord has first been notified of a lack of services and has not acted within a reasonable time. If this qualification is not in the lease then the landlord may be in breach of its covenant to provide services in circumstances where the landlord was not aware that the service had failed. Sometimes the lease will say that some services are discretionary. The question then is, should most services be discretionary or should they always be provided?

The items to be covered by the service charge should be listed in detail, as if there is any ambiguity, the courts will usually find in the tenant's favour. In Appendix B is a list of some of the more common items covered by a standard service charge; not all the items will be appropriate in every case. It is important to ensure that the service charge does cover all heads of expenditure and allows the landlord to provide further or additional services in the future – without committing the landlord now.

Service charges are often split up into separate (sub)schedules, for instance:

- **Schedule 1 Part A:** Services provided to all the occupiers within the estate/building.

- **Schedule 1 Part B:** Services provided to a class of occupiers, e.g. the retail units within the building/a mixed retail and leisure park/estate.

- **Schedule 1 Part C:** Services which the landlord may provide, but is not contractually committed to provide – often called 'discretionary' services.

In this example, the retail tenant would pay a small percentage of the Part A services and a larger percentage of the Part B services; the percentage under Part C would be determined by the benefit that that particular tenant received from that 'service' (if provided) – relative to the other tenants.

Draughtsmen often add 'sweeper clauses' to catch items which they have not (for whatever reason) covered in their detailed list. The effectiveness of these clauses will be determined in the context of the service charge provisions as a whole, but, as a general comment, they will usually be interpreted restrictively. The court will be slow to allow the sweeper to be applied so that the landlord can have a totally 'new' service; however, the clause may work where the service is in line with other services covered and is for the general benefit of the occupiers. For example, it is not yet clear whether the cost of producing the newly required Energy Perfomance Certificates (EPCs) will be caught by a 'sweeper clause' and if the landlord seeks to recover the cost, specific mention of this should be made in the Schedule of Services, so that this cost can be recovered.

Tenants will sometimes seek to impose a cap on their liability for service charges; this cap may be a fixed amount which is then subject to increase, linked, for example to the Retail Prices Index or by a stated percentage – this second option could result (if the increases are compounded) in the cap going up higher than the tenant would otherwise expect. The cap may be in for a short period of time at the start of the lease. If it is limited to a specific period of time, landlords' agents should be wary of trying to postpone works so that they arise outside the period covered by the cap, in an attempt to be able to charge the full amount to the tenant – the court may well hold that the landlord has failed to comply with its obligations to provide the 'services' within a reasonable time [*Princes House Ltd v Distinctive Clubs Ltd* [2007] EWCA Civ 374].

6.3 Items of expenditure

The general principle is that if an item is not specifically covered in the list of services (and is not picked up in the sweeper clause), then the landlord is not entitled to charge that item to the service charge.

Set out below is a table highlighting some of the matters which are sometimes not covered in service charge clauses (or which give rise to dispute) and which might be worth considering further – subject to their context.

Reference should also be made to Chapter 8, dealing with repairs, as many disputes over service charges focus on whether an item is in 'disrepair', sufficient to justify expenditure which would be covered by the service charge.

Item of expenditure	Comment	Drafting
'improvements'	Generally the service charge is there to cover repairs and this would usually extend to improvements as a result of repair, but not to improvements on their own. However, where the lease allows the landlord to charge for complying with statute and the improvement in question is as a result of compliance with statute, then the landlord may be able to charge the cost through the service charge. With new regulations requiring landlords to provide EPCs for commercial buildings at the landlord's own cost, if the landlord seeks to recover the cost of producing that report, the lease should clearly state this in the service charge provisions. Please see Chapter 16 for further details.	The clause must specify that the 'improvements' may be charged – if that is the intention. Acting for the tenant you would want to ensure that it was limited, e.g. to improvements as a result of replacing worn out equipment: 'where beyond economic repair'.
'insurance valuations'	Often not covered specifically in the lease but possibly chargeable anyway, if the landlord is entitled to charge for the cost of providing insurance services.	The lease should specifically cover this and tenants should ensure that the valuations should be no more than, say, once every two years.
'internal' management charges	Some landlords use their own internal management facilities and charge a notional cost through the service charge.	This will probably not be implied, e.g. the management fees will often refer to having been 'incurred' and if it is provided 'in house' they will not normally have been expended.
'maintenance'	This can imply pre-emptive servicing, but rarely does it go as far as substantial improvements (see *ACT Construction Co Ltd v Customs & Excise* [1982] All ER 84); tenants should not be too sceptical, as regular 'maintenance' should reduce long term costs.	Distinct from 'repair' but would normally be the same as servicing.

Item of expenditure	Comment	Drafting
'management fees'	These have to be specifically referred to in order to be chargeable. They must relate to one or more of the services being provided, as if the fees are incurred in respect of a service which is not covered, then those fees will not be recoverable.	Tenants should ensure that they do not cover the cost of enforcing or collecting payments from other tenants or the collection of rents generally.
funding charges for the cost of expenditure	If the landlord does not have the money in its account it is still obliged to provide the services and it may then need to obtain a loan, otherwise it would have to use its own monies; even if the landlord uses its own monies it would expect to be able to charge a notional interest rate. The lease should specifically cover this possibility – if it does not, then the landlord is going to be unable to recover the borrowing costs/cost of money.	Tenants should ensure that the service charge is properly funded and be given the option of paying the additional charges so as to avoid interest charges being incurred.
'expenditure incurred/expended'	Depending on its context, this may limit the service charge which can be collected to that actually spent – not something to be collected in advance.	Landlords will want to ensure that they have a fully funded service charge and tenants will want to ensure that the landlord is not building up a service charge account with no immediate intention of using it.
'services' provided	Depending on its context, this usually means 'services'; it does not mean items of repair.	Landlords must be specific if they want to be 100 per cent certain of recovering an item of expenditure.
'properly' provided	This means acting in the normal course of business, which may or may not result in a reasonable cost or reasonable item of expenditure arising.	Consider qualifying this further so that it ties in with carrying out services or incurring costs in accordance with guides to good practice; should there be prior consultation for certain items of expenditure?

Item of expenditure	Comment	Drafting
a 'fair' proportion	This may well take into account not only the relevant proportion – pro rata to other tenancies – but other aspects of 'fairness' as well. This wording could prevent a landlord charging a substantial item of expenditure to a tenant with a short term lease [*Scottish Mutual Assurance plc v Jardine* (1999) EGCS 43, QBD].	

6.4 Reserve and sinking funds and depreciation charges

Some service charge clauses allow a landlord to collect payments to be held in a reserve or sinking fund. These two terms are often confused or used interchangeably: a reserve fund is a fund set up to meet recurring items of expenditure – such as repainting the outside of the building every three years of the term; a sinking fund is a fund set up to meet the replacement of specific items and which may only be applied once or twice during a lease term – such as the replacement of the lifts.

Some leases specify what the fund is to be used for and if the lease is specific then the fund can only be applied towards the item or items so specified. Most modern leases, if they have a provision for a fund, will usually be discretionary (the landlord having the choice whether or not to set one up) and be more generally worded, to provide for greater flexibility.

With either a reserve or a sinking fund, the lease should, where possible, be drafted so as to require the landlord, or their agent, to hold the money in a specifically designated trust account (and the lease should state that the monies should be held as trust monies); if not, then tenants may have difficulty claiming that money back (assuming they have a claim) in the event of the landlord's or agent's insolvency. The Service Charge Code states that:

- monies held in a reserve or sinking fund should be held in an interest bearing trust account, separate from the landlord's own monies;

- the annual budget and reconciliation accounts should clearly state contributions to and expenditure from the sinking/reserve fund account, plus opening and closing account balances, interest earned and tax paid;

- on any sale the landlord/seller should pass all sinking fund monies together with accrued interest to the buyer/new landlord.

A few leases provide for the landlord to charge for depreciation of plant and machinery. For example, a lease may state that the landlord may charge £2,000 per annum as a depreciation charge for the lift in the building. The landlord would normally covenant to replace the lift (at its own cost) *if required* during the lease term; the tenant would still pay (via the service charge) for annual maintenance and running repairs. The point is that with a depreciation charge the money belongs absolutely to the landlord and if the lift (in our example) does not require replacement during the lease term, the landlord is under no obligation to refund the charge [*Secretary of State for the Environment v Possfund (North West) Ltd and others* [1997] 2 EGLR 56, ChD], unless the lease provides otherwise.

Reserve and sinking funds and depreciation charges may be found in leases but, in practice, sinking funds and reserve funds, are often not implemented due to the various tax, accounting and management issues which they raise. Furthermore, financially sound tenants will often prefer to pay for the costs as and when required – especially if there is the possibility that the landlord may never apply the funds received during the course of the lease.

6.5 What is a 'reasonable' service charge?

Buildings come in many shapes and sizes and what will be reasonable for one building type, location, etc. may not be acceptable for another; the actual service charge may therefore vary considerably.

The 2007 service charge analysis 'OSCARS' produced by Jones Lang LaSalle include the following data:

- **Offices** – an average of £6.86 psf, from a range of a high of £8.04 (West End) to a low of £4.77 (Midlands); the largest components of expenditure were on security and M&E services;

- **Retail** – an average of £4.45 psf, with the most expensive type of shopping centre (being one that is enclosed and air conditioned) averaging at £5.61psf;

- **Retail Parks** – an average of £0.96 psf, from a range of a high of £4.68 to a low of £0.15.

For further analysis go to www.oscar.joneslanglasalle.co.uk.

6.6 How should expenditure be apportioned?

There are various methods of apportioning the service charge; which method is chosen will depend, to a great extent, on the nature of the property and the type of services being provided. A detailed explanation of various methods of apportionment is set out in section D4 of the Service Charge Code.

The Service Charge Code's general view is that the floor area basis of calculation 'is the most common and simplest method of apportionment'. The starting point must be to consider which of the various methods is best suited to the building/estate.

The Service Charge Code provides for the service charge to be apportioned using one of a series of recognised methods of calculation, and sets out 'the most common bases for contribution for each occupier's proportion of the total service charge costs' as being:

- a fixed amount;

- a fixed percentage;

- floor area;

- weighted floor area;
- a fair and reasonable proportion;
- rateable value.

According to the terms of the Service Charge Code:

> 'Whatever the method being used, it needs to be demonstrably fair and reasonable and there needs to be a rational commentary on how the apportionment has been worked out.'

Where appropriate, the lease may well go on to state that the proportion may be adjusted during the course of the lease, where circumstances require – usually to redress an imbalance which may have arisen – e.g. where one particular tenant uses some of the services more than the others.

The most common method of apportionment is on a floor area basis. The *RICS Code of Measuring Practice* (6th edition, 2007) explains how to measure various types of building and the usual ones for commercial lettings are:

- Gross Internal Area (GIA) – applied to warehouses and various industrial buildings (including ancillary offices); and

- Net Internal Area (NIA) – applied broadly to offices and shops.

It may also be appropriate (as indicated above) to have different services charged to different tenants; the classic example of this is where there is an office building where only certain tenants use the lifts – possibly combined with the fact that the tenants on the ground floor use up more of the air conditioning (as they are larger by volume).

Another method used is to have a fixed sum for the service charge with that sum often being increased by reference to increases in a stated index. This method is simple, if a little crude, and is usually only found in short term leases where the service charge is relatively straightforward. It has the potential to be 'unfair' (to either party), especially when used in a long term lease: for instance, the index chosen may not reflect the actual increase in the cost of services and the base cost may be inaccurate – leading to a greater distortion the longer the scheme is run.

6.7   Floor weighting

When using the floor area as the basis of calculation and where the parties are dealing with substantial lettings (in particular retail leases in shopping centres), it is not uncommon to find that the service charge is 'weighted', so that the first X,000 square metres are charged at 100 per cent; the next Y,000 square metres are charged at, for example, 80 per cent, etc. The smaller tenants in the scheme may argue that this means that they are picking up more than they should; one of the counters to this argument is that the larger tenants increase the footfall – which benefits the smaller tenants; a further counter may be that the weighting fairly reflects the use of the services.

6.8   The question of reasonableness

There is no implied 'reasonableness' as to service charges in commercial leases, although there may be circumstances (to give business efficacy to the lease) in which the courts could imply a term that, in order to be recoverable, service charge costs should be 'fair and reasonable'. In *Finchbourne v Rodrigues* [1976] 3 All ER 581, although the lease required the tenants to pay by way of service charge a specified proportion of 'the amount which the [landlords] shall from time to time have expended' in providing repair and other services, the Court of Appeal ruled that the landlords were not entitled to be 'as extravagant as they chose' and did not have 'an unfettered discretion to adopt the highest conceivable standard and to charge the tenant with it'. This does not mean, however, that a landlord must necessarily accept the cheapest quotation, in all cases: consider, for example, the approach taken in *Plough Investments Ltd v Manchester City Council* [1989] 1 EGLR 244, in *Holding & Managment Ltd v Property Holding and Investment Trust plc and others* [1990] 1 EGLR 65 and in *Fluor Daniel Properties Ltd v Shortlands Investments Ltd* [2001] All ER (D) 36 (Jan).

The Service Charge Code sets out recommendations which the court is likely to take into account when considering if a cost can be recovered; for example:

- 'The services provided will be beneficial and relevant to the needs of the property, its owner, its occupiers and their customers' – paragraph 23.

- 'The aim is to achieve value for money and effective service rather than lowest price' – paragraph 24 of the guide – but see also, for instance, paragraphs 31 and 32.

- 'Service charge costs may include enhancement of the fabric, plant or equipment where such expenditure can be justified following the analysis of reasonable options and alternatives. Owners will provide the facts and figures to justify such a decision' – paragraph 30.

- 'The owner will keep costs under review and where appropriate (e.g. every three years) require contractors and suppliers to submit competitive tenders or provide competing quotations' – paragraph 34.

As mentioned above, unlike the previous guide, the Service Charge Code has an enhanced status as official

RICS material, such that when interpreting what is meant by 'principles of good estate management' or 'acting reasonably and properly' the starting point should be the Service Charge Code and the courts are likely to take a similar approach.

6.9 Shopping centres, retail and leisure parks

This chapter has been looking at service charges in general. However, shopping centres and retail and leisure parks can often have specific service charge provisions of their own, over and above the points discussed above. The list below focuses on some of the more obvious differences:

- With particular regard to shopping centres, the service charge provisions often contain an obligation on the part of the tenants to contribute towards the funding of promotional activities. The Service Charge Code urges that this should be recognised 'as a shared cost to be borne by both owners and occupiers in partnership and in such cases, consultation is considered essential' – paragraph 77. Service charge budgets should highlight the gross expenditure on promotions and the lease should, ideally, contain some form of general statement as to how much the landlord contributes towards the promotional budget; possibly the landlord should be expected to contribute more where the shopping centre (or other development) has leases linked to turnover, as the landlord is then gaining additional rental income as a result of increase in footfall.

- Service charges will often include an item for the provision and maintenance (as the case may be) of items such as public toilet facilities, public telephones and vending machines; to the extent that these items are covered in the service charge, income from these items should be treated as a service charge credit.

• With particular reference to shopping centres, landlords often provide barrows or kiosks within the common parts. Operators of those barrows or kiosks are often charged a fixed sum and there should be some obligation on the part of the landlord to apportion part of that fixed sum to the service charge account. Paragraph 40 of the Service Charge Code states that 'expenditure and income receipts will be shown separately in the service charge account with income being credited to the service charge after calculation of the management fee'. Further examples of income receipts would include: vending machine takings, selling recyclable waste, advertising space, licensed mall activities (e.g. children's rides, photo booths, etc.) and photocopying – see section D3 ('Treatment of non-core income') of the Service Charge Code.

6.10 Service charges and the short term lease

Various cases have highlighted the problems in charging tenants substantial items of expenditure; one of the better known examples is *Scottish Mutual Assurance plc v Jardine Public Relations Ltd* [1999] All ER (D) 305; EGCS 43, QBD, in which the landlord carried out substantial roof repairs and sought to charge those repairs back to the tenant under the lease. The lease did contain a clause enabling the landlord to charge the costs of the repair of the building back to the tenants, but what distinguished this case was that the landlord could have carried out patchwork repairs, rather than substantial renewal of the roof, to have achieved the same result.

The court held (noting that the lease was only originally granted for a period of three years) that the landlord had to act reasonably in choosing whether or not to carry out patchwork repairs or substantial renewal and found that the landlord had been unreasonable in electing to choose the more expensive option.

The lessons to be taken from the *Scottish Mutual* case are fairly simple:

- where there is a short-term lease, the landlord should be careful if considering whether or not to incur substantial expenditure and charge it via the service charge;

- if the only way of complying with its service charge obligation is substantial renewal (in *Scottish Mutual* it was of the roof) and the service charge entitles the landlord to charge such costs in principle, and patchwork repairs would not be sufficient to carry out the necessary works, then the landlord should be entitled to recover the costs under the service charge;

- but where there is an alternative (and there is only a short period of the lease term left to run) and that alternative is cheaper than wholesale renewal, the courts are highly likely to find in favour of a tenant if the landlord chooses the more expensive option.

Put another way, the *Scottish Mutual* case was really doing no more than applying recommendations now contained in the Service Charge Code, including:

- the service provided should be *beneficial* and *relevant* to the needs not only of the property and the owner but also the tenant (and its customers);

- service charge costs should be restricted to charges and associated administrative costs properly incurred by the owner including '...the reasonable costs of maintenance, repair and replacement (*where beyond economic repair*) of the fabric…' [emphasis added].

6.11 Exclusions from the service charge

We have covered what is included or what should be included in a normal service charge. However, service charges frequently go further than that, especially where they have been negotiated in detail by the tenants. Tenants will often expect to see an express exclusion from the service charge of certain items which would not normally (assuming a standard form of drafting) be included in the service charge in any event. The exclusions are normally there for the sake of comfort and 'for the avoidance of doubt'. They are frequently found where the lease is the first lease following the development of the building of which the lease forms part.

Some more common exclusions are noted below:

- any initial costs incurred in respect of the original design and construction and general development of the building;

- the cost of complying with any planning conditions relating to the original development;

- the *initial* provision of certain items for common benefit, such as dustbins, security systems, gates, etc;

- items which should properly be chargeable to individual tenants, such as the cost of enforcement of covenants for the collection of rent;

- improvement costs over and above normal maintenance, repair and replacement.

The list of standard exclusions can often go on for several pages; however, a well drafted service charge

provision should make it clear that many (if not all) of the exclusions would not apply in any event.

6.12 Exclusions of landlord's liability

Most leases exclude the landlord's liability to provide services where the services have been disrupted due to factors beyond the reasonable control of the landlord, i.e. the landlord's covenant to provide services is suspended. This type of exclusion is probably no more than that which would be implied if the landlord's covenant was to use 'all reasonable endeavours' and, possibly even 'reasonable endeavours'. Tenants should seek to ensure that there is an express obligation to use reasonable endeavours to ensure that the services are resumed as quickly as reasonably possible – although, again, this is probably implicit.

Another 'carve out' is that leases often state that the landlord is not liable to provide a service (such as repair) unless and until the tenant notifies the landlord of the lack of, for example, repair. This carve out is there because otherwise a landlord would normally be liable for the lack of repair, even if they were not aware of the problem. Tenants should resist becoming landlords' virtual managing agents; at the same time, landlords should not be penalised unfairly. The usual compromise is that the principle is accepted but that the landlord is not liable, provided that (and for so long as) they are not aware, or ought to have been aware, and once they know of the problem deal with it within a reasonable time; the tenant only has an obligation to inform the landlord of matters within its demise – the common parts being for the landlord to inspect and monitor.

6.13 Tax implications

The tax position of the service charge clause can be highly complex – beyond the scope of this book –

especially as much will depend upon the individual tax positions of the landlord and tenant. However, the following are by way of general comment and should cover some of the more usual points which arise.

- Service charges levied by a landlord will normally form part of the landlord's income arising from the ownership of land and will be taxed as income or corporation tax, as the case may be.

- Service charges generally follow the VAT treatment of rent, but are not chargeable consideration for SDLT purposes.

- Costs incurred by the landlord in providing the services will normally be deductible expenses.

- The same principles will usually apply to reserve/sinking fund monies received beneficially by the landlord (as opposed to where they are held in trust for the tenants, see the next point) – and it will have to offset the reserve/sinking fund monies against expenditure in that tax year: this can lead to a problem, say, a few years down the line, when the landlord actually applies the fund, as in that year the income from the service charge will be less than the actual expenditure, and unless the landlord has sufficient sources of other income, the landlord will lose out on the tax relief which would have otherwise been available to it in that year.

- To further complicate matters, some reserve/sinking funds are held under either express or implied trusts, for the benefit of the tenants and there is no clear position on how that money should be treated. The key question would appear to be: who owns the money? If it is a true trust situation, then the most consistent position would appear to be that the money so paid should be treated as a capital payment, held by the landlord as trustee and neutral in its hands; as far as the tenant is concerned, the payment of a capital contribution cannot be used as a tax deduction, as it lacks the necessary revenue nature of tax deductions.

(The previous two points (among others) highlight why both landlords and tenants tend to shy away from setting up or agreeing to reserve/sinking funds – however, in certain circumstances, they may be appropriate.)

- a depreciation charge is treated as income, in the same way as the service charge;

- capital allowances may be claimable by the landlord;

- commercial tenants can usually deduct service charges from trading profit upon payment to the landlord.

6.14 Flexibility and new legislation

The ever changing legislative framework, combined with the fact that many leases were granted years before the applicable legislation came into effect – and this will continue to be the case – means that service charge clauses, however well drafted at the time, may not cover procedures or requirements which are subsequently adopted as a result of legislation. A recent example of this is the introduction of compulsory Energy Performance Certificates (EPCs): for further information on this see Chapter 16.

The standard service charge in an institutional lease will normally contain provisions entitling the landlord to recover, via the service charge:

- the cost of inspecting, maintaining, repairing, replacing and renewing the buildings, fixtures and fittings, plant and equipment;

- the cost of complying with 'statutory requirements';

- the cost of 'any other service or carrying out any other work which the landlord acting reasonably shall think proper for the benefit of the building and/or the comfort and convenience of other occupiers' (or similar, by way of a 'sweeper' clause).

How far will these (or similar provisions) assist a landlord in charging certain costs through the service charge? From a tenant's perspective, is a landlord entitled to charge costs relating to new legislation through the service charge? The wording in the lease will be of paramount importance, but the following are some general observations which may assist.

6.15 Asbestos regulations

How do service charge provisions work when considering, for instance, the *Control of Asbestos Regulations* 2006?

The 2006 regulations, generally, continue to impose on employers and others in control of non-domestic premises, a wide range of duties in connection with the management of asbestos in premises, including risk assessment, risk management plans, monitoring, provision of information and restrictions on work undertaken, etc.

These regulations make provision for the allocation of responsibility to those in control of non-domestic property (the 'dutyholder') to ensure that the risks associated with asbestos being present in a building are 'managed'. In a tenanted building, both the landlord and the tenant may be a 'dutyholder', subject to obligations imposed by the regulations: the tenant, through its covenant to repair the premises demised; the landlord, in respect of any common parts or other areas for which they are responsible. (See Chapter 12 for further detail on these regulations.)

The regulations do not necessarily require the removal of asbestos, if found, from a building, but rather require that if asbestos is identified, it should be contained; it only has to be removed if that is the only real way of preventing potential harm to others. Accordingly, the presence of asbestos in the building does not, in itself, represent a breach of a repairing covenant or a covenant to comply with statute.

As a general comment, the landlord should be entitled to recover the costs incurred in complying with statute; this should extend to costs incurred in carrying out audits, inspections and surveys and compiling and maintaining an asbestos register.

If the asbestos has to be removed in order to comply with the regulations, then the landlord may be able to recover the cost of removal as part of the service charge obligations in the lease.

Conversely, if the asbestos does not need to be removed (in order to comply with the regulations), the landlord is unlikely to be able to recover the costs, if they choose to carry out the removal. Landlords should not fall back on the sweeper clause as a way of recovering those costs as, generally, the removal of asbestos would not fall within a definition of 'service'. It may be possible to recover the costs as part of the sweeper, where the works are for the general benefit of the tenants within the building, but again such reliance must be treated with caution.

6.16 *Disability Discrimination Act 1995 (as amended) (DDA)*

A similar method of approach can be applied when dealing with the DDA, albeit that the lines are not quite so clear cut.

The DDA and its associated regulations do not necessarily require works to be done. What they do require is that each individual 'provider of services to the public' considers how it wishes to provide its services, and, in doing so, it cannot discriminate against disabled parties. Where a landlord of a shopping centre decides that the way that it provides its services requires it to install certain additional facilities in order to comply with the DDA, then it may be able to recover those costs via the service charge, if the service charge is widely drafted.

If there is no direct way to recover, then the landlord may decide to postpone doing the works until it needs to carry out general repair, whereupon it may incorporate the required works as part of that general repair, in compliance with building regulations – this may enable the landlord to recover through the service charge, depending upon the wording of the lease.

6.17 Energy performance

Another set of regulations affecting premises has been introduced to give effect to the Energy Performance of Buildings Directive (EPBD), under which buildings with a total useable floor area of more than 1,000 square metres have to comply with certain minimum standards of energy efficiency.

The *Building and Approved Inspectors (Amendment) Regulations* 2006 implemented these requirements in the UK (subject to certain works being excluded under transitional arrangements) with effect from 6 April 2006.

Accordingly, the regulations may well require an upgrade to premises which:

- would not be a repair;
- would be an improvement.

Although the detail of the regulations needs to be worked out, it is likely that where a lease allows a landlord to recover costs incurred in complying with statute, the landlord may be entitled to recover the additional costs arising as a result of this legislation – even though, strictly, many of the costs would relate to improvements.

See also further comments on this in Chapter 12 and as to the British Property Federation's energy efficiency guidance for landlords and managing agents and on EPCs in Chapter 16.

6.18 Environmental assessments

The Building Research Establishment has devised a series of assessments for considering (and evaluating) the environmental merits of certain types of buildings such as offices, industrial and retail units; certain other types of building, such as leisure centres and laboratories, can be covered by a bespoke version. Credits are given for certain features. These assessments are a useful marketing tool for new buildings or refurbishments; as for existing buildings, managers are using them to measure the performance of buildings and develop action plans and monitor and report performance.

Carrying out such an assessment may form part of the landlord's adoption of British Standard BS EN ISO 14001:2004 (*Environmental management systems. Specifications with guidance for use*) – a voluntary initiative, which sets out the elements of an environmental management system, which includes the adoption of an environmental policy, environmental management audits and reviews.

The charges for a 'BREEAM' (Building Research Establishment Environmental Assessment Method) environmental assessment can exceed £10,000 and landlords may seek to recover these costs via the service charge but may have difficulty in doing so unless the service charge specifically covers the point or the sweeper clause is sufficiently widely drafted.

Service charge clauses often refer to the 'cost of complying with statutory requirements' as a head of expenditure, but these are voluntary initiatives. In order for the landlord to be able to recover the costs of such audits, etc. the wording would normally have to go further and refer to 'a cost of adopting initiatives such as ...'. Tenants should be advised to qualify this wording (assuming they accept the principle) by, for instance, making it a condition that the initiatives are only adopted on prior consultation with (and approval of) the tenant. This entirely voluntary position should be contrasted with the position under the DDA (discussed above); under the DDA there is a certain element of discretion as to how far a landlord chooses to provide services to the public, but having made that choice the landlord then has to comply with the statutory requirements outlined in the DDA.

More information on BREEAM (and the current pricing structure) can be obtained from the Building Research Establishment website: www.breeam.org

6.19 The Lease Code and the Service Charge Code

The Lease Code recommends that landlords 'should be aware of the *RICS 2006 Code of Practice on Service Charges in Commercial Property* and seek to observe its guidance in drafting new leases and on renewals (even if granted before that Code is effective)'. A copy of the Service Charge Code can be obtained from: www.servicechargecode.co.uk

The Service Charge Code was published by various bodies, including RICS, the Property Managers' Association and the British Property Federation. The

Service Charge Code urges property owners to adopt good business and management practices and states that they 'will procure quality service standards to ensure that value for money is achieved at all times'[paragraph 32 of the Service Charge Code]. It should be noted that the Service Charge Code is not saying that costs should be kept as low as possible; the emphasis is on value for money ('benchmarking') and transparent and fair management practices and policies.

Where there is a question mark over what is meant (in a lease) by reference to the landlord complying with the 'principles of good estate management', it is likely that the court will look first to the Service Charge Code for guidance and the introduction (section B) states:

> 'This Code can not override the lease but, if read in conjunction with it, will enable users to identify the best way forward in interpreting that lease to ensure effective services management. It benefits all users of property if those who draft lease documentation follow this Code.'

A well (and fairly) drafted commercial lease will encompass many of the suggestions in the Service Charge Code, but it is always worth reviewing the Service Charge Code and considering its applicability in individual situations; the more it is used/adopted, the less room there is for dispute.

The Lease Code suggests that:

- landlords must disclose known irregular events which would have a significant impact on the service charges;

- the tenants' repairing obligations should be appropriate to the term and the condition of the premises;

- landlords should be aware of and seek to observe the RICS 2006 Code of Practice on *Service Charges in Commercial Property*;

- insurance policy terms should be 'fair and reasonable and represent value for money, and be placed with reputable insurers'.

6.20 RICS Service Charge Code: content

The Service Charge Code was published by RICS in June 2006 and is designed to provide advice and 'best practice' guidance to its members on the practice and procedure for service charges in leases of larger commercial properties, with effect from 1 April 2007.

Although compliance with the Service Charge Code is not compulsory, its designation as an official RICS guidance note means that in any allegation of negligence against a practitioner, non-compliance with the Service Charge Code will be taken into account. The Service Charge Code is stated as representing 'the most desirable structure for service charges' and one that should be 'appropriately implemented in all new leases'. Although the Service Charge Code cannot override the terms of the lease, in managing service charges generally the aim is that it should be delivered 'as closely as possible...despite any lease constraints that might exist'.

The Service Charge Code includes provision for the following:

- *Management:* responsible management of services, with owner/manager recognising a duty of care to occupiers; the provision of services efficiently and economically; the right for reasonable challenges to expenditure; monitoring of service standards.

- *Service standards:* provision of services commercially and professionally, in accordance with written performance standards; value for money and effective service, beneficial and relevant to all affected parties; appropriately qualified people to provide the services.

- *Communication:* regular and effective ongoing communication and consultation between owners and occupiers; regular meetings; setting and communicating management policies; clear information on the delivery and costing of services to be effectively communicated by the landlord to the tenant, to minimise disputes.

- *Service costs:* services to be competitively procured on a value for money basis; service charges to be on a 'not for profit, not for loss' basis, with transparency in management fees and accounting generally.

- *Administration/mechanics:* service costs to be limited to operational management, including costs of maintenance, repair and replacement of all items necessary for the operation of the property; managers to deliver the budget with explanatory commentary at least one month before the start of the service charge year and a reconciliation within four months of the year end; significant variances to costs (above forecast figures) to be promptly notified and explained to occupiers.

- *Apportionment:* cost of services to be apportioned using one or more recognised methods: fixed amount; fixed percentage; floor area; weighted floor area; fair and reasonable proportion; rateable value.

- *Additional shopping centre services:* marketing and promotion to be agreed, monitored and reviewed with occupiers; marketing costs to be shared, with individual contributions depending on commercial factors; clear policy and transparency required in relation to non-core ('mall') income.

6.21 When will the Service Charge Code apply?

While practitioners are 'not required' to follow the Service Charge Code, RICS does regard its content as reflecting best practice and recommends that it is 'appropriately implemented in all new leases' as this 'will benefit all sides'.

Clearly, however, it will not be appropriate to follow the Service Charge Code (whether in whole or part) in the case of every lease:

- the Service Charge Code has expressly been designed for use with 'larger properties' and a 'common sense' approach as to scale and applicability (particularly as to cost benefit issues) will be called for from managers and occupiers in dealing with smaller properties;

- while the Service Charge Code is intended to represent best practice upon renewal of a lease there may be limits as to the extent to which this can be achieved in practice;

- the Service Charge Code recognises that there may be circumstances in which the Service Charge Code cannot be applied and that the parties should not be compelled by the Service Charge Code 'to an inappropriate course of action'; in such cases, a record should be kept of the reasons for not applying the Service Charge Code, shared with all the parties;

- in managing existing leases, the service charge provisions will invariably not be fully Service Charge Code-compliant; the code recommends the interpretation of such provisions in line with the Service Charge Code, subject to legally binding provisions in the lease requiring a different approach.

6.22 What difference will the Service Charge Code make?

Generally, the provisions of the Service Charge Code should inform both landlords and tenants as to the approach that is considered acceptable for service charge provisions when negotiating new leases of larger properties, and may also assist in future disputes over the operation of existing lease provisions.

In any event, it does appear that the Service Charge Code is here to stay and that RICS is determined to use these 'voluntary' measures as a springboard to facilitate the transformation of the traditional approach to service charge recovery. While it 'is not intended to override existing leases', managers are expected 'to emulate and match their delivery as closely as possible to the Service Charge Code, despite any lease constraints that might exist'.

However, given the continuance (in many cases long-term) of existing leases with service charge provisions which do not reflect the aims of the Service Charge Code, coupled with the (sometimes) major changes in landlord's practices that will be called for and the potential compliance cost burden on landlords, it remains to be seen to what extent, and at what pace, the fairer and more transparent approach to service charges envisaged will take hold in the market.

6.23 How will the Service Charge Code affect lease drafting?

To what extent will the drafting of new commercial leases of larger properties be adjusted and come to reflect the recommendations of the Service Charge Code? Some landlords have already adopted some of the provisions; indeed, standard draft leases covered some of the provisions before the Service Charge Code was published.

Going forward it is likely that key elements of the Service Charge Code will increasingly be incorporated into newly negotiated leases, as tenants and their advisers push for the inclusion of such provisions as reflecting accepted 'best practice'.

Just how far this process will go (and how quickly it will be adhered to) will, to some extent, depend on market conditions and on the circumstances and negotiating position of the parties. For example, it may prove to be commercially impracticable to insist upon Service Charge Code-compliant service charge provisions in new leases being granted in respect of (say) units in a multi-let development where a number of leases are already in place containing non-compliant service charge provisions and where the practical arrangements for the provision of services on a particular basis are already in operation. Even in such cases, however, the landlord will be under increasing pressure to waive or vary (subject as appropriate to tenants' agreement) non-compliant provisions, to bring the service charge scheme into line with the Service Charge Code.

6.24 Service Charge Code-compliant drafting: some suggestions

Set out in Appendix A are some suggested additional/alternative drafting clauses for possible inclusion in service charge provisions, which are designed to reflect the aims of the Service Charge Code. These are drafting extracts, representing part only of what may be included in a comprehensive service charge provision and further drafting would be required to cover other aspects not dealt with here. In any event, it should be noted that these clauses may, perhaps, go somewhat further than some institutional landlords may be willing to concede, at least in the short term.

6.25 Points to consider

- When acting for a tenant taking a short-term lease, consider whether or not the service charge should be capped at a fixed sum or whether the rent should be 'all inclusive' (but note that there may be an increase in Stamp Duty Land Tax if the rent is 'all inclusive'), with there being no separate liability for service charges; alternatively, try to exclude or reduce the potential liability for material structural repairs and/or inherent defects and other 'major' items of expense.

- Just because a lease states that 'x' can be recovered, courts can be reluctant to find in favour of a landlord, especially where the lease is for a short term or only has a few years left to run. Pause before incurring material expense when acting for a landlord, where there are short term leases; consider, especially in these circumstances, whether there is a more economic way of carrying out the work.

- When acting for a tenant, consider whether the service charges actually charged are the same as those covered in the lease.

- Are the services which the landlord provides appropriate or sufficient for the property concerned and how are the service charges to be best or most fairly apportioned?

- If there are reserve or sinking fund provisions in the lease, are they appropriate; what are the tax and management issues? Do the funds belong to the tenants, if not expended by the landlord during the course of the lease? Is the fund account fully funded and should it be moved into a specifically designated account?

- If taking over an existing lease, make sure that the existing tenant has paid all its service charges and, if there is any doubt, ensure that there is a retention or deposit made by the existing tenant to cover any shortfall which may be confirmed after completion, once the service charge accounts have been finalised.

- How much flexibility is there for the landlord to add to the service charges – is the sweeper clause widely drafted?

- If the service charge is on the high side – relative to the age of the building and the type of services provided – this is likely to have an adverse impact on rent review, as the premises will, in comparison to others, be less attractive to tenants in the open market.

- Where the service charge sets out particular steps to be taken by the landlord before the landlord can recover monies from the tenant, the landlord should take care to follow and fully comply with all such requirements and equally tenants should check that there has been such compliance before making service charge payments. For a recent example of the problems that can arise where procedural conditions for recovery of the service charge were not met, see *Leonara Investment Company Limited v Mott Macdonald Limited* [2008] EWCA Civ 857.

Insurance

7

7.1 Overview

Normally, the landlord will insure the building/estate against damage by the 'usual' insured risks (covered by a comprehensive insurance policy) and the landlord's insurance cover will extend to such items as demolition costs, professional fees and loss of rent for a fixed maximum period of time, following damage.

The costs and premiums incurred by the landlord in maintaining the insurance (including, usually, any insurance valuations) will be charged back to the tenant, either as part of the service charge or, more usually, as a separate (annual) cost.

7.2 Definition of 'insured risks'

We would suggest that 'best practice' is for the 'insured risks' to be specifically defined; one example of such a definition is as follows:

> 'Insured risks means (to the extent that property of the nature of the Premises can be insured against each such risk in the market at commercially acceptable rates and subject to such exclusions and limitations as are imposed by the insurers and which are normal in the insurance market at the time) the risks in respect

> of loss or damage by fire, lightning, explosion, aircraft and other aerial devices or articles dropped therefrom, earthquake, subsidence heave, landslip, riot, civil commotion, terrorist acts, malicious damage, storm, tempest, flood, bursting or overflowing of pipes, boilers, water tanks and other apparatus and equipment and such additional risks as the landlord may from time to time (acting reasonably) require or which the tenant (having given at least ten working days written notice) may reasonably require.'

In addition to the defined 'insured risks', the lease will usually go on to provide that the landlord includes loss of rent insurance for a specific period in the insurance policy, normally for no less than three years and no more than five years; the exact period of time will depend upon the length of time reasonably envisaged for the particular property to be rebuilt in the event of total demolition – taking into account the fact that planning consent may be required. (Complex structures and listed buildings, for instance, are likely to take longer to rebuild than a building of standard design/construction.)

The insurance should also extend to professional fees, demolition and shoring up costs and local authority and other fees and charges, e.g. planning and building regulation fees and third party and occupier liability cover.

7.3   Plate glass

A lot of time is spent arguing over plate glass insurance and whether the tenant should be provided with a letter of waiver, excluding the tenant from having to comply with the obligation to insure plate glass, providing a copy of the policy to the landlord, etc. We feel that much of the time, this is a waste of time: plate glass is usually part of the demise to the tenant and covered by the tenant's repairing liability; the landlord's insurance policy for the building should exclude plate glass and it should be up to the tenant to decide whether or not it wishes to insure the plate glass separately – always assuming the building has any plate glass. There should not be the need for a specific clause, for example, in the lease of a normal high street 'shop'.

However, where the building contains a glass frontage, careful consideration will be needed as to who is liable for the insurance and whether the plate glass is part of the actual structure. If it is part of the structure and the tenant has taken a lease of part then the repair of the plate glass is likely to fall on the landlord, via the service charge, and the landlord will also be liable for its insurance.

7.4 Parties' mutual responsibilities

7.4.1 *Rent suspension*

If there is damage by an insured risk, then the landlord is usually under a responsibility to apply the insurance proceeds received towards repairing the building/unit and, whilst those works are being carried out, the rent, or an appropriate proportion of the rent, is suspended (the 'rent suspension period').

The insurance provisions will normally provide for the rent to be suspended where there has been damage to the premises (or the access to the premises) by an insured risk – either in whole or in part, depending upon the nature and extent of the damage. If the premises (or access) are totally unusable as a result of damage by an insured risk then it will be normal to expect the rent to be suspended in full.

Accordingly, it is important to ensure that adequate loss of rent insurance is in place at all times. For instance, if there has been a recent rent review which has resulted in an increase in the rent, the landlord's loss of rent insurance cover should be increased in line with the revised rent. If this is not done and there is damage by an insured risk then it is entirely possible that the insurers will only pay out a proportion of the actual loss suffered and the landlord will be unable to reclaim the shortfall from the tenant, as it is the landlord's responsibility to ensure that adequate loss of rent insurance is in place at all times.

Tenants should ensure that their lease requires the landlord to refund any rent paid in advance (or an appropriate proportion) following damage by an insured risk, for the period from the date of damage until the next quarter day – when the rent suspension will 'kick in'. If there is no express statement to that effect, the landlord is entitled to keep the rent and, as they have not suffered a loss at that point, the landlord is unable to claim loss of rent under the insurance policy for that period. (If the landlord has to refund part of the rent they will be able to reclaim under the policy.)

From a tenant's perspective, it is always important to ensure that the rent suspension lasts for as long as it takes to carry out the relevant reinstatement works. This is not always agreed by landlords, but the compromise in these circumstances is usually that the tenant is provided with a break clause upon expiry of the loss of rent period so that it can terminate the lease if the premises have not been reinstated by the expiry of the rent suspension period. (In any event, it is usually appropriate to have a cut out date at some point in time in the future – enabling the lease to be determined if the reinstatement has not been completed by then.)

The landlord should ensure that the tenant's ability to break does not come into effect before the expiry of the loss of rent period – although there is no particular issue with the tenant serving notice during this period. If the break is exercisable and 'completed' during the loss of rent period, then the landlord may well lose the right to continue to claim under the loss of rent provisions of the insurance policy – as the lease will have been terminated, resulting in there being no 'lost' rent.

7.4.2   Reinstatement

The landlord usually covenants to insure the property to its full reinstatement value. It is common under commercial property insurance to have a policy on a 'day 1 reinstatement basis' which means that if the reinstatement costs of the building were £100,000 at the start of the insurance policy, the insured value would be increased by an agreed figure (e.g. 25 per cent to £125,000) to allow for increases in building costs where reinstatement spans several insurance years. Therefore, this increased value is a prudent way to ensure that there is enough money available for the rebuild. (If there is a shortfall (not being the excess under the policy), then, subject to the wording of the lease, the landlord will usually be liable to pick up that shortfall out of its own monies – some leases expressly state this, to avoid argument.)

If there is damage covered by the policy then the landlord will normally be obliged to endeavour to obtain all necessary consents and, subject to having done so, to reinstate the premises as quickly as reasonably possible. The lease will usually expressly state that the tenant will be liable for making up the excess on the policy.

Tenants should note that the reinstatement obligation will not normally extend to the tenant's own plant, fixtures, fittings and stock – the tenant should have those items covered under their own policy, and will have to refit and pay rent at the same time – albeit they may well be able to claim the rent back under their own business disruption policy.

Some tenants are now starting to insist that the landlord's reinstatement obligation includes, where appropriate, an obligation to procure warranties in favour of the tenant from the consultants and contractor involved in the reinstatement works – the form of warranties being in line with the then industry standard, approved by the tenant, approval not to be unreasonably withheld or delayed. As the reinstatement works, once completed, will become the responsibility of the tenant (under its repairing covenant) this is a perfectly fair requirement.

7.5 Uninsured risks: flood and terrorism

There has been much recent discussion over terrorist insurance cover and who should carry the risk of any uninsured loss if terrorist cover ceases to be available in the insurance market. However, the focus on terrorist activity has obscured the 'uninsured risk' more likely to be encountered – flooding. Cover for flooding is still available for areas classed as 'low' and 'moderate' risk, as well as high risk areas where there is a commitment to improve flood defences: areas are usually classified by their postcode and their current status can be checked on the Environment Agency flood plan: www.environment-agency.gov.uk. In other areas, there is no guarantee that insurance will continue to be available.

As to terrorist cover, there are two basic issues: insurance cover for terrorist action may not be available in the future; secondly, the cover currently available may not cover 'all risks' as there are two different definitions of a terrorist act used in the market, one affording wider coverage than the other.

The narrow definition is in section 2 of the *Reinsurance (Acts of Terrorism) Act* 1993:

> 'acts of persons acting on behalf of, or in connection with, any organisation which carries out activities directed towards the overthrowing or influencing, by force or violence, of Her Majesty's Government in the United Kingdom or any other de jure or de facto.'

The wider definition is in section 1 of the *Terrorism Act* 2000:

> '(1) . . . the use or threat of action where–
>
> (a) the action falls within subsection (2),
>
> (b) the use or threat is designed to influence the government or to intimidate the public or a section of the public, and
>
> (c) the use or threat is made for the purpose of advancing a political, religious or ideological cause.
>
> (2) Action falls within this subsection if it–
>
> (a) involves serious violence against a person,
>
> (b) involves serious damage to property,
>
> (c) endangers a person's life, other than that of the person committing the action,
>
> (d) creates a serious risk to the health or safety of the public or a section of the public, or
>
> (e) is designed seriously to interfere with or seriously to disrupt an electronic system.'

Crown Copyright material is reproduced with the permission of the Controller of HMSO and the Queen's Printer for Scotland.

Although primary insurance is now usually based on the 2000 Act, reinsurers still tend to use the 1993 definition so there can be 'gaps' in the insurance cover.

The basic issue is that there may be circumstances where 'all risks' are not covered under a landlord's insurance policy, in which case they will not be 'insured risks', but uninsured risks.

If the lease does not expressly address the point, if damage is caused by an uninsured risk the rent still has to be paid by the tenant, rent suspension will not apply, and the tenant is likely to be liable to carry out the reinstatement works at its own cost, under the repairing covenant – at least that used to be the position, until recently. Over the last three to four years, some tenants have taken an increasingly hard line and many sizeable tenants will now no longer be prepared to be a landlord's insurer of last resort – the landlord, in these cases picking up the risk and if there is damage by an uninsured risk then the rent is suspended, as if there had been cover, and the landlord is obliged to reinstate using its own monies, or may be able to terminate the lease, if it chooses not to reinstate.

See section 7.8 for further comment on this point.

7.6 Noted interests, non-invalidation and subrogation

Tenants will often require the landlord to ensure (as far as possible) that the tenant's interest is noted on the policy and, again where possible, that the insurance policy contains a tenant's non-invalidation clause and a provision whereby the insurers agree to waive all rights of subrogation.

Notation: having the tenant's interest 'noted' on the policy is of questionable effect. The insurers are not under any contractual obligation to inform the 'noted' tenant if a policy is not renewed; if there is a claim under the policy the insurer is unlikely to consult the tenant. However, notation may serve to help a tenant defend an action by an insurer against the tenant where the tenant caused the damage – as it would argue that it has an 'interest' under the policy by virtue of that 'notation'.

A 'non-invalidation clause': is a statement to the effect that the policy is not invalidated by an act or default of a tenant. The point of concern in relation to 'non-invalidation' is that, if it is not covered, then there is a possibility that the insurance may be invalidated by an act or omission of the tenant; as the tenant is a potential beneficiary of the policy (for instance, because of the loss of rent payments) we would argue that it would be inequitable for the insurers to avoid paying out on the policy as a result of such act or default. Put another way, the very purpose behind arranging insurance is to ensure that cover is available in certain circumstances, including where the damage is a result of the tenant's negligence.

Insurance is a contract requiring full disclosure of all relevant information. If a landlord is aware of a material fact relating to the tenant but fails to disclose this to the insurers, the landlord may not be able to rely on a non-invalidation clause [*Ansari v New India Assurance Limited* [2008] EWHC 243 (Ch)].

A waiver of rights of subrogation: is a statement to the effect that the insurance company will not pursue a tenant where the tenant caused the damage. A waiver of rights of subrogation is also of concern to a tenant: there is a general principle of insurance law that, if an insurer pays out under a policy, it can step into the shoes of the insured and seek to recover any payment made to the insured from the third party that caused the loss in the first place. Obviously, as it may be the tenant's action which has given rise to the loss, the tenant does not want to find itself being sued by the insurer. Where the policy has a waiver this problem should not arise.

If the landlord accepts an obligation in the lease to procure a waiver of subrogation rights, the obligation should be limited to using reasonable endeavours. This is because a letter of waiver may need to be issued at the start of each insurance year and insurers may not always be willing to issue such a letter.

7.7 Interrelationship with other lease terms

The insurance covenant ties in with the tenant's repairing covenant: the tenant's repairing covenant will usually be qualified in that, if there is damage by an insured risk, then the tenant's repairing liability is effectively suspended and the landlord's obligation to reinstate that damage comes into play.

As noted above, it is important to make sure that the definition of the insured risks is as wide as appropriate and that all items that one would expect to have insured are either covered under the landlord's insurance policy (in which case if there is damage the landlord is responsible) or the tenant can take out its own insurance (which it can then claim upon in reinstating the damage – in compliance with its obligations to keep the premises in good and substantial repair and condition). Where there are two separate policies, one held by the landlord and the other by the tenant, the tenant must ensure that there is no risk of double insurance – its policy should only apply to matters not covered by the landlord's own policy – and there is usually an express requirement to that effect in the lease.

The insurance covenant also links in with some of the more general covenants contained in the lease relating to compliance with statute, fire regulations and user. If a tenant does not comply with fire regulations then this might have an adverse effect on the landlord's insurance policy and could result in the insurers not accepting a claim under the insurance policy – the potential effect of that being that the damage caused by the loss (not covered by the insurance policy) would fall upon the tenant. Another example of this would be where the tenant stores highly combustible items on the premises without keeping them in a fire-proof container; there will almost certainly be issues under the insurance policy in these circumstances if a fire occurs and the flammable material explodes as a result of it being kept in the open.

7.8 The Lease Code

The Lease Code suggests:

> 'If the whole of the premises are damaged by an uninsured risk [so] as to prevent occupation, tenants should be allowed to terminate their leases unless landlords agree to rebuild at their own cost.'

The Lease Code therefore promotes a 'sharing' of the risk of damage by an uninsured risk and there are various compromise positions surrounding this allocation of risk, such as:

- the landlord is obliged to reinstate at its own cost;

- possibly coupled with the tenant continuing to pay rent;

- or the tenant paying rent after, say, six months;

- unless the landlord has elected to terminate the lease within six months of damage.

The market now contains a sufficient number of leases which broadly follow the recommendations of the Lease

Code for this risk-sharing to be viewed as an 'institutionally' acceptable position, although certain institutions may still not be prepared to accept such a compromise, unless they have to! Risk sharing remains something that should be negotiated specifically between the parties at the heads of terms phase. The Lease Code contains a standard form set of heads of terms, but these do not deal with responsibility for damage by uninsured risks.

The Lease Code also promotes the following:

- landlords 'must always' disclose the insurance commission they receive and provide full insurance details upon request;

- if premises have not been reinstated by the end of the loss of rent period either party should be able to terminate the lease.

7.9 Points to consider

- Check that the landlord's insurance policy covers all 'usual risks' as, otherwise, for instance, the tenant may find itself liable under its repairing covenant to repair damage which should normally be covered by an insurance policy; if there are any 'gaps' in the landlord's policy then the tenant should ensure that either the landlord changes its policy or that they are covered under the tenant's own policy.

- The wording in the lease should be checked to make sure that the landlord's insurance covenant relates to the whole of the 'building' including any common areas, access roads, car parking areas, etc. as well as the landlord's plant machinery and equipment – albeit that the landlord's plant, machinery and equipment may be covered under a totally separate insurance policy to that of the buildings. (Note that the tenant's repairing liability will be qualified to the extent that an item is damaged by an insured risk and therefore, from the tenant's perspective, it is important to ensure full cover is in place.)

- Check that the 'loss of rent insurance' is adequate and that it is for an appropriate minimum rent suspension period (three years is considered the norm for a 'standard' building); if not, then the tenant should consider taking out additional cover (at its own cost) or seeking an amendment to the lease to cover the point as, otherwise, it may find itself paying rent for a damaged property once the rent suspension period has expired. Conversely, landlords should check that the amount of rent cover is correct.

- The tenant will get the premises back with the landlord's building reinstated, at which point the rent will become payable again – the tenant will then need to reinstate its own required fitting out works; the tenant should ensure that the rent payable during the refit and the refit itself is covered by its own insurance.

- Where the lease has fixed (sometimes, fixed minimum) increases in rent, check that the insurance brokers have covered this in the loss of rent insurance cover, i.e. that the total amount of cover reflects the fact that the rent will go up to a (minimum) stated figure.

- If the damage cannot be reinstated within the period covered by the loss of rent insurance, then the lease should provide for either party to be able to terminate the lease on the expiry of the rent suspension period (as, otherwise, again the tenant could find itself liable for rental payments for a building which has been destroyed).

- The amount of the insurance cover should also be checked as, although any shortfall is not usually the tenant's responsibility, if the landlord does not have adequate insurance, the landlord may not be able to afford to reinstate the property in accordance with its contractual obligations.

- Review the tenant's proposed use of the unit/building and, if appropriate, the insurers should consent to the proposed use; in addition, any alterations proposed by the tenant may need the insurer's approval.

- If the insurers have certain conditions (and what may look like a requirement could well also be a 'condition') then the tenant will have to comply; failure to comply with a condition in an insurance policy will often invalidate the policy, even when the failure had no bearing on the particular claim.

- Do the insurers have any particular requirements – if so, will they need to be complied with?

- If the tenant stores any 'high risk' items, are they stored in appropriate containers, in compliance with any regulatory requirements, as well as any insurer's requirements, which could be more onerous?

- Frequently, buildings policies will not cover plate glass and it may be appropriate to take out a separate policy if this is not covered under the landlord's policy.

- Tenants should take out separate insurance in relation to loss or damage in respect of contents and tenant's fixtures and fittings as well as appropriate business disruption insurance (covering loss of profits, rental payments, etc.) public liability cover, employer's liability insurance and any other risks not covered by the landlord's policy or policies.

- The lease should make it clear (if possible) that the insurance premiums are 'reasonable' as, under general contract law, there is nothing to prevent the landlord from recovering all the costs, even if they would normally be viewed as 'excessive'.

8 Repairs, decoration and dilapidations

8.1 Overview

The repairing clause is one of the keystones of a lease: it is inextricably linked to the description of the property, the subject matter of the demise. Not only does it impose a material obligation (and liability if not complied with), it can impact on the rent review and insurance provisions. If the clause is onerous or badly drafted (or if it has not been complied with), it can severely restrict the tenant's ability to assign.

For a standard repair covenant to bite (whether on the landlord providing the services or the tenant covenanting to repair), there must be actual disrepair: just because a building becomes unusable as a result of damp, for instance, it does not follow that there is any disrepair. Even if there is an element of deterioration, there may still need to be deterioration sufficient to produce an adverse effect, before the repairing covenant will apply. As one judge noted: 'In a sense all structures start to deteriorate the moment they are constructed.' [*Janet Reger International Ltd v Tiree Ltd* [2006] EWHC 1743 (Ch)].

Furthermore, an item is not in disrepair simply because it is old: a boiler may have reached the end of its life expectancy in accordance with recognised guides – such as those produced by The Chartered Institution of Building Services Engineers – but this does not mean that it has fallen into disrepair. If the boiler is in working order (albeit obsolete), it is not necessarily in disrepair. Clear wording will need to be used for a tenant to be required to replace functioning, but obsolete, equipment with new equipment.

8.2   Lease of whole

If the tenant occupies the whole building, then the tenant is usually responsible for all of the repairs, maintenance and decoration of the building, including the repair of the main structural elements, plant and equipment (such as air conditioning and lifts) internal fittings (including any carpets) and services.

8.3   Lease of part

Where the tenant occupies just part of a building, then the following is the usual scenario:

- The tenant is responsible for those internal (non-structural) parts of the property including the plant, equipment and internal fittings (including any carpets, plate glass in a shop front and external doors) within the property itself.

- The landlord is responsible for the repair and maintenance of the main structure, exterior and common parts of the building and outside areas and the plant and equipment which serve the whole building.

- The individual tenants within the building will then contribute an appropriate proportion of those total costs via the service charge provisions in their leases.

8.4 An example of some standard wording in a lease

'The Tenant covenants to keep ["put" is implied] the Property [is it clearly defined and does this extend to fixtures and fittings?] in good and substantial ["substantial" and other similar wording does not add much, but is frequently encountered] repair [includes many inherent defects] and condition ["condition" is more than just repair and can impose a material additional burden], and when necessary rebuild, reconstruct or replace the Property [these can often be considered as areas going on beyond repair] (damage by Insured Risks [these need to be clearly defined and include all standard risks] excepted ...)'

8.5 Review of the wording in a repairing covenant

The word 'repair' goes much further than mere maintenance and, depending on the exact wording in the lease, can also cover replacement of major parts of the building and, as noted below, the 'repair' of inherent (i.e. hidden) defects in the design and construction of the property.

An obligation to 'repair' usually gives rise to an (implied) obligation to put the property into a good state of repair, even if it is in poor repair at the start of the lease.

Reference to an obligation to keep the property 'in good and substantial' repair, or similar, does not add to the general obligation 'to repair'. [*Simmons v Dresden* [2004] EWHC 993, TCC] Also, reference to 'substantial repair' does not mean that the property has to be kept in pristine condition, or perfect repair and the expression 'renew' adds little to 'repair' [*Collins v Flynn* [1963] 2

All ER 1068]. The standard of repair is that of an intending occupier who judges repair reasonably by reference to its intended use of the property.

If the disrepair is caused by an inherent defect, then, in many cases, the tenant will be required to make good the inherent defect [*Ravenseft Properties Ltd v Davstone (Holdings) Ltd* [1980] QB 12]. In one leading case on this point, the tenant had to repair defective cladding even though the disrepair was caused by the absence of expansion joints and effective ties. It was irrelevant to the point to distinguish between defective design and workmanship; the key was that there was disrepair [*Post Office v Aquarius Properties Ltd* [1987] 1 All ER 1055]. Contrast this with where there is a design fault, but no disrepair – the tenant will not normally be in breach.

Including wording along the lines of 'when necessary rebuild, reconstruct or replace' will normally be viewed as onerous, going beyond the normal covenant to repair and may well result in a discount being applied on rent review – 27.5 per cent in one case [*Norwich Union Life Insurance Society v British Railways Board* (1987) 283 EG 846]. Often, tenants will qualify this by including 'where beyond economic repair' after 'where necessary', which will normally neutralise the effect of the additional obligation.

Some repairing covenants refer to 'maintain'; this is a rather vague word and is not necessarily distinguished from 'repair' but, in some contexts, may have a wider meaning which may extend to other operations.

An obligation to repair does not, without more, impose an (implied) obligation to keep a property safe [*Alker v Collingwood Housing Association* [2007] All ER (D) 98 (Feb)].

8.6 Repair or replacement?

There can be various different ways of effecting repairs:

- The tenant has the choice and does not have to choose the most expensive;

- Replacement can only be required if repair is not reasonably or sensibly necessary [*Dame Margaret Hungerford Charity Trustees v Beazeley* [1993] 2 EGLR 143; *Ultraworth v General Accident First and Life Assurance Co* [2002] EGLR 115];

- If patch repairs 'do the job' the landlord should not be able to insist upon replacement [*Carmel Southend Ltd v Strachan & Henshaw Ltd* [2007] EWHC 1289].

8.7 Other matters

The tenant's repairing liability will usually (and should) be qualified by reference to the landlord's insuring liability: if (and to the extent) there is damage by an 'insured risk' then the landlord is responsible for reinstatement, but otherwise the tenant is to repair.

In considering the repairing covenant, one should also look at the definition of the property/demise, as it is that which is the subject matter of the repairing obligation. One common issue is whether the definition extends to the tenant's fixtures and fittings; if it does, then they may well be caught by the obligation on the tenant to keep the property in repair and to yield up the property at the end of the term in good repair. There may also be an implication on the rent review: does the hypothetical lease (being considered at review) include (i.e. rentalise) tenant's fixtures and fittings?

8.8 The standard of repair

The appropriate standard of repair depends upon two points:

- The nature of the area in which the property is situated and the type of building in question. Is it in a post-industrial hinterland with decaying buildings or a newly constructed business park?

- Applying the circumstances as at the date on which the lease was granted (as opposed to any other date).

Therefore, as Lord Esher MR said in *Proudfoot v Hart* [1890] 25 QBD 42, 'the state of repair necessary for a house in Grosvenor Square would be wholly different from the state of repair necessary for a house in Spitalfields' (albeit that Spitalfields has changed dramatically since the nineteenth century!).

It should be emphasised that there must be some state of disrepair; just because something is old, provided it works, there is usually no implied requirement to carry out preventative works [*Mason v TotalFinaElf* [2003] 3 EGLR 91]. This should also be considered in the light of the position on inherent defects.

8.9 Inherent defects

There is a common misconception that where there is an inherent defect in a building the tenant is not responsible (either directly, or indirectly via the service charge). This misconception may have arisen from the (perfectly correct) proposition that, where an inherent defect is not causing any damage, the tenant does not have to remedy the inherent defect – in the absence of any specific wording to the contrary. Secondly, it is often associated with another (again correct) principle that, in complying with the repairing covenant, the tenant should not be required to 'improve' the property, to give back to the landlord more/something better than that which the landlord demised. In the leading case on this point [*Post Office v Aquarius Properties Ltd* [1987] 1 All ER 1055], a basement was flooded due to defective tanking, but the tenant did not need to remedy the defective tanking as there was no actual damage caused by the flood. However, if there has been damage, the tenant will normally be required to remedy the actual damage, but not necessarily the cause – unless the only way to remedy the damage is to remedy the inherent defect as well.

So, the tenant will normally be required to remedy inherent defects where this is required in order to effect a repair, even though it could be argued that the tenant is 'improving' the demise. Where there is no disrepair then, normally, the tenant will not be under a liability to remedy an inherent defect save, possibly, where there is an obligation to keep the property in good condition, as discussed in section 8.10 below.

Applying these points to contamination existing at the start of the lease: a normal repairing covenant would not require a tenant to clean up any such contamination, (but there may be other provisions in the lease which could require clean up, regardless – see Chapter 12), as any remediation would result in the tenant 'improving' the demise and, just because the land/buildings may be contaminated, this does not mean that they are not in 'repair'.

Similar rules apply where a landlord has an obligation to repair common parts. Where the landlord has no contractual obligation to carry out such repairs, and assuming there are no express words in the lease to the contrary, there will be no claim in this regard in nuisance. Therefore, where the inherent defect (such as water ingress) causes damage to demised premises the landlord will not be liable [*Jackson v JH Watson Property Investment Limited* [2008] EWHC 14 (Ch)].

8.10 Repair contrasted with 'condition'

Many repairing clauses refer to the tenant keeping the property in 'good condition'. This is not the same as 'good repair'. A property can be in good repair, but in poor condition. A property could be very damp and suffer from condensation; this would not trigger the repairing obligation but the damp condensation would have to be treated where the tenant has to keep the property in 'good condition' [*Quick v Taff-Ely Borough Council* [1986] QB 809].

In other words, the obligation to keep in good condition can require works to be carried out even if there is no disrepair.

8.11 Decoration

In addition to the repairing covenant, in most leases there will be a specific covenant to decorate the property.

A typical decoration covenant may be:

> 'The tenant will once in every fifth year and also during the last year of the term (however determined) paint all the inside walls, ceilings, wood and metal work and other inside parts of the Property and all additions with [two coats of] good quality paint.'

The covenant will often go on to require the tenant to:

> 'clean and treat the inside walls and all doors and windows and grain varnish and colour the inside wood of the Property previously so grained and varnished.'

Anomalies do arise where the draughtsman has paid little attention to the design of the building; for instance, reference is often made to 'painting' and 'staining' property which is neither painted nor stained in the first place.

Many decoration covenants are specific as to how regularly the property must be decorated and, strictly speaking, failure to decorate, when required, will be a breach of covenant.

Some leases may link the decorating year to the rent review dates, so as to gain the benefit of the assumption that the hypothetical lease premises are newly redecorated. A more pragmatic approach is just to state that redecoration must be 'as often as reasonably necessary' and 'in any event in the last [3] months of the term'.

The standard of decoration required by a decorating covenant would generally be judged by reference to similar factors which govern the standard of repair, i.e. the standard of workmanship and materials will depend on the age, character and locality of the building.

8.12 Power of entry to repair

The lease will usually contain provisions enabling the landlord to serve a notice requiring the tenant to comply with its repairing obligations, and failure to do so can result in the landlord entering the property and carrying out those works, charging the cost of those works to the tenant. This is known as a 'Jervis v Harris' clause.

8.12.1 *Jervis v Harris clauses: enforcing repair*

Given the expense and uncertainty of dilapidations claims (particularly in respect of the quantum of damages recoverable – see the 'Limitation on dilapidations damages' section of this chapter), landlords may consider not waiting until the end of the lease and, instead, threaten to exercise their right of entry to carry out material works and (if they do so) to charge the costs incurred back to the tenant as a debt (rather than as a claim for damages), assuming the lease has been so drafted to allow for this option: many are so drafted.

This option (a 'Jervis v Harris' clause) enables the landlord to avoid arguments over whether the value of its interest has diminished and the amount of damages – see below as to why this is important – but timing is crucial, as the initial notice has to be served so as to allow enough time for the tenant to comply and for the landlord then to be able to do the works before the end of the term if the tenant fails to do so.

Depending on the wording of the landlord's right of entry to carry out repairs:

- The statutory ceiling on damages imposed by section 18(1) of the *Landlord and Tenant Act* 1927 (damages limited to the effect of the breach on the value of the landlord's interest) may not apply to the cost of the works carried out by the landlord, enabling the landlord to avoid this statutory 'cap' – as the landlord's claim is for a debt, not damages.

- The landlord is not caught by section 146 of the *Law of Property Act* 1925 and so the clause can be used (subject to the above), at any time during the lease, without having to comply with the various notice procedures, which are described in Chapter 14.

However, this self-help remedy is not without its issues and risks:

- It imposes a duty on the landlord to take reasonable care to see that visitors and tenants are reasonably safe from personal injury (or damage to property) caused by the lack of repair, of which the landlord is, or ought to be, aware – section 4(4) of the *Defective Premises Act* 1972.

- The tenant could refuse to allow the landlord to use the utility supplies.

- The tenant may subsequently argue that the landlord did works badly and/or they were outside the extent of the repairing covenant.

For these (and other reasons), although the provision is in most leases, in practice it is more often threatened than applied.

8.13 Yielding up and reinstatement

The 'yielding up' covenant should be considered in conjunction with the repairing and alterations covenants – although it is a distinct obligation. Secondly, licences for alterations often try to expand on these obligations. The reinstatement obligation may be inferred from the wording of the 'yielding up' covenant or expressly covered in a separate clause.

An example of some standard wording for the 'yielding up' covenant:

> 'The Tenant will at the expiration or sooner determination of the term quietly yield up to the Landlord the premises (including all additions and improvements made to the premises) in such good and substantial repair and condition consistent with the due performance of the covenants in the Lease to repair and decorate.'

The yielding up covenant imposes obligations specific to the end of the term (however the term ends, e.g. by actual expiry of the term granted, forfeiture or surrender). A yielding up covenant may impose two separate obligations on the tenant. The first would be to deliver up vacant possession and the second is that, at that time, the property must be repaired and decorated in accordance with the tenant's obligations in the lease. This is despite that fact that a repairing covenant will apply throughout the term: however, a decorating covenant will often only 'bite' on specific dates (e.g. every three years).

The yielding up covenant (which may also be repeated or extended in a licence for alterations) may well extend to a requirement that the tenant reinstates any alterations made to the property during the lease term – whether or not consent was required or obtained at the time they were carried out.

As a general point, unless there is an express statement to the contrary, a tenant is not normally under an obligation to remove 'fixtures'. (The obligation to yield up vacant possession does imply an obligation to remove 'chattels' – as opposed to fixtures – being loose items, including carpets, which belong to the tenant.) This general point can cease to apply where the tenant has to reinstate alterations – where the fixture is caught by the interpretation of the covenant relating to alterations.

Sometimes the requirement to reinstate will be introduced by 'if the landlord reasonably requires' – what is reasonable will depend upon the circumstances: if the alterations add to the value of the property or the cost of reinstatement is wholly disproportionate to any increase in value which would result from the reinstatement are two examples of where it may be considered to be unreasonable to require reinstatement – where the landlord has to act reasonably.

The requirement to reinstate will often be linked to the landlord serving a notice on the tenant requiring reinstatement. In such circumstances, although the legal position is far from clear, the common sense advice would be that the landlord should serve such notice within a reasonable time, so as to provide the tenant with enough time to reinstate before the expiry of the term. (If the landlord leaves service of notice to the last day of the term, say, does the tenant have rights to remain in the premises after the term to do the works?

Serving notice in good time avoids this and other issues arising.) The Lease Code suggests that the landlord should provide at least six months prior notice.

As noted in 8.15 below, a claim by a landlord for breach of a covenant to reinstate is not covered by a pure dilapidations claim (they are often confused) and, therefore, is not subject to the limitations imposed on dilapidations claims.

The claim will be based on a damages claim under common law – the actual loss suffered by the landlord and whether it is reasonable for the landlord to carry out the reinstatement works. The question of 'reasonableness' will be viewed in the context of the reduction in value (if any) of the landlord's reversionary interest.

The Lease Code states that, as a general principle, 'tenants should only be obliged to give the premises back at the end of their lease in the same condition as they were in at its grant'.

8.14 Dilapidations

A landlord can serve a schedule of dilapidations at any time during the lease term (as well as for a while afterwards), itemising repair works required so as to ensure compliance with the repairing covenant.

The Lease Code suggests that landlords should serve a schedule of dilapidations (where applicable) at least six months before the end of the lease and notify the tenant of any further dilapidations as soon as practicable thereafter. This time period ties in with the suggestion, in the Lease Code, that tenants should only be required to remove alterations at the end of the lease, where it is reasonable to do so and that the landlords should provide notice of their requirements at least six months before the end of the lease.

The cost of compliance with a schedule cannot exceed the sum representing the decrease in value of the landlord's interest in the property relating to the lack of repair. However, that limitation does not apply, for instance, to the costs associated with the reinstatement of the property at the end of the lease (by the removal of tenant's fixtures and fittings and alterations) and general redecoration.

Depending on the original length and unexpired term of the lease and on the nature of any disrepair, there may be statutory restrictions on the landlord enforcing repairing obligations against the tenant. An order for specific performance of a repairing covenant is available in principle but is rarely granted, especially where the landlord has alternative remedies [*Rainbow Estates v Tokenhold* [1998] 2 All ER 860].

The *Leasehold Property (Repairs) Act* 1938 provides that where there is 'a lease for a term of no less than seven years with three years or more remaining unexpired at the relevant time', the landlord must serve on the tenant a notice pursuant to section 146 of the *Law of Property Act* 1925. Such a notice must inform the tenant that it may serve a counter-notice. If the tenant does serve a counter-notice within 28 days, leave of the court must be obtained by the landlord before it can forfeit or sue for damages.

When considering a dilapidations clause, the first stage is to establish the nature and extent of the tenant's breaches of the repair/decorations/alterations covenants; then establish the appropriate remedy for each breach; the third stage is to consider the breaches and the proposed remedies and work out what is reasonable in the circumstances. This process will include considering:

- the age, character and locality of the premises at the date of the lease – is what is being required reasonable?

- the relative costs of the alternatives;

- the practicalities of repair;

- compliance with current statute; in particular the Building Regulations.

Most schedules of dilapidations are served towards, or shortly after, the end of the lease. Each case will be decided on its facts, but some general principles can be highlighted:

- as with the standard repairing obligation, there has to be an element of 'disrepair', e.g. the fact that premises have an asbestos roof does not, of itself, justify total replacement of the roof;

- replacement can only be reasonably required where repair is not reasonably practicable – although some leases try to get around this point by having an express covenant to replace 'old' fixtures with new at the end of the term;

- if a covenant can be observed in two ways, the tenant can choose the cheaper option; the same principle applies to the landlord where it undertakes matters which the tenant should have done before expiry of the term – the landlord does not have to do works in the cheapest way possible;

- the Dilapidations Protocol and RICS Guideline Notes should be followed – see below;

- where possible, mediation or other dispute resolution procedures should be explored.

8.15 Limitation on dilapidations damages

Under section 18(1) of the *Landlord and Tenant Act* 1927, the damages for breach of a *repairing* covenant [emphasis added] shall not exceed the reduction in the value of the landlord's interest as a result of the breach.

If the evidence is that the premises are likely to be redevelopeed, the tenant's liability for repairs will be limited to the amount that an incoming developer is likely to spend on necessary remedial repairs when carrying out its redevelopment [*Ravengate Estates Ltd v (1) Horizon Housing Group Ltd (2) Persons unknown* [2007] EWCA Civ 1368].

Similarly, where the tenant's subtenant remains in occupation following the end of the tenant's lease (and where the subtenant is subject to the same repairing obligations as the tenant), the landlord will not be entitled to substantial damages for breach of the tenant's repairing obligations in the head-lease [*Lyndendown Ltd v Vitamol Ltd* [2007] EWCA Civ 826], on the basis that the landlord will have a full dilapidations claim against the subtenant.

It should be noted that the statutory protection afforded by this section does not apply to a covenant to reinstate alterations, as opposed to repair, or to remove fixtures. Furthermore, the limitation extends not just to the cost of works but also VAT costs, and fees and loss of rent; none of which will be recoverable save to the extent that they are reflected in the diminution in the value of the landlord's reversion.

No damages can be recovered where it is likely that the premises will be demolished or substantially altered so as to render any repair work irrelevant.

Damages for breaches of non-repairing covenants are limited to the amount actually lost by the landlord. However, the cases on dilapidations do not always make a clear distinction; in some cases the award of damages will be the actual cost of doing the work and in others the drop in value.

This tension can be explained by a quotation from Dowding and Reynolds: *Dilapidations: The Modern Law and Practice* (3rd revised edition, 2004):

'If the court is satisfied that the works have been or will be done, it may be ready in practice to draw the inference that this is the reasonable course, so that damages will be assessed by reference to the cost incurred or to be incurred. Conversely, where the claimant has not done the work for which he claims and does not intend to do so, the burden may in practice be on him to show why the cost should nonetheless be awarded.'

The above quote from page 703 of Dilapidations: Modern Law and Practice, by Nicholas Dowding and Kirk Reynolds, published by Sweet & Maxwell in 2004, is reproduced with permission.

Ultimately, it will generally come down to a matter of evidence: if a landlord spends £x on repairs which a tenant should have carried out, that will be an actual loss and a sound basis for a claim. However, where a landlord has no intention to carry out the repair works, the courts will place little or no reliance upon a costed schedule of works as it is of little relevance to establishing the diminution in the value of the landlord's reversionary interest – valuation evidence should also be provided.

In addition, the landlord may be able to claim for loss of rent for the period during which the landlord is carrying out the remedial works – the success of this claim will depend upon the market circumstances: where the market for that particular property is over supplied or otherwise sluggish the courts will be slow to countenance such a claim – the point being that even if the property had been returned in good repair it would not have been let any earlier [*Marchday Group plc v BT plc* [2003] EWHC 2627 (TCC)].

8.16 Dilapidations protocol at the end of the lease

Some of the problems arising in respect of dilapidations are addressed in the latest edition of the Property Litigation Association's protocol, which was published in May 2008. The protocol sets out a 'standard' timetable for exchanging information relevant to a claim for dilapidations at the end of a lease. It also outlines a basic process that should be followed by the professionals in these circumstances. Whilst the timetable is not mandatory (and, like many other protocols has not been formally adopted by the government), there can be adverse cost implications for a defaulting party in any subsequent court proceedings. Reference should also be made to the RICS *Dilapidations* guidance note, the most recent edition of which was published in June 2008 and which provides further guidance on dealing with claims at any time during the lease.

The aim of the protocol is to set standards for the content of schedules and claims, and, in particular, the conduct of pre-action negotiations, thereby increasing the number of pre-action settlements. If the protocol is not followed it could result in an adverse costs order. The basic time frame and structure of the protocol can be summarised as follows:

- the schedule of dilapidations should: (i) set out the breaches of covenant (distinguishing between works of repair, reinstatement and redecoration), (ii) detail the works required to comply with the lease and (iii) set out the landlord's costings of the works;

- the schedule should include an endorsement by the surveyor who prepared the schedule confirming that: (i) all works set out are reasonably required in order to put the premises in repair; (ii) full account has been taken of the landlord's intentions for the property at or shortly after the termination of the lease; and (iii) the costs quoted for such works are reasonable;

- the claim (this is different to the schedule) should set out and substantiate the monetary sum the landlord is claiming as damages for the tenant's breaches of covenant and should be limited to the landlord's actual loss;

- the schedule and claim should be served within 56 days of the end of the lease – if a schedule has been served before the end of the lease, the landlord should confirm at the end of the lease whether that schedule stands and, if not, serve a further schedule;

- the tenant should respond within 56 days of service and the parties should meet within 28 days of the response – the protocol promoting alternative dispute resolution as a means of resolving any issues, with court proceedings viewed as a last resort;

- if proceedings are likely then a 'section 18 valuation' will need to be prepared (although this is not usually necessary if the landlord has already done the works) – this valuation assesses the landlord's losses relating to the breach of the repairing obligations, capping them at the diminution in value to the landlord's reversionary interest;

- the tenant should respond to the landlord's section 18 valuation within 56 days of receipt;

- court proceedings issued.

8.17 The Lease Code

The Lease Code suggests that the repairing liability should be 'appropriate to the length of the term and the condition of the premises'.

What this points at is, for instance:

- agreeing a schedule of condition, so that the tenant only has to keep the property in the condition as evidenced by that schedule – the Lease Code goes so far as to state that 'unless expressly stated in the heads of terms, tenants should only be obliged to give the premises back at the end of their lease in the same condition as they were in at its grant';

- excluding liability for certain 'major' repairs, e.g. the replacement of plant or of a roof. This is especially the case where dealing with short term leases.

8.18 Points to consider

- Check that the wording and lease plan clearly define and describe what is covered by the 'demise'!
- Some leases include tenant's fixtures and fittings in the demise – should the tenant be under an obligation to the landlord to repair their own items?
- Always consider whether the client should have a survey of the property carried out before proceeding. If a survey is carried out, then consider whether a schedule can be prepared which can be incorporated in the lease ('a schedule of condition'); the tenant's repairing liability could then be qualified by making it clear that the liability does not extend to keeping the property in any better state and condition than it is in, as evidenced by the schedule of condition. The schedule can be a photographic or written schedule, or both.
- Schedules of condition may well lose their effectiveness when linked to a long lease – for instance, at some point during the lease patch repairs of an already defective part of the demise will become uneconomic and more material work will be required, regardless of the schedule.
- If advising a tenant taking an assignment of a lease (especially where the lease only has a few years left to run), a survey will be a useful way to establish the tenant's potential liability under the repairing covenant and may enable the purchaser/tenant to negotiate a reduction in the price or a payment from the seller/tenant.

- The landlord's insuring responsibility should extend to the full list of 'insured risks'; (an example of some standard wording is set out in Chapter 7). If there is a gap (for instance because the definition only covers fire or does not extend to acts of terrorism), then the tenant will normally be responsible; see Chapter 7 (Insurance) for more information. Where there is a gap then the parties should ensure that the insurance arrangements are clarified.

- Advise the client to obtain an engineer's report where the tenant's repairing obligation extends to the repair and maintenance of any expensive plant and equipment, e.g. lifts and air conditioning. If so, the client should also take out its own insurance policy for such items where appropriate, provided that the landlord is not obliged to insure them under the buildings policy.

- Where negotiating an FRI lease, consider whether the lease should specifically oblige the landlord (where the landlord repairs) or the tenant to repair inherent defects.

- Under the terms of the lease the tenant will be expressly or implicitly responsible for any asbestos related issues in respect of the property – the landlord will be liable for the common parts. The basic responsibility (which is imposed via legislation, if not directly in the lease) is to 'ensure that a suitable and sufficient risk assessment is carried out as to whether asbestos is or is liable to be in the premises'. The first step is, therefore, to check that an appropriate assessment has been carried out and any appropriate action taken.

- Assess and advise the client on the potential cost or charge of complying with legislative requirements (bearing in mind much of the legislation is new and still not fully understood), e.g. adapting the building to ensure satisfactory access for the disabled and compliance with asbestos regulations.

- Where the client is taking a lease of a recently constructed building, it may well be appropriate to obtain warranties (or acknowledgements of third party rights) from the building contractor and professional team involved, as well as product guarantees for such items as lifts and boilers, or advise the client's solicitors to ensure that the lease specifically excludes any liability for 'inherent defects' arising in respect of the original construction of the building. If this is not done then the tenant may find itself liable to repair a defect in the original construction of the building.

- At the end of the lease, the landlord will prepare a 'schedule of dilapidations' which will list all outstanding items of repair and which will either require the payment of compensation or that the tenant carries out the works itself. If advising a client taking up a lease which only has a few years left to run, always consider what potential liability there may be in respect of such a schedule.

- In preparing a schedule of condition, landlords should not rely only on estimated costs schedules, especially where it is difficult to identify the actual repair costs (where the landlord subsequently does works) or where the actual repair work is not carried out – clear valuation evidence must be provided.

9 Alterations

9.1 Overview

Most leases distinguish between structural and non-structural alterations and exterior and internal alterations. Generally (especially where dealing with retail units), tenants are not able to carry out any structural alterations and certain types of external alterations, although leases of larger buildings are becoming more flexible over structural alterations.

Internal non-structural alterations, alterations to any shop fascia and alterations to signage and electrical wiring are usually permitted (sometimes, subject to the landlord's consent, such consent not to be unreasonably withheld or delayed). As noted below, the Lease Code promotes a more relaxed position, with no consent being required for internal non-structural alterations.

The general trend now, in particular with more sophisticated tenants, is for leases to permit certain types of alteration without the landlord's consent: usually this will cover internal demountable partitioning but often it will go further and allow internal non-structural alterations to be carried out and signage and shopfronts in accordance with the tenant's corporate image/style to be installed, without consent. However, the tenant should still be required to remove these alterations at the end of the lease and provide details of the works before they start.

The temptation for the landlord may be only to allow for minor alterations but an unduly restrictive lease could have an adverse effect on rent review, with the tenant arguing for a discount.

The landlord will usually be able to recover its professional costs incurred in considering any application for consent.

Leases normally require the tenant to remove any alterations carried out by it at the end of the term (whether or not those alterations required consent). Tenants may well seek to qualify this by making it clear that the reinstatement should only be where and to the extent it is reasonable, i.e. reflecting the true position under statute [as provided by section 19(2) of the *Landlord and Tenant Act* 1927] and also bringing the lease into line with section 8 of the Lease Code. An absolute obligation to reinstate may well have an adverse impact on rent review – unless expressly disregarded at rent review.

The alterations covenant should not be considered in a vacuum; there are other clauses which may need to be considered at the same time:

- the covenant relating to planning applications often requires the landlord's approval prior to the application being lodged and, sometimes again, prior to implementation – this could mean that although the alterations themselves do not need approval, the planning application for them does!

- the tenant covenants to comply with the building insurer's requirements: the insurer may have issues with the alterations which have to be addressed;

- the tenant will, in any event, have to ensure that the works comply with health and safety and building regulations.

9.2 Standard wording

There is a danger here in stating that there is such a
thing as 'standard' wording – in the case of the
alterations covenant, as with many others, much will
depend upon the type of property and the landlord's
management intentions, but the following wording
follows a form often encountered:

'(A) Not without the consent of the Landlord (such
consent not to be unreasonably withheld or delayed)
to make any erections, alterations or additions to the
Premises, save that consent shall not be required for
the following ('Permitted Alterations'):
(i)   internal non-structural alterations or
        additions or removals (which shall include
        but not be limited to the installation,
        alteration or removal of non-structural
        demountable partitioning or check-out
        counters or other readily removable
        equipment);
(ii)   the alteration, removal or installation of
        signage, placards, flags, poles, advertising
        hoardings or billboards on the exterior of the
        Premises;
(iii)   the replacement of shop fronts and fascias
        with a new shop front and/or fascia of similar
        quality to that being replaced and which is in
        line with the Tenant's national corporate
        identity where there are no structural
        alterations required;
(iv)   alterations and additions to the internal
        electrical installations, air conditioning,
        heating, cooling and ventilation systems and
        electrical circuits and equipment;
where the following provisions are complied with.

(B) To deposit with the Landlord detailed drawings and specifications (including any variations) showing any significant revisions to the layout of the Premises not later than seven days prior to commencing any Permitted Alterations and within twenty-one days of their completion to deposit with the Landlord two sets of 'as built' drawings (and, if required, in respect of the works undertaken, a copy of the updated health and safety file).

(C) Unless the Landlord directs otherwise in writing, to remove any alterations and additions made to the Premises before the end of the Term and reinstate the same.

(D) To carry out all erections, alterations, additions and installations in a good and workmanlike manner with good quality and suitable materials strictly in accordance with all licences, approvals, permissions and consents causing as little nuisance, damage or inconvenience to the Landlord or the owners or occupiers of any neighbouring property as reasonably possible.'

'Alteration' has to be interpreted in the context of the clause and the lease itself; in many cases a restriction on 'alterations', on its own, will not prevent a sign being affixed to the exterior of the property, nor would it prohibit replacement of plant within the property. Fixing signage will however be prevented if the clause prevents the tenant from 'cutting or maiming' the walls of the property and preventing 'additions' may also prevent signage and could extend to, say, the installation of an ATM in the frontage.

9.3 What is meant by structure?

There is no settled legal definition as to what constitutes the 'structure' of a building; in the absence of clear and unambiguous wording in the lease, the meaning will be determined, in each case, as a matter of fact and degree, depending on the terms of the particular lease, viewed in the overall context. There is case law indicating that it is not limited to the load bearing elements of the building, but includes elements which are material or significant in the overall construction; the structure extends to most parts of the building which provide it with its essential appearance, stability and shape. [*Irvine v Moran* [1991] 1 EGLR 261].

For example, plate glass might not normally be considered as part of the structure, but where a modern building has been built using glass on a steel frame, the glass forming the outside walls of the building – although not being used in any load-bearing capacity – will still be part of the main 'structure'.

9.4 Landlord's consent

If a lease does not prevent a particular alteration being made, then the tenant is free to carry out that alteration. However, any well drafted lease will make it very clear what can and cannot be done. The lease will contain an absolute prohibition against certain alterations and will then state that certain alterations require landlord's approval. If that is all the lease states (i.e. that landlord's consent is required), then it is implied that that approval cannot be unreasonably withheld – section 19(2) of the *Landlord and Tenant Act* 1927 – and this implied term cannot be excluded by the lease. Where there is an absolute prohibition against alterations, the terms implied by statute will not apply.

The Lease Code suggests that a landlord should normally request any additional information required from tenants within five working days of receipt of the application. Furthermore, the landlord should 'make decisions on consents for alterations within 15 working days of receiving full information'.

9.5 Reasonable refusal

There are very few cases providing guidance as to the circumstances where a landlord can be reasonable in withholding consent, but the following general principles may assist.

- If the proposed alterations affect the parts of the building outside the tenant's demise then the landlord can refuse consent simply on the ground that the tenant does not have the necessary right of access or the actual area otherwise under its control.

- If the proposed alterations could have a detrimental effect on the structural integrity of the building, then the landlord would be reasonable in refusing consent. However, this may well not be the case if the tenant is able to provide structural engineer's evidence to the contrary – which the landlord is able to rely upon.

- Where the application relates to alterations under the DDA some additional points should be considered – see, for instance, the commentary in Chapter 12 below.

One of the few recent cases [*Iqbal v Thakrar* [2004] EWCA Civ 592] on reasonableness and consent for alterations has set out some further general principles:

- The requirement for the consent is to protect the landlord from the tenant carrying out alterations which damage the landlord's property interests.

- A landlord is not entitled to refuse consent on grounds which have nothing to do with its property interests.

- It is for the tenant to show that the landlord has unreasonably withheld its consent to the tenant's application and the tenant has to provide full details of its proposed works so that the landlord has sufficient information to come to an informed decision.

- The landlord does not have to justify its conclusions which led it to refuse consent if they were conclusions which might be reached by a reasonable landlord in the particular circumstances.

- It may be reasonable for the landlord to refuse consent to an alteration for the purpose of converting the premises for a proposed use, even if that use is not forbidden by the lease. Whether such refusal is reasonable or unreasonable depends on all the circumstances.

- A landlord need usually only consider its own interests but there may be cases where it would be disproportionate for a landlord to refuse consent having regard to the effects on itself and on the tenant respectively.

- Consent cannot be refused on grounds of pecuniary loss alone: the proper course for the landlord to take in these circumstances would be to grant consent subject to compensation being paid.

- In each case it is a question of fact depending on all the circumstances whether the landlord, having regard to the actual reasons for refusal, acted reasonably.

9.6 Statutory provisions permitting alterations and compensation for improvements: the 1927 Act

Even where a lease seemingly prevents the tenant from carrying out certain alterations, statutory provisions may help a tenant, faced by a refusal.

The statutory provisions are set out in section 3 of the *Landlord and Tenant Act* 1927 and override any contrary provisions in the lease. The section is seldom applied in practice, although it is sometimes used as a way of putting pressure on the landlord to agree to alterations.

If the tenant wishes to carry out 'improvements' it can serve a prior notice on the landlord of its intention and, if the landlord objects, the tenant can apply to the court for authority to carry out the improvements. The court can authorise the improvements if:

- they are likely to add to the letting value of the property at the end of the term;

- they are reasonable and appropriate to the property; and

- they will not reduce the value of any other property owned by the landlord.

The court can make modifications and impose conditions.

If the landlord does not object to the proposed improvements within three months of the notice, the tenant can carry out the improvements without the need for any further landlord's consent, regardless of the wording in the lease. Alternatively, the landlord can offer to do the works itself in return for a reasonable increase in rent.

The 1927 Act also enables a tenant to claim compensation for improvements carried out under section 3 of the 1927 Act. The reason for its lack of use may be, in part, because tenants who claim capital allowances for qualifying improvements could be subject to a balancing charge for tax on any compensation received at the end of the term under the 1927 Act. In order for a claim to be made, the tenant:

- should hold a certificate confirming that the improvements were properly completed at the time – this certificate would have been issued by the

landlord, failing that the court – however the lack of
a certificate may not, of itself, prevent a claim being
made;

- must be able to show that the right was not excluded
by any licence for alterations – although the 1927
Act itself cannot be excluded, the drafting of the
licence – for instance by requiring reinstatement at
the end of the term – may result in the
'improvements' falling outside the terms of the 1927
Act;

- as noted above, must show that the improvements
(which have to be physical) add to the letting value
of the property at the end of the term, are reasonable
and suitable to the character of the property and do
not diminish the value of any adjacent property
owned by the landlord;

- must be able to establish that the improvements were
not carried out under a contractual obligation for
valuable consideration;

- must be in possession of the property at the end of
the term and (probably) not applying for a new lease
– there are strict time limits for making the
application, which depend on how the lease is
terminated; forfeiture of the lease will not preclude
an application for compensation under the 1927 Act;

- must be able to establish that the 'improvements'
were carried out in accordance with the 1927 Act
and the notice provisions were complied with.

The amount of compensation claimable is the lesser of
the net value directly attributable to the improvement at
the end of the term or the cost of carrying out those
works at the end of the term. The amount claimable may
be substantially reduced (if not nullified) if the landlord
intends to carry out material alterations after expiry of
the lease.

9.7 Other statutes

There are other statutes and statutory provisions which can require or enable a tenant to do works (and empower the court to vary a lease), including the *Regulatory Reform (Fire Safety) Order* 2005 and the *Disability Discrimination Act* 1995, as amended by the *Disability Discrimination Act* 2005 (DDA).

Under the DDA there are specific provisions (which override anything to the contrary in the lease) whereby it is to be implied that a tenant can make reasonable alterations with the landlord's prior written consent, such consent not to be unreasonably withheld.

A landlord is required to give its consent within 21 days of a proper/complete application or, if the landlord has to obtain the consent of a superior landlord, then 14 days after receipt of the superior landlord's consent. If the landlord fails to comply with this requirement, they are deemed to have refused consent.

The landlord is able to refuse consent if it can establish reasonable grounds for refusal. The reasonable grounds for refusal are limited. Four conditions are stated to be reasonable, and these relate to planning, to approval of plans, inspection by the landlord and payment of the landlord's reasonable costs for providing its consent.

There is neither direction as to how the works should be treated on rent review nor any mention of the payment of costs for inspection by the landlord (only costs for approval), nor provisions for reinstatement.

We suspect that it would be deemed to be reasonable for the landlord to be able to charge for inspection fees, bearing in mind the fact that the condition of inspection is expressly stated to be reasonable. The obligation to reinstate may be viewed as unreasonable unless the alterations are 'individual' – linked to that particular tenant – and would be of no use to another tenant. The issue of rent review will be determined by reference to the actual wording in the rent review provisions: most rent reviews assume that the tenant has complied with statutory obligations and disregard tenant's improvements – so it may be difficult for a tenant to argue for a discount on the grounds that DDA works would need to be carried out – under the hypothetical lease – and therefore there should be a discount.

9.8 Construction (Design and Management) Regulations 2007

The *Construction (Design and Management) Regulations 2007* (CDM) replaced the previous (1994) regulations with effect from 6 April 2007. Anyone who enters into a project (being a project which is, or includes, construction work) carried out in Great Britain, which includes construction work in the course of their business, needs to be aware of the burden falling upon them as a result of the regulations. Construction work is defined very widely and includes any building, civil engineering, or engineering construction work.

The regulations apply to works of maintenance, alterations, repair and fitting out. Depending on whether or not a project is 'notifiable' under the regulations, more onerous obligations may be placed upon the parties involved.

A key feature of the regulations is the duty on the 'client' (i.e. persons who retain others to undertake construction work, or who do the work themselves) to appoint a competent person as CDM coordinator, to manage the health and safety risks in respect of the project. In default of such appointment, the client is deemed to be the CDM coordinator.

A further requirement of the regulations is that a health and safety file is maintained for the works – essentially, a set of plans, manuals, papers and information relating to the building, the plant and the equipment.

Where the regulations apply, the landlord is no longer able to make the tenant fully responsible for all obligations under the regulations and needs to be aware of its own obligations as 'client' for any works undertaken.

9.9 The Lease Code

The Lease Code recommends that the landlord's control over alterations be no more than is necessary to protect the value of the property and any nearby premises belonging to the landlord. It then goes on to state that:

> 'Internal non-structural alterations should be notified to landlords but should not need landlords' consent unless they could affect the services or systems in the building.
>
> Landlords should not require tenants to remove permitted alterations and make good at the end of the lease, unless reasonable to do so. Landlords should notify tenants of their requirements at least six months before the termination date.'

9.10 Points to consider

- If acting for a tenant, ensure that the works which need to be done are fully within the property: if the works involve areas outside the property (e.g. the installation of air conditioning where the condensers are on an exterior wall outside the property boundary or lift plant and machinery on a flat roof where the definition of the property does not include the airspace), then the lease must contain the necessary rights for that equipment to be placed there and subsequently maintained.

- When advising on the acquisition of an existing lease, always ensure that the lease plan accurately reflects the internal layout. If not, refer back to the lawyers, so that they can check that the appropriate consents were obtained for any alterations at the time as, otherwise, the landlord may require the removal of the alterations and reinstatement of the property.

- Conversely, acting for an investor buying property subject to a lease, ensure that all alterations have been properly documented and that there is no potential claim for compensation at the end of the lease term.

- Make sure that the landlord's consent to any proposed alterations (especially if they are structural alterations) has been or is obtained before proceeding.

- Before the client pays for any alteration ensure that either the Construction Industry Scheme does not apply or that the client is able to comply with it. This is a scheme which (in many circumstances) requires a contractor who obtains 'construction services' to contact HM Revenue and Customs (HMRC) before making any payment for such services. HMRC will then direct the payer how much tax should be deducted and accounted for in respect of the payments.

- Even if the tenant obtains the landlord's consent to the proposed alterations, the tenant may still need to obtain other consents, such as the building's insurer's consent, fire officer's approval, listed building consent and planning permission (which the landlord may also have to approve), before being able to start the works.

- As a 'rule of thumb', a tenant should allow for at least three to four weeks (from the time that the landlord receives full details of the proposed alterations) to put the licence for alterations in place – frequently it takes much longer.

- Even if consent to alterations is given, the lease (or licence for alterations) may allow the landlord to require the reinstatement of the property to its original configuration at the expiry or sooner determination of the lease – this can be costly (see the section on dilapidations in Chapter 8).

- A landlord may well seek to retain tight control over alterations which link in with adjacent premises – common examples are sprinklers, fire alarm systems and telecommunications cables which link into a 'communal' system.

User

10

10.1 Overview

The lease will only permit certain specified uses; the tenant should ensure that the permitted use is wide enough to cover the tenant's uses and that the permitted use clause does not conflict, and dovetails in, with any clauses dealing with planning and alterations, bearing in mind the fact that often a change of use will require planning consent and necessitate alterations to the property. (The tenant's solicitor should also check that there are no user (or other) restrictions on the landlord's title, including any superior lease.)

For instance, if a lease has a wide user clause, but an absolute prohibition against the tenant making or implementing any planning consent, the benefit of the wide user clause is reduced – if not nullified – where the change of use requires planning consent. By way of further example, if the lease allows structural subdivision (subject to consent), it may also be appropriate to allow change of use (subject to consent not to be unreasonably withheld), as well as subletting of part (subject to consent); if it only allows one without the others, the one permitted may be of very limited use.

Some leases have a very restricted permitted use clause and, although the permitted use may be sufficient for the tenant, the restrictions may make it very difficult for the tenant to assign or sublet the lease to a third party.

Provisions relating to use may also appear, in a slightly different guise, elsewhere in the lease: clauses preventing the tenant from committing a nuisance, annoyance or disturbance are common, as well as obligations to comply with regulations issued by the landlord from time to time – the regulations further limiting what can be done in the property.

If the lease refers to the tenant being able to change the use of property with the landlord's prior written consent, then the lease must state that the consent cannot be unreasonably withheld as, otherwise, the landlord can refuse consent to change of use for any reason.

Generally, from a tenant's point of view, it is best to have a certain amount of flexibility in the user clause so as to enable an assignment or sublease to proceed without too much difficulty and to take into account any possible changes in the operational requirements of the tenant.

10.2 Some standard wording

'Not to use the Property otherwise than for [ ] and/or for any other use or uses falling within use class(es) [   ] of the *Town and Country Planning (Use Classes) Order* 1987 (as enacted at the date of this Lease) as may have been previously approved by the Landlord, such approval not to be unreasonably withheld or delayed (the 'Permitted Use') and as ancillary to the Permitted Use, [storage, offices and staff canteen facilities].'

This wording is taken from a modern lease. However, some leases (especially those from 10 to 15 years, or more, ago), take the approach of listing out specific uses (as being the 'permitted use') and then stating that the tenant cannot use the property for any other purpose. They often then go on (usually, rather pointlessly) to list prohibited uses.

In interpreting what a particular use means, the courts will try to work out what the word would have meant to a commercial person who would have entered into that type of lease at the time the lease was completed – not the current meaning. The courts will prefer an ordinary meaning over a technical one. If there is still any doubt the courts will normally favour the tenant. [*Joint London Holdings Ltd v Mount Cook Land Ltd* [2005] EWHC 507 (Ch)]. For instance, 'victualler' in the 18th and 19th centuries referred to someone providing food; by the 1950s the term was normally applied to someone who ran a pub: so, depending upon the date of the lease, the term could prevent premises being used as a sandwich shop.

10.3 Ancillary uses

Some user clauses refer to certain specified ancillary uses: these uses are those which are incidental to the permitted use. As a general rule, this reference adds little, as it is normally implied that such uses would take place, e.g. a shop would normally have some back office and storage space and a staff toilet; however, where there is any doubt, there is no harm in making an express statement as to what ancillary uses may take place – especially where one would not normally expect that use: for instance, a private cinema/screening room in offices.

There is no definition of what is meant by 'ancillary use': something which takes up 10 per cent or less of the premises is likely to be considered as ancillary; if it takes up (say) 60 per cent or more it will almost certainly not be ancillary – and therefore could be in breach of the user clause.

10.4 The Use Classes Order and planning consent

The *Town and Country Planning (Use Classes) Order* 1987 (as amended) and the related provisions of Part 3 of The *Town and Country Planning (General Permitted Development) Order* 1995 (as amended) identify those changes of use for which a grant of planning permission will not be needed. While the Schedule to the 1987 Order sets these out in greater detail, the Use Classes are broadly as follows:

PART A

Class A1. Shops – retail sale of goods (other than hot food) and other similar specified 'retail-type' uses, in all cases provided to visiting members of the public.

Class A2. Financial and professional services – provided principally to visiting members of the public (to be contrasted with B1(a), which covers general offices).

Class A3. Restaurants and cafes – sale of food and drink for consumption on the premises.

Class A4. Drinking establishments – public house, wine bar or other drinking establishment.

Class A5. Hot food takeaways – sale of hot food for consumption off the premises.

PART B

Class B1. Business – offices (other than A2), research and development, and industrial processes, where any such uses can be carried on in a residential area without detriment to the amenity of the area.

Class B2. General industrial – industrial processes (other than B1).

Class B8. Storage or distribution – use as storage or distribution centre.

PART C

Class C1. Hotels – hotel, boarding house or guest house, without providing a significant element of personal care.

Class C2. Residential institutions – includes hospitals, nursing/care homes, residential schools and colleges.

Class C2A. Secure residential institutions – includes prisons, secure hospitals and military barracks.

Class C3. Dwelling houses – occupancy by single person, family, or up to six persons living as a single household.

PART D

Class D1. Non-residential institutions – includes nurseries, schools, museums, libraries, exhibition halls and places of public worship.

Class D2. Assembly and leisure – includes cinemas, bingo, concert and dance halls and other sports facilities.

There are a number of specific uses which are not within a Use Class and any change to such use will require planning permission; included among such uses are the sale of fuel for motor vehicles, motor vehicle sales showrooms, theatres, nightclubs and casinos (although a change from casino use to D2 is now permitted under the 1995 Order – see below).

As well as being able to switch (under planning law) between uses contained within any particular Use Class without the need for planning permission (although the lease may require landlord's consent to be obtained), the 1995 Order also makes specific provision for changes of use between certain of the Use Classes (in some cases, subject to restrictions (for example, as to the extent of the area affected) and/or fulfilling conditions). A summary of the permitted changes follows.

Permitted development: changes of use allowed between Use Classes		
FROM	*TO*	*Subject to specific restrictions/ conditions?*
A1	• Mixed A1 and single flat	Yes
A2	• A1 (where ground floor window display)	Yes
	• Mixed A1 and single flat (where ground floor window display)	Yes
	• Mixed A2 and single flat	Yes
A3	• A1 • A2	No No
A4	• A1 • A2 • A3	No No No
A5	• A1 • A2 • A3	No No No
B1	• B8	Yes – limited to or under 235 m² of floor space
B2	• B1 • B8	No Yes – limited to or under 235 m² of floor space

Permitted development: changes of use allowed between Use Classes		
B8	• B1	Yes – limited to or under 235 m² of floor space
Casino use	• D2	No

10.5 Lease drafting and the Use Classes Order

Although the Use Classes Order is part of the statutory framework governing the permitted use of a property under the planning legislation, it is also often used as a convenient shorthand to describe the use(s) that will be permitted under the terms of the lease itself (as illustrated in the standard wording above).

Where this is the case, care should be taken to ensure that the reference to the Use Class is expressly linked to the timing of the grant of the lease (see the approach taken in the standard wording above), since the scope of the Use Class referred to might change significantly as a result of any subsequent amendment made to the Order, which could seriously prejudice the landlord or the tenant, depending upon the circumstances.

(The draft standard wording set out above refers to the *Town and Country Planning (Use Classes) Order* 1987 and this was updated on 21 April 2005).

Where the lease refers to the 1987 Order, the first thing to consider is whether it is referring to the original 1987 Order or to an updated version of the Order (i.e. the 1987 Order taking into account the 2005 changes).

As covered in the draft standard wording above, many leases, either in the user clause itself or in the interpretation clause at the start of the lease, amend the standard position: normally a reference to legislation is taken to be the legislation as in force from time to time; however, with Use Classes landlords tend to prefer the certainty of tying that reference down to the Order in place at the time the lease was granted – so that subsequent legislative change does not have the effect of narrowing (or widening) the scope of the lease user clause.

Some leases do not make this distinction, in which case you could come across a lease where the reference is to, for example, Use Class A3, as in place from time to time: if the property was a pub at the time the lease was granted and the lease was granted before the 2005 changes to the Order, then technically the tenant will be in breach if it is continuing to use the property as a pub – which use is now within new Use Class A4. Commercially, the landlord is unlikely to take the point and will probably be keen to agree to a variation of the lease, widening the user clause to include A4 and thus reducing (if not avoiding) the potential negative effect on rent review.

10.6 Planning consent or lease consent?

A further obvious, but easily overlooked, point to note is that a clear distinction should be made between the use to which any planning permission (as supplemented by the operation of the 1987 and 1995 Orders) may allow the property to be put, and the use permitted under the terms of the lease.

The existence of a wide planning permission does *not* mean that that the tenant can necessarily put the demised premises to all such uses, since the lease user covenant may be more restrictive; conversely, a wide lease use covenant does not of itself imply or warrant that all (or indeed any!) such uses may be undertaken as a matter of planning law; for good measure, from a landlord's perspective, it is common to see an express provision excluding the possibility of any such warranty by the landlord in the lease.

10.7 Landlord's consent

If the lease refers to the tenant being able to change the use of property with the landlord's prior written consent, then the tenant should ensure that the lease states that the consent cannot be unreasonably withheld as, otherwise, the landlord can refuse consent to change of use for any reason. However, in these circumstances, statute states that a proviso will be deemed to apply (unless there are structural alterations involved) that a landlord (who has the ability under the lease to refuse consent but is minded to consent) cannot demand a premium or increase in rent for providing its consent; all the landlord can recover are its costs and a reasonable sum to cover any reduction in value in the premises, or any adjacent premises it owns [*Landlord and Tenant Act 1927* section 19(2)]. These provisions cannot be excluded.

If a lease is very restrictive, the tenant may be able to argue for a discount on rent review (as the lease is onerous). In one case, there was a highly restrictive user clause which stated that the premises could only be used as offices in connection with the tenant's business of consulting engineer. Accordingly, only consulting engineers could be hypothetical tenants: this reduced the rent from £130,000 pa to £89,000 pa [*Plinth Property Investments Ltd v Mott, Hay & Anderson* (1978) 249 EG 1167].

If the user clause is 'open', then this may result in a higher rent upon review (as a hypothetical tenant would be prepared to pay a higher rent for a more flexible lease).

10.8 Landlord's reasonable withholding of consent?

Assuming that the lease states that the landlord's consent is not to be unreasonably withheld (remember, there is no statutorily implied provision that where there is reference to consent it is not to be unreasonably withheld), when will it be reasonable for the landlord to withhold such consent? It is difficult to answer this question with any degree of certainty. The landlord does not have to give reasons for refusing consent (unlike for an assignment application), but in considering the application might have to consider the tenant's interests – see the example of the *Sportoffer* case below.

The onus is on the tenant to prove that the landlord is being unreasonable – and it is not enough to show that some landlords would provide their consent; the tenant has to show that no reasonable landlord would have acted in the way that that particular landlord was acting; this is a hard test to prove.

10.9 Securing a collateral advantage

At the same time, the landlord is not entitled to withhold consent in order to secure a 'collateral advantage' for himself; for instance, just because a landlord would prefer to see a retail use in a unit is not (*of itself*) enough to refuse change of use from a travel agency to building society – for example see the *Anglia* case below. However, if there are good estate management reasons for refusing consent, this will not necessarily be viewed as conflicting with that general principle.

The leading case on consent (although dealing with assignment, it is regarded as an authority for cases on change of use) is *International Drilling Fluids Ltd v Louisville Investments (Uxbridge) Ltd* [1985] EWCA Civ 3, where it was stated that a landlord is not entitled 'to refuse his consent … on grounds which have nothing to do with the relationship of landlord and tenant …'. As a general comment, the general principles governing 'reasonable refusal' for alterations and assignment can be extended to user.

10.10 Some examples

The following cases may provide some guidance when considering this point on behalf of a client – but they are of illustrative value, as each case will depend upon its own facts and the question of reasonableness will be one of 'fact', i.e. the facts of that particular case; for this reason, some of the examples below appear to be at odds with others. It also emphasises the danger of quoting case law when dealing with an application for change of use – for every case where it was reasonable for a landlord to refuse consent, there is usually a similar case where it was held to be unreasonable.

Background reasons	Case	Result
Lease allowed the business of precision engineering. Tenant wished to sublet part to a printing firm. Lease stated that consent would not be treated as being unreasonably withheld if proposed use conflicted with the landlord's interpretation of good estate management.	*Berenyi and another v Watford Borough Council* [1980] 2 EGLR 38	Unreasonable to refuse consent – the only reason given by the council was the (unjustified) ground of traffic difficulties. No evidence that the proposed use was considered or that it conflicted with good estate management.
Existing use as a travel and employment bureau or theatre and ticket agency. Proposed assignees wished to use the premises as a building society.	*Anglia Building Society v Sheffield City Council* [1983] 1 EGLR 57	Unreasonable to refuse consent – the council was trying to secure a collateral advantage by attempting to force a retail use on the premises in an effort to increase the rental value of the landlord's building.

Background reasons	Case	Result
Existing use as a doctor's surgery with residence. Proposed assignee travel agents occupied adjacent premises which had a shop front and wished to use the premises in question as offices for their retail business, by relying on a planning permission granted for retail use. The landlord objected as the premises were not suitable for retail use due to lack of street frontage leaving them potentially unmarketable.	*Warren and another v Marketing Exchange for Africa Ltd* [1988] 2 EGLR 247	Reasonable to refuse consent – no certainty that once use changed to retail, planning consent would be granted for a return to office use. Clearly, this would damage the landlord's reversionary interest.
Change of use from restaurant to an amusement hall with ancillary snack refreshments. The landlord was concerned that the change would reduce the value of the property – attracting vandals and detracting from the economic fabric of the immediate area.	*Tollbench v Plymouth City Council* [1988] 1 EGLR 79	Reasonable to refuse consent. Contrast this case with *Anglia* (above) – the change of use would have had a negative impact on the landlord's interest in the actual premises demised – rather than a positive impact on adjacent premises.
Proposed expansion of user to allow sale of electrical appliances as well as gas appliances already permitted. Landlord objected as it interfered with its background letting strategy and maintenance of a good tenant mix which was designed to benefit the tenants as well as protect the landlord's reversionary interest at rent reviews.	*Chelsfield MH Investments Ltd v British Gas plc* [1995] NPC 169	Reasonable to refuse consent – but note that the court indicated that its decision rested greatly on the presented legal arguments. Had the tenant actually challenged the reasonableness of the landlord's specific tenant mix policy the ruling might have been different.

Background reasons	Case	Result
A ground floor Regent Street unit was being used for retail use and proposals for assignment, change of use and alterations would subdivide it into retail and non-retail use.	*Crown Estate Commissioners v Signet Group plc and another* [1996] 2 EGLR 200	Reasonable to refuse consent – the Commissioners were entitled to consider the three proposals together and to pay attention to general estate management considerations relevant to the improvement of the (Regent Street) estate. A reduction in shop frontage was not in line with their desired, and published, long term policy aims.
Existing use as a golf club – application to change of use and alter to include swimming pool.	*Sportoffer Ltd v Erewash Borough Council* [1999] 3 EGLR 136	Reasonable to refuse consent – the landlord operated two fitness centres nearby and the proposal would compete. Estate management considerations were relevant. This case expands *Tollbench* (above) to where the proposed user would negatively impact the landlord's interest in adjoining premises. But note that the reasoning did not focus on the collateral advantage principle but rather on whether or not the refusal would result in 'sterilisation' of the tenant's business, so as oblige the landlord to take into account the tenant's interests. (The court felt this was not made out on the facts).
Premises used as a nightclub. Landlord refused consent to a subletting and change of use as a gym and health club as it was believed this use would diminish the value of the reversion.	*Luminar Leisure Ltd v Apostole* [2001] 3 EGLR 23	Unreasonable to refuse consent – whilst the ground for refusal (protection of a reversionary interest) was not challenged, the valuation report which the landlord relied upon was unsound, causing the refusal to be unreasonable.

Background reasons	Case	Result
The premises had previously been used as the University of Westminster's Students' Union. Previously, the landlord had refused consent for an application for planning permission for the premises to be used as offices, preferring educational use. (This refusal was found unreasonable but in the event, the planning application failed.) Subsequently, the tenant requested consent to use the premises for D1 use, it being clear that educational purposes were intended. The landlord owned a number of mixed use properties in the area and refused consent on the basis that the noise and disruption of an influx of students would damage its business interests and that an office development would be more suited to the area.	*London & Argyll Developments Ltd v Mount Cook Land Ltd* [2003] All ER (D) 104 (Jun)	Unreasonable to refuse consent – whilst the court indicated that the noise and disruption could be a relevant factor, the landlord had not requested enough information about the intended type of educational facility to sustain the argument. Further, the evidence did not support the objection that the area was an established office area. The landlord's general (inconsistent) conduct was also a factor.

Background reasons	Case	Result
Use of a new extension would compete with landlord's adjacent business – tenant wanted to extend hotel to cater for weddings and landlord ran an adjacent golf club which held weddings. In giving consent to alterations, the landlord attempted to impose a restriction limiting the use to management training conferences to protect their current weddings business and also to protect the future potential business avenue of holding conferences in general.	*Sargeant v Macepark (Whittlebury) Ltd* [2004] EWHC 1333 (Ch)	Unreasonable to refuse consent – the court accepted that the landlord was entitled to be protected against competition (weddings and functions) but here the required restriction on use went further than was reasonable as it precluded the tenant from pursuing activities which formed part of its usual (and already permitted) business. The landlord was not entitled to prevent the future possibility of the tenant entering into competition by running conferences. Significantly, the court interpreted *Sportoffer* (above) as holding that a landlord's trading interests were a 'reasonable concern'. It was merely the extent of the limitation which made it unreasonable in this case. The reasoning in this case takes very little account of the collateral advantage principle. This might be because it relies on the adapted version of the *International Drilling* principles articulated in the case of *Iqbal v Thakrar* [2004] EWCA Civ. 592 (on consent to alterations) which waters this down to a landlord not being able to refuse consent on a ground which has 'nothing to do with his property interests'.

So, assuming consent cannot be unreasonably withheld, the following general principles can be extracted from the above cases:

- A landlord cannot withhold consent on grounds which have nothing to do with the relationship of landlord and tenant – although this principle may now be limited, so that consent cannot be refused on grounds which have nothing to do with the landlord's property interests; (the distinction between the two may be difficult to spot, in many cases).

- If the requirements of the first principle are met, the question of whether the landlord's conduct is reasonable will be a question of fact – you should not rely upon old cases.

- The landlord's obligation is only to show that its conduct was reasonable – a landlord does not need to justify its decision, it only has to show that it is a decision that a reasonable landlord would have made – the argument that another landlord may have granted consent is not relevant.

- A refinement of the previous point is that the withholding of consent by the landlord on the grounds of protecting its reversionary interest will usually be held to be reasonable, provided the concern is reasonable, justified and supported by the evidence.

- 'Reasonable' should be given a broad common sense meaning, taking into account the wording used in the lease, where applicable.

10.11 Keep open covenant

Retail leases, especially in shopping centres, sometimes have a clause which requires the tenant to keep the premises open during stated hours and days. Such a clause provides little benefit to a landlord with only one unit in a high street and really should only be found where a landlord has a vested interest in promoting an active shopping centre or block of retail units or, say, a trade park, in each case where footfall is likely to have a positive effect on rent. (It should not appear in an investment lease, where the tenant is the investor and is not trading from the property, nor are they normally relevant to office leases.)

The courts will not grant an order for specific performance if the tenant fails to comply with the clause but they will consider a claim for damages arising as a result of a breach and the landlord would normally be able to forfeit the lease, subject to the tenant's ability to apply for relief from forfeiture.

Any well advised tenant will resist accepting such a clause but this may be difficult, especially where the rent under the lease is linked to the tenant's turnover from the premises or where the tenant is there to act as a 'draw' to the scheme – an 'anchor tenant' – such as a department store in a shopping centre or a multiplex cinema next to a leisure complex.

Certain compromises may be accepted by the landlord on this point, such as:

- the obligation being suspended for any refit of the premises by the tenant – the landlord may seek to limit this to a maximum period of time (in aggregate) over a set period;

- the obligation being suspended (for a maximum period) whilst the premises are being marketed for disposal;

- the clause not being breached by the tenant not opening, to allow for staff training – at set times;

- the clause not applying where the rent is suspended as a result of damage by an insured risk;

- the clause only applying for a limited period of time – to enable the scheme to become fully let and well known/established; and

- the clause ceasing to apply if the scheme is not fully let within a set time frame.

If the clause has to be accepted by the tenant it might have an adverse effect on rent review. Furthermore, if such a clause is imposed, then the tenant should make sure that the planning permission and any related planning agreement do not prevent opening for the required times.

10.12 The user clause and rent review

As noted above, there is a close relationship between the permitted use under a lease and the rent review clause: the more open the user clause, the more it enables the landlord to argue for a higher rent at rent review – the hypothetical tenant is likely to pay more for flexibility.

Where a lease allows for a specific use (such as a restaurant) but allows for any other use within, for example, A1 (retail) and A3 (restaurant) subject to landlord's consent, such consent not to be unreasonably withheld, does this mean that there is a wide permitted use and that the rent on review should be adjusted accordingly?

Sometimes a lease will state that, at rent review, the assumed use is to be that permitted by the lease and a landlord may argue that, as consent is not to be unreasonably withheld, the assumed use should take into account any possible permitted use – where, in this example, retail use achieves a higher rent than restaurant use, notwithstanding the fact that the premises are, at the time of the rent review, being used as a restaurant. Subject to the exact wording of the lease, the answer to this question would usually be 'no': the use to be assumed is that actually permitted at the time, not all possible uses to which the landlord may give its consent at some future time. [*Faucet Inn Pub Co plc v Ottley Corporation* [2006] EWHC 1170 (Ch)].

10.13   The Lease Code

The Lease Code suggests that a user clause should not be more restrictive than is necessary to protect the landlord's interest in the property and any adjacent premises belonging to the landlord.

10.14   Points to consider

- Does the proposed use cover all likely uses and is it sufficiently flexible?

- Does the permitted use tie in with the permitted use under planning law?

- If the lease allows the tenant to change uses, are those other uses likely to be permitted under planning law; if they would require planning consent, does planning policy conflict?

- In interpreting a user clause, the language used will be considered based on the time the lease was granted, not today's usage.

- Do not just look at the user clause – there will be other clauses in the lease which will have an influence over the uses, e.g. the alterations, planning, dealings and signage clauses and the covenants against causing a nuisance.

- Where possible, the landlord should be required to give reasons for its refusal for an application for change of use within a reasonable time and there should be a covenant from the landlord not unreasonably to withhold its consent for change of use – there is no implied obligation to provide reasons or reply promptly and there is no claim for damages (absent such a covenant) if the landlord is found to have been unreasonable.

- Conversely, a landlord should be careful – if they do not give any reasons for its refusal, the court is more likely to infer from this that the landlord was acting unreasonably [*Luminar Leisure Ltd v Apostole* [2001] 3 EGLR 23].

- If a tenant carries out potentially dangerous activities, have the building's insurers been fully informed and their requirements complied with (e.g. a hot food shop may have hot cooking fat to dispose of, or a newsagents may store fireworks)?

Transfers, underleases and other dealings

11.1 Overview

The lease will contain various restrictions against dealing with the lease; some of the restrictions will be 'absolute', with the landlord having an absolute discretion as to whether or not to consent to the relevant transaction; other restrictions will be subject to a 'qualified' covenant, whereby it will either be expressed or implied that before the transaction can proceed the landlord's consent needs to be obtained, such consent not to be unreasonably withheld or delayed.

Usually a tenant will be permitted to transfer or sublease the whole of the property subject to the landlord's prior consent, such consent not to be unreasonably withheld or delayed. Assignment of part is very rare and should not be permitted.

The tenant will normally also be permitted to charge the lease and may be able to sublet certain parts of the lease (perhaps whole floors where possible), again subject to the landlord's consent, such consent not to be unreasonably withheld.

Depending on the type of use, tenants will also normally be allowed to share occupation with franchisees and enter into concession arrangements and in most leases tenants are permitted to share occupation with group companies – provided (in all instances) that no tenancy is created by these arrangements.

In considering what is 'reasonable' the parties must take into account the size and use of the property; for instance, there is normally little point in allowing a tenant to grant subleases where its demise is of a 500 square feet shop unit or where the tenant has a larger unit but that unit has a small shop frontage; there is also little to be gained from allowing the tenant of an office to grant concessions. Equally, a tenant of a 10,000 square feet unit will want to have the flexibility to underlet part – the argument then moves on to the number of underleases, the minimum floor areas for underleases and other conditions.

Where a unit lends itself to underletting or the permitted use would be ideal for franchises, if the landlord keeps to a restrictive lease this may well impact on the landlord upon rent review. At the same time, the landlord will want to ensure that the alienation provisions are not so widely drafted so as to create management issues, such as starting off with a single-let building which ends up as a multi-let building with numerous tenants and other interests, which may, or may not, have security of tenure at the end of the lease term and which may impact upon the value of the landlord's reversionary interest.

The bottom line is that the landlord will seek to maintain control and the tenant will want flexibility so as to be able to adapt the unit to different trading conditions and occupational requirements over the lease term.

This chapter looks at how these competing aims and issues are addressed in a 'standard' lease when it comes to dealings – although for a complete picture, the provisions relating to use and alterations may also have a bearing.

A 'standard' lease will cover the following:

- **Assignment of part or whole**

Normally there will be an absolute prohibition against assignment of part – assignment of whole being allowed subject to prior consent.

- **Underletting of whole or part**

  This will be dictated by the type and size of the property being let.

  Underletting in some form is normally allowed subject to prior consent; leases of smaller areas will often prohibit subleases of part.

  If underletting is allowed, the lease will also often consider how many subleases can exist at any one time, whether the subleases should have security of tenure, whether further subunderleases can be created and what other preconditions should apply.

- **Charging of part or whole**

  Normally there will be an absolute prohibition against charging part – whether there will be a restriction against charging whole is another matter: often leases will allow this (without consent) where the charge is to a clearing bank or is otherwise to a third party providing a business loan.

- **Sharing occupation and parting with possession**

  Normally prevented, save to the extent expressly permitted.

- **Group companies**

  Normally allowed to share occupation (without consent) provided no tenancy is created.

- **Concessions and franchises**

  Normally allowed (without consent) in retail leases subject to certain preconditions and no tenancy being created; where a tenant operates solely through franchises this will often be extended to allow the tenant to grant leases to its franchise operators (without consent) provided that the franchise lease terminates when the franchise arrangement terminates and certain other preconditions are met.

● **Licences**

Sometimes allowed provided no tenancy is created and subject to similar restrictions as apply to concessions (which are themselves often a form of licence).

● **Registration**

Normally the tenant will have to register any approved transaction with the landlord (providing a copy of the relevant document) and pay a small registration fee.

Ultimately what is or is not permitted under the terms of the lease will be influenced by such factors as the type of property being let, its location and use, the tenant's operational requirements, the landlord's management policies and, ultimately, the negotiating strengths of the parties. Assuming that the above issues are covered in a commercially sensible manner, the problems arise when the tenant seeks the landlord's consent – the following sections deal with some of the more common issues in these circumstances.

11.2 Considering the application for consent to assign/sublet

Acting for a landlord in considering a tenant's application (and leaving aside the fact that a prompt response has to be provided and a request for further information has to be made in a timely manner), it is important to ensure that consent is not given inadvertently. The lease may state that any consent has to be by way of a formal deed but this may not be enough to protect an agent or lawyer's actions being treated as conferring consent.

To address this, the first letter dealing with any application should contain some wording along the following lines:

> 'Finally, neither any letters issued by us, nor the [submission,] negotiation and in due course agreement of any draft licence is to constitute consent to the proposed [assignment/underletting] and Landlord's consent will be given only upon delivery and completion of a formal licence by way of deed. We have no authority to give consent on behalf of the Landlord.'

11.3 Landlord's consent and privity

When considering an application for consent to an assignment or a sublease, the landlord will require financial references for the proposed new tenant or subtenant and any proposed guarantor. It is important (from the current tenant's point of view) to ensure that the prospective tenant or subtenant is of sufficient financial strength to be able to observe and perform the obligations in the lease (as otherwise it may find itself liable in the event of a default).

It should be assumed that landlord's consent to a transaction will take at least four weeks to be granted (calculated from the date that the landlord is supplied with all relevant financial and other information) – frequently it can take much longer.

11.4 Pre-1996 leases

Where the lease was completed before 1 January 1996, or a contract for that lease was entered into before 1

January 1996, the doctrine of 'privity of contract' will apply to that lease: the original tenant (and guarantor) will remain liable for the tenant's obligations in the lease notwithstanding any future transfer of the lease to a third party. This is obviously a critical factor in assessing whether or not to take a transfer of an existing lease where that lease has a considerable amount of time left to run and the landlord is insisting (possibly unreasonably but certainly legally) upon a covenant from the new tenant to comply with the lease terms until the expiry of the lease.

Subsequent tenants/guarantors would also be and remain liable as they would be required to provide direct covenants in the licence to assign which would mean that they too would be liable for the residue of the term, notwithstanding any subsequent assignment.

11.5 Post-1995 leases, AGAs and preconditions

Where the lease was entered into on or after 1 January 1996 (without any previous obligation to take up that lease), the doctrine of 'privity of contract' does not apply and the general principle is that the tenant is released from any future obligations upon a transfer of that lease.

However (depending upon the terms of the lease), the tenant (and its guarantor through its guarantee) will usually find itself under an obligation to enter into an 'authorised guarantee agreement' (often abbreviated to AGA) whereby the tenant guarantees the subsequent tenant's obligations in the lease, but that guarantee will automatically cease when the lease is next transferred with landlord's consent.

AGAs can require the outgoing tenant to take a new lease on disclaimer – but not where the lease has been forfeited, as is often the case under a standard contractual guarantee. A provision in an AGA which requires the tenant to be liable for lost rent following forfeiture is also unlikely to work, again because this would appear to fall outside the statutory requirements for an AGA [*Active Estates Ltd v Parness* [2002] 36 EG 147].

There is also a question mark over whether an AGA will automatically subsist in relation to matters arising after the expiry of the contractual term, including any interim rent – it is best to make sure that the drafting expressly covers these matters where it is intended that the contractual obligations under a lease are to continue beyond the contractual term [*Herbert Duncan Ltd v Cluttons* [1993] 2 WLR 710].

Post-1995 leases will also usually contain a list of preconditions which will have to be satisfied before the landlord will be required to grant consent, such as financial solvency tests, the provision of a guarantor and jurisdiction requirements (as well as the provision of an AGA) and often there will be no qualification that the landlord has to act reasonably in respect of these preconditions and, if properly drafted – as absolute preconditions – these cannot be challenged on the grounds of reasonableness.

If, however, the conditions are worded in such a way as to provide the landlord with a discretion (e.g. 'in the opinion of the landlord …') they should also expressly state that that discretion shall be exercised reasonably; if they do not, the tenant is given the right to have the determination reviewed by an independent person [s. 19(1C) of *the Landlord and Tenant Act* 1927].

It remains a moot point whether the outgoing tenant's guarantor can be required to enter into the AGA, but it is not uncommon for alienation covenants to require this or for the point to be covered expressly in the actual guarantee; the general position appears to be for landlords to seek this where it is permitted under the terms of the lease.

One point which has been settled is that on the renewal of a pre-1995-Act lease landlords are not able to insist on an AGA being automatic on lease renewal – it should only be required where reasonable and the principles of the *O'May* case [*O'May v City of London Real Property Co Ltd* [1983] 2 AC 726] will not assist – at least that was the decision in *Wallis Fashion Group Ltd v CGU Life Assurance Ltd* [2000] L&TR 520.

Where a tenant has provided an AGA and there is a subsequent default by the assignee, the landlord will need to ensure that it serves a 'section 17' notice on the tenant who provided the AGA within six months of the rent becoming due – otherwise it will be out of time – see Chapter 15 for further discussion. Where a tenant faces such a demand they can call for an overriding lease, which puts them in greater control of the situation and enables them to be able to recover VAT (where an election has been made), which would not be the case in relation to payments made as a result of the assignee's default.

The Lease Code tries to steer landlords away from a long list of preconditions and urges landlords only to consider an AGA when the incoming tenant is of lower financial standing than the tenant at the date of the assignment (or, alternatively, is resident or registered overseas). However, at the time of writing, this has yet to be accepted by many landlords, who still insist on an AGA regardless of the covenant strength of the assignee.

11.6 Implied and express consent

The lease will normally state that the landlord's consent is required before an assignment or underletting can proceed; many leases now expressly state that such consent is not to be unreasonably withheld or, in many cases, delayed.

Even if there is no such express statement, if the lease just says that consent is required for an assignment, underletting, parting with possession or charge, statute [s. 19 *Landlord and Tenant Act* 1927] implies a term (which cannot be excluded in the lease) that such consent is not to be unreasonably withheld.

11.7 The *Landlord and Tenant Act* 1988

Under this Act, where the landlord's consent is not to be unreasonably withheld, the landlord is under a statutory duty to give a written decision on an application for consent to an assignment, underletting, charging or parting with possession within a reasonable time and, if refusing consent must give its reasons, and, if imposing conditions, must set out those conditions; some examples of 'standard' conditions are set out below.

The onus is on the landlord to show that it has acted reasonably. If the landlord is in breach of these statutory duties, the tenant will be entitled to claim damages arising as a result of the breach.

In addition to the actual damages incurred, the tenant may be able to claim 'punitive damages', although to do so, the landlord is likely to have taken a deliberately obstructive stance to gain some pecuniary advantage for itself; one possible example is of a landlord, who is keen to get back possession so as to be able to re-let at a higher rent, being slow to respond and asking for more and more information, in the hope that the assignee will lose interest, leaving the tenant to negotiate a surrender with the landlord [*Design Progression Ltd v Thurloe Properties Ltd* [2004] EWHC 324 (Ch)].

11.8 Reasonableness – general principles

There are numerous cases dealing with whether a landlord is being reasonable in withholding its consent – some of them apparently conflicting. However, there are some simple points which can be taken from the case law.

- The landlord is not entitled to refuse consent for matters which have nothing to do with the relationship of landlord and tenant.

- The landlord is only required to consider its own interests, save where a refusal would be disproportionate in relation to the respective effects on the landlord and the tenant.

- Whether a landlord is being reasonable or unreasonable is a question of fact – in each case.

- The landlord does not have to establish that its conduct was correct or justifiable and the tenant will not win just because they can point to an example where a landlord granted consent in the same circumstances: what the landlord has to show is that a reasonable landlord could have come to the same decision as the actual landlord did, i.e. that there was a genuine concern.

- Refusal of consent based on change of use may be reasonable, but this will depend on the circumstances.

- A 'reasonable time' will depend on the facts of each case but as a rough guideline, if an application has not been dealt with once all the information is to hand within about 21 days, then there is a good chance that any further delay would be viewed as unreasonable; there are some instances where a court may feel that a shorter time frame would be appropriate, but we suspect they would be rare, in practice.

In the case of subletting, some would assume that the landlord should not be able to refuse consent on the grounds of lack of financial strength, as the tenant is still going to be there paying the rent. Although there is a certain logic to this point, if the subtenant is weak and the subtenant could end up being the occupational tenant at the end of the lease, applying for a new lease from the head landlord, then the (head) landlord may well be justified in withholding consent to the grant of the sublease – the landlord's position may not be so clear cut if the sublease is to be excluded from the rights of renewal under the 1954 Act [*NCR Ltd v Riverland Portfolio No 1 Ltd* [2005] EWCA Civ 312].

11.9   Preconditions to assignment

The landlord and tenant can agree, in advance, circumstances in which the landlord may withhold consent, and conditions subject to which consent to an assignment may be given which, in either case, would therefore not be subject to challenge on the grounds of reasonableness.

There are some landlords/lawyers who draft long lists of preconditions/circumstances, possibly for sound estate management reasons, but this approach can result in long disputes with the tenant in initial negotiations and could impact on rent review. Others keep to as few as one condition – the usual one being the completion of an AGA – relying on the general ability to impose other conditions where 'reasonable'. Possibly, the best approach is generally the 'middle line'. Where the lease requires 'management', such as a shopping centre store, then a list of conditions/circumstances serves a sound purpose; where the lease is of an office in the high street, maybe the simple approach is better?

Here are some of the more common circumstances or conditions:

Circumstances	Comment
rent and/or other payments due and outstanding under the lease	Qualify so that it only relates to principal rent and VAT, as the other elements may be being disputed?
there is a material breach of covenant	This is unreasonable from a tenant's point of view: it is not determinative of the assignee's ability to comply with lease obligations; and the landlord has the assignor (and perhaps its guarantor too) liable under an AGA. In addition, there are at least some cases that – applying the usual reasonableness tests – suggest that, other than for a very serious breach of a major obligation (e.g. repair), it may be unreasonable to withhold consent for breaches generally, especially where they can be remedied relatively easily.
inability to comply with tenant's covenants	Reasonable, but adds little to the 'standard' position.
assignment will have a detrimental effect on value of reversion	This is very subjective and potentially onerous and difficult to assess; a possible compromise is to have a provision to the effect that in the landlord's reasonable opinion the assignee is not likely to be able to comply with the tenant covenants following assignment.
non-compliance with a financial and profits test	This is usually an objective set of criteria but it could be onerous on the tenant and could rebound on the landlord – a potential tenant could satisfy the tests but otherwise not be acceptable for good reason: the landlord would need to be able to pick up that reason under the general provisions, i.e. consent not to be unreasonably withheld.
group company or associated company	The landlord's concern is that the group/associated company may be substantial at the time but could be stripped of its assets at a later date and then apply to assign – the AGA given at the first assignment would then fall away – assuming the landlord had to grant consent. One possible compromise is to obtain a guarantee from the parent company. The tenant could equally point to the fact that the group company still has to satisfy other tests, why should the group company assignment be treated differently?
other consents outstanding/not given	This should be subject to the refusal being justified.
overseas company	There could be issues regarding enforcement – the compromise is to allow those overseas companies where there are no such issues – such as one based in the EU.

Circumstances	Comment
an AGA is provided	The question is, whether this should be automatic or only where reasonable?
new guarantor	Only where reasonable.
rent deposit to be provided	Only where reasonable.
later withdrawal of consent	This looks innocent but what if there is inadvertent non-payment of rent (for instance) during the process, would the tenant have to start over again? In practice, unlikely to be a major issue one way or another.
the tenant has first to offer to surrender the lease back to the landlord	This often appears in shopping centre leases, where control/management is an important factor for the landlord – the clause is only effective if the lease itself is excluded from the rights of renewal under the 1954 Act – otherwise a stalemate could be reached where the landlord cannot force the tenant to surrender and the tenant cannot assign, as a result of the anti-avoidance provisions in the 1954 Act.

11.10 Release criteria

There are often discussions over new lease terms and assignment terms whereby the outgoing tenant (in an AGA) and/or its guarantor try to secure some form of contractual release from their liabilities, if certain criteria are met. An example of the drafting of such release criteria, is as follows:

'"The Release Criteria" shall be the production by the [Tenant/Guarantor] to the Landlord of true copies of the audited accounts of [the [new] tenant] for the [three] immediately preceding financial years which shall disclose for each of those financial years:
(a)   a pre-tax profit on ordinary activities (excluding extraordinary items) of not less than [three] times the [Principal Rent]; and
(b)   net assets of not less than [ten] times the [Principal Rent].'

If the criteria are satisfied then the (previous) tenant or the guarantor would be released from any ongoing liability.

11.11 Subleases – preconditions to subletting

In the case of a proposed sublease of either the whole or (assuming this is permitted) part of the property, the landlord will often impose an additional set of preconditions which need to be satisfied before the subletting can proceed; examples of some of the preconditions usually imposed are set out below. There is no implied term that the preconditions have to be reasonable.

- The sublease has to contain similar rent reviews and similar (if not identical) terms to those contained in the main lease.

- No premium is to be accepted or paid for the grant of a sublease – as this would affect the 'market rent'.

- The sublease has to be granted at no less than the higher of the market rent at the time or the apportioned rent under the main lease. This can result in making the lease very difficult to dispose of in a depressed market (as no prospective tenant will want to pay above the market rent), even where the tenant is prepared to pay a premium to the new tenant. This is not as common as it used to be.

- Alternatively, the sublease rent has to be at no less than the open market rent – this and the last point are considered further below.

- The undertenant has to enter into an AGA with the head landlord upon the undertenant assigning its interest in the underlease – this is quite 'harsh'.

- There should be no more than a stated number of subleases in place at any time.

- The tenant should not accept the surrender of part of a sublease and if there is to be a surrender of whole the landlord's prior consent is obtained; this is designed to avoid, for instance, the situation in a lease which only allows subletting of whole – the tenant subletting whole and taking a surrender back of part would otherwise be a possible way around the restriction; the restriction would also help prevent a tenant accepting a substantial premium for the surrender from a subtenant and then the tenant going insolvent, not having first shared the premium with the landlord, for example.

- The sublease must exclude the security of tenure provisions in the *Landlord and Tenant Act* 1954, i.e. prevent the subtenant from being able to obtain a new sublease upon expiry of its sublease.

- Subleases of part should be of an area which can sensibly be subdivided and (independently) serviced, with provision for the collection of a service charge.

- Leases of retail premises often contain a particular set of restrictions designed to ensure that any sublease has a minimum shop front and/or floor layout.

The requirement to underlet at no less than the rent payable under the lease (pro rata in respect of a lease of part) has been the subject of much discussion. It can often result in difficulties when the tenant wants to sublet and the market rent has dropped below the rent payable by the tenant under the lease, as it would require the tenant to sublet at a higher than market rent. Even if that is not likely in the immediate future, the tenant taking a 20 year lease will be concerned that it could happen at some time during the term.

As a result of this issue (and the political pressure surrounding it) 20 leading landlords issued a declaration in 2005, through the British Property Federation, that all new leases granted by them would require that the rent on the grant of sublease would have to be at no more than the market rent. They also stated that they would waive the requirement in existing leases, so as only to require subleases at a market rent (no higher), save in exceptional circumstances.

There is a balancing act with these restrictions: where they are too onerous, they may prevent the tenant from being able to sublet in accordance with the lease, leading the tenant to argue for a discount upon review. If the provisions are too generous to the tenant, the landlord may end up with a building in multiple occupation, all the leases being on different terms, making it difficult for the landlord to secure vacant possession at the end of the lease – the adverse effect on the investment value could be material.

11.12 Subletting and side agreements

Where the lease has restrictive provisions, tenants have sometimes tried to find ways around the lease or ignored them altogether. In one case a tenant granted a sublease which did not comply with the preconditions contained in the lease – it relaxed the repairing obligation and this contradicted the precondition that the terms of the lease had to be in a 'like' form – the judge held that this was a material difference. The deliberate action of the parties was enough, in this case, to enable the judge to order the surrender of the lease and damages in favour of the landlord; see *Crestfort Ltd and others v Tesco Stores Ltd and others* [2005] EWHC 805 (Ch).

Totally ignoring preconditions is one matter, but can a side arrangement work – whereby the tenant and subtenant have a side agreement to relax the terms of the sublease, the terms of the sublease however being compliant with the preconditions? This used to be one way that tenants avoided restrictive subletting terms but *Homebase Ltd v Allied Dunbar Assurance plc* [2002] EWCA Civ 666 held that the sublease and side agreement were interdependent and should be viewed together. Accordingly, the lease preconditions relating to subletting were breached and the landlord was not under a duty to respond to the application within a reasonable time.

The *Allied Dunbar* case related to variations between the parties to the sublease. *Crestfort* indicates that the court may not come to the same decision where the parties are different: the tenant and subtenant enter into a fully compliant lease; at the same time an associated company of the tenant provides the subtenant with an indemnity in respect of some of the liabilities under the sublease; this structure may well not breach the lease. This position has yet to be fully tested and even if it is held to be robust, there are issues over whether or not the associated company entering into the collateral agreement can show sufficient 'corporate benefit' for the collateral agreement to be enforceable against it.

Another possibility, where the lease does not prohibit the grant of a sublease in return for a reverse premium (being paid by the landlord to the tenant) and the lease requires any sublease to be granted at the higher of the passing rent and the open market rent, is to comply with the lease; at the same time the tenant/landlord pays the subtenant a reverse premium – equivalent to the rent the subtenant would otherwise have paid [*NCR Ltd v Riverland Portfolio No 1 Ltd* [2005] EWCA Civ 312]. This suggestion is not ideal, as it does not deal with what would happen if the subtenant then became insolvent and paying a reverse premium by instalments (as a possible alternative) is likely to be viewed as a sham.

11.13 Occupation and possession and holding on trust

In addition to specific prohibitions on assignment and underletting, the alienation provisions will ordinarily contain some broader general wording intended to catch any type of occupation, possession or sharing of the premises.

Parting with possession and occupation are often (and generally wrongly) considered to be the same thing. Parting with possession connotes some transfer of control of the property; it is not the same as allowing, for instance, a group company to share occupation, although it is possible to share possession and part with occupation!

The simple point is that a well drafted lease will exclude any sharing or parting with possession or occupation of the whole or any part – there will then normally be certain stated 'carve outs' subject to conditions, e.g. group companies sharing occupation, as discussed in section 11.14 below. This wording would prevent the granting of a licence that would normally be treated as a sharing of possession. For futher consideration of what is a licence and the concepts of occupation and possession see section 11.15 below.

A broadly drafted lease will also exclude holding the lease on trust – partly because a beneficiary under a trust carrying on business is treated as equivalent to occupation by the tenant, so the beneficiary could acquire the right to new lease under the 1954 Act. (This wording would normally be breached by the tenant contracting to assign the lease – at exchange the tenant would be holding the lease on trust for the assignee – subject to the terms of the contract.)

11.14 Franchise, concessions and group companies

Retailers, especially department store operators but also retailers such as booksellers and chemists, often trade by allowing other companies to use part of the sales floor under a concession agreement; restaurant chains and car dealerships, for example, often operate via franchise agreements. Often this arrangement will be documented by commercial agreements which are not leases and these tenants will want to ensure that the standard lease restrictions preventing the 'sharing of occupation' or 'parting with possession' are not breached by these arrangements – which, if not expressly dealt with, would be in breach of a properly drafted lease.

A landlord should not be too restrictive – it is in its interest to ensure that its tenants can trade in their normal way. The following are the basic preconditions which should be covered:

- the arrangements do not create a tenancy;

- the arrangements cease automatically upon expiry of the franchise or concession arrangement or the company ceasing to be a group company (as the case may be), or if, earlier, the termination of the lease.

Clauses dealing with concession and franchise arrangements will also often contain the following additional provisions:

- the onward appearance of the unit is as a single store in the occupation of one party;

- no more than a stated number of concessions can exist at any time; and

- no more than a stated floor area can be occupied by concessions at any one time.

(The last two restrictions may be considered restrictive, given that the other restrictions would normally be enough to protect the landlord's interest, but they are common, in practice.)

A 'group' company is usually defined by reference to section 42 of the 1954 Act: 'two bodies corporate shall be taken to be members of a group if and only if one is a subsidiary of the other or both are subsidiaries of a third body corporate or the same person has a controlling interest in both'.

A sophisticated lease may also allow associated companies to share; associated being defined by reference to whether the tenant 'controls' the other company, 'control' and 'associate' being considered with reference to section 416 of the *Income and Corporation Taxes Act* 1988, which provides as follows:

> **'416 Meaning of "associated company" and "control"**
>
> (1) For the purposes of this Part, … a company is to be treated as another's "associated company" at a given time if, at that time or at any other time within one year previously, one of the two has control of the other, or both are under the control of the same person or persons.
>
> (2) For the purposes of this Part, a person shall be taken to have control of a company if he exercises, or is able to exercise or is entitled to acquire, direct or indirect control over the company's affairs, and in particular, but without prejudice to the generality of the preceding words, if he possesses or is entitled to acquire:
>
>> (a) the greater part of the share capital or issued share capital of the company or of the voting power in the company; or

(b) such part of the issued share capital of the company as would, if the whole of the income of the company were in fact distributed among the participators (without regard to any rights which he or any other person has as a loan creditor), entitle him to receive the greater part of the amount so distributed; or

(c) such rights as would, in the event of the winding-up of the company or in any other circumstances, entitle him to receive the greater part of the assets of the company which would then be available for distribution among the participators.

(3) Where two or more persons together satisfy any of the conditions of subsection (2) above, they shall be taken to have control of the company.

(4) For the purposes of subsection (2) above a person shall be treated as entitled to acquire anything which he is entitled to acquire at a future date, or will at a future date be entitled to acquire.

(5) For the purposes of subsections (2) and (3) above, there shall be attributed to any person any rights or powers of a nominee for him, that is to say, any rights or powers which another person possesses on his behalf or may be required to exercise on his direction or behalf.

(6) For the purposes of subsections (2) and (3) above, there may also be attributed to any person all the rights and powers of any company of which he has, or he and associates of his have, control or any two or more such companies, or of any associate of his or of any two or more associates of his, including those attributed to a

company or associate under subsection (5) above, but not those attributed to an associate under this subsection; and such attributions shall be made under this subsection as will result in the company being treated as under the control of five or fewer participators if it can be so treated.'

Crown Copyright material is reproduced with the permission of the Controller of HMSO and the Queen's Printer for Scotland.

Again, tenants will want to be able to allow group companies to occupy without being in breach of the lease. Landlords should be sufficiently protected provided that no tenancy is created and the arrangement ceases if and when the occupying company moves outside the group structure.

The flexibility for allowing franchises, concessions and group companies should normally be available to subtenants as well.

11.15 Lease or licence?

While this book deals with commercial leases, the difference between a lease and a licence should also be considered, not least because it is not uncommon for parties to enter into what they think is a licence when, at law, it is a lease. Even if a tenant grants a licence to a third party, this will normally trigger a breach of the provisions in the lease preventing 'sharing occupation', discussed in section 11.13 above, unless the landlord has granted its prior consent.

A licence is not much more than a personal right to use space in someone's property; it does not create an interest in land and it does not confer exclusive possession of the space – others can use it as well. However, if the document does confer exclusive possession, then it is likely to be a lease – regardless of any label which the parties give to it and even if the parties state in the main body of the document that they do not intend to create any form of lease. If it is, in fact, a lease, then the tenant may well have rights of security of tenure under the 1954 Act – which was probably not the intention of the parties at the time of completion.

A lease is the grant of a right to the exclusive possession of land for a fixed period of time; exclusive possession is the ability to exclude both the landlord and third parties from the property (except to the extent that the landlord has reserved rights of entry, for example, to carry out works) – it goes further than 'occupation', as possession is effectively the right to receive the rents from the property, so a tenant may have possession by virtue of being entitled to the rents (reflecting the right of ownership), while the person in occupation may, for example, be an undertenant. Accordingly, a document which reserves rights of entry to a landowner is likely to be a lease, as the reservation of rights would not be needed if the document was a licence – the rights reserved would only be needed if the other party otherwise had exclusive possession.

In considering whether a document is a lease or a licence, the court will look at the actual substance of the document – as a whole. It may well have elements of both a licence and a lease, but if it grants exclusive possession for a term then it will almost certainly be a lease. We set out in the table below some general points to act as a guide (but no more than that) if you have to consider whether a document is a lease or licence:

Term in question	Lease or licence?
Grants exclusive possession	Lease

Term in question	Lease or licence?
For a term	Could go either way, as a 'term' could equate to licence period. A lease has to be for a term certain (that is certain or capable of being made certain and which is for a shorter term than any superior lease) and if the document does not provide for this then it is likely to be a licence. A 'licence' for a fixed period of (for example) 10 years is likely to be viewed as a lease, as a right to occupy for a long period is strongly indicative of it being a lease
At a rent	May be either a lease or licence, as 'rent' could equate to a licence fee (or vice versa)
Reserves rights of entry in favour of the landlord	Lease
Allows others to use the same space, without any particular restriction	Licence
Limits the hours of use	Could go either way, but may suggest that the party does not have exclusive possession – n.b. a shopping centre lease will also have certain hours restrictions
Provides for a covenant of quiet enjoyment	Likely to be a lease
Stated to be a licence/not confer a tenancy	Could still be a lease if the other provisions point to this
Contains various detailed restrictions and onerous obligations	Likely to be viewed as a lease, subject to other points moving in that direction

11.16 Inadvertent surrender

Managing agents are often concerned that they may accept a surrender of a lease without intending to. Surrender is usually effected by the parties agreeing the terms upon which the lease will be surrendered and then the lease is handed back to the landlord, along with the keys, and, in return, the landlord releases the tenant from its liabilities under the lease. Often this will be formally documented.

Sometimes a surrender can happen without the parties intending it to occur. However, this is rare. As a general rule a landlord would have to act in such a manner which is inconsistent with the continuation of the lease to be found to have accepted a surrender; doing nothing is not enough to effect surrender. Also a landlord can accept keys on a 'without prejudice' basis without being found to have accepted a surrender and a landlord who has failed to demand rent/service charge or has failed to pursue arrears will not – on those points alone – be held to have accepted a surrender.

The key point for the managing agents is to ensure that they make it clear that nothing they do should be treated by the tenant as accepting a surrender – and make sure that that is confirmed in writing.

11.17 Liability post-assignment

Where that Act applies, the *Landlord and Tenant (Covenants) Act* 1995 has provided for the automatic release of tenants; however, the lease can require the tenant to enter into an authorised guarantee agreement on assignment. If a tenant has assigned its lease, it will be liable where it has provided an authorised guarantee agreement and the new tenant defaults and it will be liable where the tenant held a lease granted before the 1995 Act came into force, i.e. where 'privity of contract' still applies and it is either the original tenant or it has otherwise provided a direct covenant to the landlord.

However, there are various statutory protections which, for instance, require the landlord to serve notice of such a liability within a stated time frame and enable the previous tenant to call for a new lease to it so that it can regain control of the property, albeit subject to the defaulting tenant's lease. Professional advice should be taken very promptly in these circumstances to minimise or see if the liability can be avoided. These provisions apply to all leases – pre- and post the 1995 Act.

11.18 The landlord's position: liability post-sale and recovery of rent

11.18.1 Landlord's release under statute

Under the terms of the 1995 Act, the landlord is not automatically released from its obligations upon a transfer of its reversion (unlike the tenant), but may apply to the tenant at any time before or within four weeks after such transfer for a release of the landlord covenants; where the tenant resists this by serving a notice of objection, the landlord can apply to the court for a declaration that it is reasonable for the covenant to be released.

Where the landlord fails to make an application for release to the tenant within the time limit, the opportunity to apply for such release is lost until the next assignment of the lease, when the right again arises, subject to the same timing constraints.

There has been some debate about whether a landlord should apply for a release from the landlord covenants in the new leases to which its interest is subject when it assigns the reversion. Experience so far suggests that landlords do not often seek to use this release mechanism.

- If there is a single tenant in the property there may be a reasonable case for attempting to obtain a release. There will be no release unless the outgoing landlord asks for it, and, if the tenant does not respond, the release will be granted automatically.

However, it is unlikely to be worth pursuing the matter if the tenant objects, mainly because in a single occupancy building, the landlord's liabilities are likely to be much smaller than in a multi-let building, possibly only relating to insurance (although that is an important covenant).

- There may be dangers in obtaining releases when selling a multi-let building or estate. Where the landlord has obtained a release from some tenants and not from others, he will still be liable to the tenants who have not released him for, say, provision of services. The 1995 Act provides that if the landlord is released from all the landlord covenants in a tenancy, he ceases to be entitled to the benefit of the tenant covenants in the tenancy from the date of the assignment. He cannot therefore recover any of the costs from the tenants who have given him a release, but presumably can do so in relation to tenants who have not given him a release.

11.18.2 *Landlord's release under the lease*

Until recently, it was considered that the anti-avoidance provisions in s. 25 of the 1995 Act were of such wide application that any contractual attempt to limit or release the landlord from its covenant obligations before the lease came to an end (other than via the mechanism provided by the 1995 Act) would not be effective.

The position has been changed by the House of Lords' decision in *London Diocesan Fund v Phithwa (Avonridge Pty Co. Pt 20 defendant)* [2005] UKHL 70. In that case the court held that an express clause in a lease releasing the (original) landlord on assignment was effective; there is nothing in the judgement to indicate (if the clause is so drafted) that a subsequent landlord could not also be released upon assignment – but the case was not dealing with such a point.

Tenants should ensure that where the landlord is providing material covenants, any provision for automatic release should be qualified, at the very least, by a requirement that the tenant's consent should be obtained to any release, such consent not to be unreasonably withheld.

11.19 Assignment of reversion – recovery of rent arrears

There is an important distinction to be drawn between old and new tenancies in terms of recovery of outstanding rent arrears.

In respect of 'old' tenancies (those pre 1 January 1996) the rent reserved by a lease and the benefit of the tenant's covenants runs with the reversion; as a result, any outstanding arrears of rent (and the right of recovery) will pass automatically to the new landlord [s. 141 of the *Law of Property Act* 1925].

Upon the assignment of the reversion to a 'new' lease by the landlord, the right of action for any arrears outstanding at completion of the assignment remains with the assigning landlord, unless that right is expressly assigned to the new landlord. Although [s. 23 of the *Landlord and Tenant (Covenants) Act* 1995] the benefit of tenant covenants passes to the new landlord upon assignment, this is only in relation to the period from the date of the assignment and the new landlord does not have any rights 'under the covenant in relation to any time falling before the assignment'.

It is open to the parties to agree to an express assignment of such rights, but in the absence of an express assignment of the benefit of those rights, the new landlord cannot seek recovery of pre-assignment arrears, the rights to which will remain with the assignor. However, the assigning landlord will lose its self-help remedies under the lease, as only the landlord for the time being can distrain (see Chapter 15 for comments on forthcoming changes in this area) and the right to forfeit (even for arrears accruing pre-assignment) passes to the new landlord.

Assignment of the reversion does not affect the assigning landlord's liability for pre-assignment breaches – whether or not the landlord is released: the release relates to post assignment breaches.

11.20 The Lease Code

The Lease Code states that there should not be any specific preconditions to an assignment, other than landlord's consent, such consent not to be unreasonably withheld or delayed. The only exception to this would be a condition that on a group company assignment, the assignee and any guarantor must be of equivalent or greater financial strength than the outgoing tenant (and its guarantor).

The Lease Code goes on to promote the point that AGAs should only be automatically required where the assignee is resident or registered overseas or is (with any guarantor it offers) of lesser financial strength than the outgoing tenant/guarantor.

It is fair to say that these provisions mirror the last edition of the Lease Code and (in particular on the AGA point) they have not been adopted in the market in any material way. Certainly, there will, as often as not, be no major advantage in having a long list of preconditions to consent to an assignment in a lease of an office; there is greater justification for this approach in leases where management is a key issue, such as a unit in a shopping centre or a leisure unit in a park.

The Lease Code also promotes:

- smaller tenants being able to provide rent deposits rather than enter into an AGA;

- sublettings being at the open market rent at the time (i.e. not the higher of the open market rent and the rent payable under the superior lease);

- where subleases are excluded from the 1954 Act, they should not have to be on the same terms as the superior lease.

11.21 Points to consider

- Ensure that the lease is flexible, taking into account the possibility that the tenant may not need all the space all the time and may want to underlet at some time in the future, the tenant's current proposals and that flexibility should complement the design and layout of the building and its uses.

- Try to limit the preconditions to an assignment so that in all cases the landlord has to be reasonable, including where the requirement is for an AGA – although it has to be accepted that this is an 'ideal' which will often not be achieved.

- If a lease of retail premises, consider altering the lease to allow for franchise and concession agreements (or franchise leases) without the need for consent from the landlord or, at least, on the basis of a less restrictive set of conditions.

- Does the lease allow group companies to occupy the property with the tenant without the need to obtain the landlord's consent? If the lease is silent then usually only the tenant itself is able to occupy and any 'sharing' of occupation would be in breach of the lease.

12 Planning and statutory matters

12.1 Overview

During the course of the lease the tenant will have to comply with all statutory provisions relating to the property, including those relating to planning and use, environmental matters, health and safety, fire and building regulations requirements, as well as any obligations imposed upon the tenant as a 'service provider' under the DDA. Such legislation normally imposes a primary obligation for compliance on the tenant as occupier, save where there are 'common parts' where the responsibility for compliance will normally rest with the landlord. (In some cases the courts may apportion the cost of compliance between those having an interest in the property and, if so, the court's decision will override the lease.)

Leases tend to have several clauses which refer to the tenant having to comply with statute, often, unnecessarily, listing out (by way of example) various statutes which have to be followed. The covenant to comply is then supported by a covenant to indemnify the landlord against any breach of, or non-compliance with, statute. In addition, there will normally be various references to the tenant having to obtain the landlord's consent before following a particular course of action, providing the landlord with copies of any statutory notice received and taking any action (reasonably) required by the landlord in respect of such notices and informing the landlord of anything in the property/common parts which could affect the landlord.

Below is brief overview of some of the more common legislative provisions which affect both the landlord (as an owner of property and often as the person directly in control of the common parts within a building and the provider of services to the building) and the tenant (as an occupier).

12.2 Planning

Normally, there will be clauses in the lease making it clear that the tenant has to obtain the landlord's consent before making any planning application relating to the property. (Note that there is no implied term that the landlord has to act reasonably. Accordingly, whether for planning applications for alterations or change of use, the lease should make it clear that consents cannot be unreasonably withheld.)

Often leases also make it clear that before any planning consent is implemented, the landlord's approval to that actual planning consent has to be obtained. Some of the more tightly drafted leases also require the tenant to appeal against a planning refusal or a condition which the landlord considers adversely affects its interest.

The main reason behind this is that the landlord will want to avoid the property being blighted either by an (implemented) planning consent which contains an onerous condition or a planning refusal. We would suggest that an obligation to appeal should generally only be required where planning for a particular property is 'sensitive'; it should not be viewed as 'standard'.

In many cases, the tenant is only going to need planning consent for signage/shopfront, as the user clause will be limited to a particular type of use and the tenant will only have a very limited ability to carry out alterations.

However, where the lease is more flexible as to permitted use, planning consent for change of use may be required before the use can be implemented, assuming the landlord has consented to the change.

The basic position should be that the restrictions on planning should link in with the user and alterations clauses in the lease: where there is an absolute prohibition against change, that should be duplicated in the planning clause; where there is flexibility that also should be mirrored in the planning clause.

12.3 Listed buildings

Some properties will be listed buildings, being buildings of special architectural or historic interest. If a building is listed, it is likely to be a Grade II listed building; about 4 per cent of listed buildings will be Grade II* – buildings of more than specialist interest – and about 2 per cent of listed buildings will be Grade I – buildings of exceptional interest.

Listed buildings are covered under the *Planning (Listed Buildings and Conservation Areas) Act* 1990; demolition of a listed building, or alterations which would affect its special architectural or historic interest, will require consent under the Act. Consent is not required under that Act for a material change of use, which will be covered by the *Town and Country Planning Act* 1990. Note:

- the listing applies/extends to any object or structure within the curtilage that forms part of the land and did so before 1 July 1948;

- the listing may be as a result of a particular part of the building but it applies to the whole building;

- consent is not usually required for repair works, provided they match the original details.

12.4   Conservation areas

Under the *Planning (Listed Buildings and Conservation Areas) Act* 1990, local authorities must formulate and develop policies to preserve and enhance conservation areas. If a property falls within a conservation area then consent for demolition will be required under the Act – the Act does not apply to consents to change of use or other building works, which will be covered by the *Town and Country Planning Act* 1990, but in determining an application for planning permission, the local authority will take into account the need to preserve and enhance the conservation area.

12.5   Contaminated land

This is principally covered by the *Environmental Protection Act* 1990.

Most leases make it clear that, as between the landlord and tenant, the tenant is liable for any contamination on the property, i.e. where the contamination is caused by the tenant (or a subtenant). This may be done in a specific clause in the lease dealing with contaminated land, or may be covered by a clause requiring the tenant to comply with statute.

The position on historic contamination is not so clear; the starting point under the legislation is that the 'polluter pays' so the tenant would argue that it is not liable; however, the tenant may be liable at law where the original polluter is no longer in existence. An owner or occupier can be liable for contamination if no one can be found who caused or knowingly permitted the historic contamination. Liability would normally be split between all owners and occupiers in the proportions in which they share the capital value of the land. An occupier may be excluded from liability if it is only liable to pay a rent which is equivalent to a full market rent for the land and holds no beneficial interest in the land other than the tenancy to which the rent relates. Tenants who hold a beneficial interest in the land and therefore risk being liable for historic contamination at law often try to make the landlord pick up responsibility for that historic contamination through the wording of the lease. Many tenants will insist upon a clause specifically excluding them from liability to the landlord for any historic contamination.

Where the lease makes the tenant liable and the contamination is historic, the remediation notice is likely to be served on the landlord (who will pass it on to the tenant) and if the tenant fails to comply, it is the landlord who will incur criminal liability. The tenant may also be liable under statute (leaving aside the position under the lease) – such as health and safety legislation.

Where there is the possibility of historic contamination, a tenant should:

- try to avoid taking up any liability for historic contamination by an express exclusion of liability (backed by an indemnity from the landlord for pre-lease contamination) and/or by taking a lease of the building but not any subsoil (assuming the contamination is in the soil, rather than the actual building) and if this does not work seek to agree a cap on its liability;

- exclude any liability to pay for remediation costs via the service charge;

- where the tenant's own use could result in contamination it may be prudent to agree to document the condition of the land at the date of the lease by way of an invasive audit/survey;

- failing this, carry out a survey and ensure that warranties are available from the consultants for the benefit of the tenant and its assignee;

- try to obtain a warranty from the landlord that there is no contamination, coupled with an obligation to comply with any remediation notice if the warranty is proved to have been incorrect.

Some further points to consider are set out in Appendix C.

Where the contamination is caused by the tenant, the remediation notice will normally be served on the tenant and both the law and the lease will make the tenant liable and require the tenant to clean up any contamination.

12.6 Disability discrimination

There has been much written about the DDA, some of it inaccurate, especially with reference to the DDA's imposition of obligations to carry out alterations to premises to ensure that the disabled can use the services provided from those premises, and the duty not to discriminate; this duty is not always translated into a duty to take positive action.

For instance, in considering whether a landlord is reasonable in refusing a request to carry out alterations, the court will consider the landlord's reasons for refusal, not whether or not it will make access, for instance, easier – the reasons for refusal should not be connected with disability. [*Richmond Court (Swansea) Ltd v Williams* [2006] EWCA Civ 1719]

For the purposes of this guide, we would emphasise that the overriding principle behind the DDA is one of 'reasonableness' and that the DDA relates to the provision of 'services' from premises.

Since 4 December 2006, landlords and property managers have been under a duty to make reasonable adjustments to address a person's disabilities, where requested to do so (section 24 of the DDA) – although this appears to be positive, the action which is required will be governed by what is considered 'reasonable'. Since 1 October 2004 (section 21of the DDA), a service provider has been under a (positive) duty to take reasonable steps to remove or alter a physical feature that makes it impossible or unreasonably difficult for a disabled person to use the service. Since October 1999, the service provider has been under a duty to provide a reasonable alternative way of making the service available.

Some factors which should be considered with an application under the DDA:

- the length of the lease and the practicality and cost of the proposed measures;

- any statutory and regulatory issues;

- objections and comment from other tenants within the building;

- alternative ways of dealing with the issue: any tenant covenants/management policies/rules/regulations which could be introduced or amended;

- the existing tenants' covenants – can they be altered?

The overriding question will be: is the reason for refusal the same as it would be if the application had been made by a non-disabled party?

12.7 Asbestos

With effect from 13 November 2006, The *Control of Asbestos Regulations* 2006 revoked previous regulations and replaced these with a simplified and consolidated UK legislative framework, imposing on employers and others in control of non-domestic premises a wide range of duties in connection with the management of asbestos in premises.

Regulation 4 requires a 'dutyholder' to carry out the necessary risk assessment to determine whether asbestos is present, or likely to be present, in a building and to manage the risk from any asbestos that is or is likely to be present.

'Dutyholder' is defined broadly, as:

'(a) every person who has, by virtue of a contract or tenancy, an obligation of any extent in relation to the maintenance or repair of non-domestic premises or any means of access thereto or egress therefrom; or

(b) in relation to any part of non-domestic premises where there is no such contract or tenancy, every person who has, to any extent, control of that part of those non-domestic premises or any means of access thereto or egress therefrom.'

These regulations make provision for the allocation of responsibility to those in control of non-domestic property (the dutyholder) to ensure that the risks associated with asbestos being present in a building are 'managed'. The definition of dutyholder extends to include all owners of non-domestic property, landlords, tenants, licensees, and, potentially, managing agents. There can be several dutyholders – both the landlord and its tenants, the freeholder being liable for the common parts. In addition, the landlord may also be responsible in respect of disrepair arising from a breach of covenant by the tenant, where the landlord has reserved the right (as is commonly the case in commercial leases) to enter and repair in the event of such default.

It is commonly thought that the dutyholder has to carry out an asbestos audit/survey and has to remove any asbestos found. In practice this may be the case in some circumstances, but not always; asbestos only has to be removed if that is the only real way of preventing potential harm to others. Accordingly, the presence of asbestos in the building does not, in itself, represent a breach of a repairing covenant or a covenant to comply with statute.

With modern buildings (built within the last 15 years or so) it is highly unlikely that there will have been any asbestos used in their construction – there are three main types of asbestos commonly known as brown, blue and white asbestos, brown and blue asbestos being banned from use in 1985 with white asbestos banned (with a few minor specialist exceptions) in 1999; a review of the construction contract and planning and building regulations approvals, coupled with a visual inspection, may be more than sufficient for such buildings.

Even if there is asbestos, it may be of a type or in a location where it is safer to keep it in place, 'managed', e.g. identified, with warning signs and restricted access.

If asbestos is in the common parts the landlord will have to 'manage' it; this may or may not require its removal and the removal may, or may not be chargeable to the tenants via the service charge.

As a general rule, the landlord should be entitled to recover the costs incurred by it in complying with statute; this will extend to costs incurred in carrying out audits, inspections and surveys and compiling and maintaining an asbestos register. If the asbestos has to be removed in order to comply with the regulations, then the landlord should be able to recover the cost of removal as part of the service charge obligations in the lease – subject to the drafting of the lease. For further discussion on this point, see Chapter 6.

12.8 Fire prevention

Until 1 October 2006, certain types of building required a fire certificate (issued by the local authority fire officer) confirming that the property complied with the applicable fire regulations, and the *Fire Precautions Act* 1971. Under the 1971 Act, a fire certificate was only required in respect of premises designated by Order for that purpose and there were exclusions for premises of certain types or where only a small number of people worked; further fire fighting and emergency escape arrangements were imposed on 'workplaces' by 1997 Regulations.

The *Regulatory Reform (Fire Safety) Order* 2005 consolidated existing fire safety legislation for most workplaces and other non-domestic premises in England and Wales into one composite Order, replacing fire certification under the 1971 Act with general duties to ensure safety from fire risk. Both the 1971 Act and the 1997 regulations were revoked and replaced upon implementation of the 2005 Order. Fire certification was abolished, and replaced by a new risk assessment regime, imposing on the responsible person (the employer, owner or person in control of the premises – which in the case of an occupational lease will generally be the tenant, but may also be the landlord in respect of those parts of the building over which it retains control) duties of ongoing risk assessment, prevention and mitigation. Among those new duties is a requirement that the responsible person ensures the proper installation and maintenance of safety equipment and the taking of precautions by appointing at least one appropriately qualified and trained 'competent person' to assist in undertaking the required preventive and protective measures.

It is important to appreciate that the new regime is of wider application than the old certification arrangements. In particular, the new risk assessment provisions are not subject to the same limitations as to property type or number of workers; the new regime extends to cover all non-domestic premises, subject to a limited number of exceptions and applies to 'any place', i.e. not just buildings, but also open land, installations and other moveable structures. In addition, a wider range of persons now enjoy protection under the legislation, with 'relevant persons' extending both to persons lawfully on the premises and others in the immediate vicinity of the premises at risk from a fire on the premises concerned.

12.9 Energy performance

In 2006, revised Building Regulations and other provisions introduced certain new minimum energy performance building requirements, in accordance with European law.

The *Energy Performance of Buildings (Certificates and Inspections) (England and Wales) Regulations* 2007 (as amended) implemented further European law energy efficiency requirements in England and Wales, including five-yearly inspections of, and reports on, air conditioning systems. The new requirements were introduced, in stages, for residential property in 2007 and for commercial buildings during 2008. They now apply to the letting or sale of most commercial buildings.

The energy performance certification provisions require the production of an Energy Performance Certificate (EPC) for buildings constructed, sold or rented out for most domestic and (subject to conditions) commercial buildings and a Display Energy Certificate (DEC) in respect of certain larger public buildings over 1,000 m² (likely to be extended to other (private) buildings, such as shopping centres and hotels).

Whilst the economic impact of the introduction of EPCs remains uncertain, it is possible that a high rating may have an impact on the yield and capital values of an investment.

See Chapter 16 for more detail on EPCs.

12.10 The Five Steps to improve energy efficiency

This legislation is now being supported by the BPF's guide to landlords and managing agents: *The Five Steps to improve energy efficiency and reduce CO_2 emissions in rented office buildings*, which was published in May 2007. The 'five steps' are:

1 Taking stock – this would include collating reports and extends to reviewing leases to confirm what the contractual requirements are with respect to services requiring energy – such as the provision of heating, air conditioning and lighting.

2 Planning – e.g. monitoring, reviewing and analysing data.

3 Making initial savings – e.g. changing hours when services are provided, carrying out simple repairs and effecting technical upgrades where appropriate.

4 Working with tenants – discussion, review and motivation – the guide promotes 'no cost' actions which result in savings.

5 Making improvements routine – by continued dialogue and review.

The basic aims of the guide are to standardise reporting by promoting what the BPF describes as landlords' energy statements (there is a suggested template) and to reduce energy use.

There may be some fear on the part of tenants that the costs involved will be picked up by the tenants via the service charge; however, the thrust of the guide is that by promoting what could be termed as 'energy awareness' (possibly at some administrative cost), both landlords and tenants will benefit – a building will achieve a positive rating and there will be cost savings, to the benefit of the service charge.

12.11   Smoke-free premises

Legislation contained in Part 1 of the *Health Act* 2006 provides for the creation of 'smoke-free' premises in England and Wales, by prohibiting smoking in most 'enclosed or substantially enclosed' areas in workplaces and other such places to which the public has access, with further powers to designate additional smoke-free places. These provisions were substantially commenced in Wales on 2 April 2007 and in England on 1 July 2007.

12.12   CDM Regulations 2007

Another issue to consider is the impact of the *Construction (Design and Management) Regulations* 2007 in relation to the management of health and safety risks in carrying out works/alterations (for more on this, see Chapter 9).

12.13   Liability to third parties

Occupiers Liability Act 1957: imposes a duty on an occupier in respect of dangers due to the state of the premises or to something done, or not done, on the premises. (The common parts of a building will be 'occupied' by the landlord.) The duty is to take such care as is reasonable to ensure the reasonable safety of visitors; visitors, for these purposes, are those persons to whom the occupier gives (or is treated as giving) permission to enter or use the premises – in other words, the occupier's invitees or licensees. Furthermore, in certain circumstances, provisions in the *Occupiers Liability Act* 1984 may also extend the occupier's duty to trespassers, where the occupier is aware that such persons are in, or may come into, the vicinity of such dangers, against which the occupier might reasonably be expected to offer some protection.

Defective Premises Act 1972: imposes duties on a landlord in respect of defects in the premises (the existence of which the landlord knows or should have known about) arising through the landlord's non-compliance with its repair obligations. The definition of 'repair obligations' extends to the situation where the landlord has right of entry to effect repairs, as a result of the tenant's default. The duty

- is to take such care as is reasonable in the circumstances to ensure that persons to whom the duty is owed are reasonably safe from personal injury or from damage to their property caused by the lack of repair;

- is owed to all persons who might reasonably be expected to be affected by defects in the premises (and so may extend to trespassers) – but not the tenant where the lack of repair arises as a result of the tenant's failure to comply with its repairing obligations; and

- arises where the landlord is first able to exercise the right of entry.

12.14 Telecommunications code

Schedule 2 to the *Telecommunications Act* 1984 provides a framework (code) governing telecommunications equipment and enables telecommunications operators with code powers to retain their equipment on premises following expiry of the lease term. It is something which, while not often enforced, a landlord needs to be aware of, particularly where a tenant is seeking landlord's consent to enter into arrangements with such an operator.

12.15   Points to consider

- Before taking up a lease, check that the property has the appropriate planning consent for the proposed use and that any alterations which have been carried out comply with the applicable health and safety, planning and building regulations requirements. It is important to ensure that the property complies with these requirements, as otherwise the tenant may find itself liable for carrying out any required works at its own expense. (It is also possible that those additional works (notwithstanding the fact that they are carried out at the tenant's expense) will be taken into account in any future rent review under the terms of the lease.)

- Check that no alterations or additions are required in order for the property to comply with fire, disability and health and safety regulations. The insurers may also have some requirements and/or recommendations and these must be passed on to the tenant.

- In some circumstances, even if the lease specifically prohibits certain alterations, it may be possible to obtain a court order permitting the alterations but the landlord can then offer to carry out the alterations itself in return for an increase in the rent.

- Make sure that any health and safety file (which should have safety procedures and general information on the maintenance of plant and equipment) is complete and handed over at the time of taking possession of the property. When taking the property back, e.g. following a surrender, or the exercise of a break clause or at the end of the term – the tenant should be required to hand over a complete file. From a tenant's point of view, it should ensure that where it appoints the CDM coordinator, the appointment makes it clear that it is the coordinator's responsibility to ensure the preparation of the health and safety file.

- If the property is listed and/or in a conservation area, check that all appropriate listed building/conservation area consents have been obtained and complied with.

- The planning requirements should tie in with the alterations and user clauses, so that where consent cannot be unreasonably withheld under one, the same applies to the other clauses.

- Consider whether contamination is an issue, especially where the definition of the property includes the ground below; in certain circumstances the tenant could find itself liable for contamination caused prior to the date of the lease.

13 Security of tenure

13.1 Overview

Commercial leases can broadly be spilt into two categories: those that have the protection of a statute called the *Landlord and Tenant Act* 1954 (the 1954 Act) (often referred to as 'protected tenancies' or as having security of tenure) and those which do not ('unprotected tenancies'). Most commercial leases are by default protected tenancies (with security of tenure) and so, in this chapter, we deal predominantly with those, but we also provide some comment about how to grant a unprotected tenancy.

Most commercial leases are granted for a specified length of time (as opposed to being periodical). When that period has expired, the tenant can normally continue to occupy the property (essentially on the same terms and conditions as under the lease). In these circumstances, the tenant is described as 'holding over' and continues to remain liable until the lease is either renewed or terminated in accordance with the provisions of the 1954 Act. The lease can be brought to an end by either the landlord or the tenant serving a statutory notice.

A landlord can serve a 'section 25 notice' to determine the lease on or after the expiry of the contractual term. Such a notice can either state that the landlord does not oppose renewal, or that it does. If a landlord wants to oppose renewal then it can only rely on certain specified grounds (which are summarised below – see 'Grounds for a landlord to oppose renewal').

If the landlord does not take any action terminating the lease, the tenant can request a new lease (which the landlord may oppose, again, on one or more of the grounds specified below) by serving a 'section 26 request'.

In certain circumstances, the tenant may be well advised to apply to the court for a new lease as early as possible, so as to pre-empt any action which the landlord may otherwise take.

The procedures outlined above have to comply with the relevant provisions in the 1954 Act and are governed by very strict time constraints and prescribed forms must be used. It is important that initial professional advice is obtained by both the landlord and tenant over a year before the expiry of the lease and at all times during the course of proceedings, as otherwise the respective rights may be prejudiced.

13.2 Leases which do not entitle the tenant to apply for renewal

The following leases do not confer on the tenant security of tenure under the 1954 Act:

- Those leases which are expressly excluded from the ambit of the security of tenure provisions conferred by the 1954 Act, in accordance with the 1954 Act – see section 13.11 below.

- Leases which satisfy the provisions contained in section 43 of the 1954 Act and which can be summarised as:

    - certain leases of agricultural holdings

    - mining leases

- farm business tenancies
- leases where the tenant occupies by reason of an office or employment by the landlord and the rights can cease when the employment/office comes to an end
- Leases granted for a term certain not exceeding six months unless

  (a) they contain provision for renewing the term or for extending it beyond the initial six months or

  (b) the tenant (including any predecessor in the same business) has been in occupation for more than twelve months (periods of occupation under a tenancy at will have not been taken into account).

  In relation to the exclusion of six-month leases, under limb (b), initially, a tenant can safely be granted a lease for a fixed term not exceeding six months without creating any rights of security of tenure under the 1954 Act. This can then be followed by a further lease for a term of just less than six months. Potentially, this could stretch to a third lease term, not exceeding six months, provided that the third tenancy was granted within twelve months of the tenant first taking occupation of the premises – however this third lease is not one we would recommend as it is not without its risks.

13.3 The procedure for renewal and opposing renewal

Where the security of tenure provisions of the 1954 Act have not been excluded (see section 13.11 below), or the lease is not one covered in section 13.2 above, the lease renewal and termination procedures set out in the 1954 Act have to be followed.

The main points are briefly set out below, but the procedures are complex and rely to a great extent on using prescribed forms and following set time lines – this is not a comprehensive review of the intricacies of the 1954 Act. The flowcharts on pages 215–216 provide an overview of the procedures described below.

If the procedures are not followed, then the tenant will forfeit its statutory rights of renewal or the landlord will forfeit its rights to oppose renewal, depending on the circumstances. However, the parties are always free not to start the statutory procedures – in which case nothing is certain until a new lease is completed.

13.4 Acting for the landlord

13.4.1 *Acting for the landlord – landlord initiating renewal*

Where not opposed to the grant of a new tenancy, the landlord may serve a section 25 notice on the tenant indicating that it does not oppose the grant of a new tenancy in order to initiate renewal of the lease.

The notice

- A section 25 notice cannot be served where the tenant has already served a section 26 request (see below).

- The notice must be in prescribed form and set out the landlord's proposals as to the terms of the new lease – although the landlord is able to change the terms subsequently.

- The notice must be served not more than twelve months or less than six months before the termination date specified in the notice. The notice must inform the tenant that if it wants a new lease it has to apply to the court for a new tenancy, by the termination date specified in the notice.

Next steps

- The next step in the process is for either the landlord or the tenant to apply to the court. There is no requirement for the tenant to serve a counter-notice, as was necessary under the previous regime.

- The court application must be made before the termination date specified in the landlord's section 25 notice.

- The parties can, however, agree in writing to extend the date for making an application to the court provided that they do so before the deadline expires – the extensions may be as long as the parties choose, but they must not be open-ended. The parties may agree as many extensions as they choose.

- The landlord's section 25 notice will be treated as terminating the tenancy at the end of the last extension period agreed.

- Once the landlord has made an application for the renewal of a tenancy, the landlord cannot withdraw it without the tenant's consent.

13.4.2 Acting for the landlord – landlord opposing renewal by service of a s. 25 notice

If the landlord does not want the tenant to be granted a new lease, then the landlord can initiate its opposition to the grant of a new lease by serving a section 25 notice on the tenant, opposing renewal.

The notice

- As stated above, a landlord cannot serve a section 25 notice if the tenant has previously served a section 26 request.

- The section 25 notice must be in prescribed form and make it clear what ground of opposition the landlord is relying on. Further it must specify that:
  - The tenant does not need to serve any counter-notice.
  - The landlord is opposed to the grant of a new tenancy.
  - If the tenant wishes to ask the court for a new tenancy, it must do so by the termination date specified in the notice, unless the landlord has previously agreed to a later date.
  - The court may order the termination of the tenancy and that the landlord may (in certain circumstances) have to pay compensation.
  - The tenant cannot stay in occupation after the specified termination date (or any later date agreed with the landlord) unless the tenant has previously applied to the court for a new tenancy, or the landlord has applied for the termination of the tenancy without renewal.

Next steps

- The landlord can apply to the court for termination of the lease as soon as it has served a section 25 notice.

- If an application is not made to the court (by either the landlord or the tenant) before the termination date (or any later date agreed between the parties), the lease will automatically come to an end and the tenant will lose its right to a new lease.

- If the landlord establishes any of the grounds for opposition (provided in section 30(1) of the 1954 Act), the court will make an order terminating the current tenancy. The date of termination of the tenancy will be three months after the proceedings are finally disposed of. If the landlord does not succeed, the court will order a new tenancy and the court will settle the terms of the new lease, unless the parties agree these between themselves.

13.4.3 Acting for the landlord – landlord opposing renewal by responding to tenant's s. 26 request

Where the tenant has initiated the 1954 Act procedure with a section 26 request, which the landlord wishes to oppose:

- The landlord will have to serve a counter-notice within two months of service of the section 26 request, setting out the grounds for opposition before it makes its application to the court. There is no required form, but it should use the same wording as is set out in section 30(1) of the 1954 Act.

- If the landlord does not serve the counter-notice within two months of service of the section 26 request, it cannot oppose renewal and will have to grant the tenant a new lease.

- An application can then be made to the court. This must be made before the new lease commencement date (specified in the section 26 request) unless the parties have agreed in writing beforehand to a later date. As with applications for renewal, further extensions are allowed provided that the parties agree them in writing before expiry of the then current deadline.

13.5 Acting for the tenant

13.5.1 *Acting for the tenant – tenant initiating renewal*

The tenant can remain in occupation (holding over) after the lease has expired without serving a section 26 request. However, before the term of a new lease can begin (and assuming no section 25 notice has been served), the tenant needs to serve a section 26 request on the landlord requesting a new tenancy.

The notice

- A tenant cannot serve a section 26 request where the landlord has already served a section 25 notice.

- The notice must be served at least six months, but no longer than twelve months, before the suggested term start date for the new lease (which cannot be before the expiry of the current lease).

- The section 26 request has to be in a prescribed form (similar to a landlord's section 25 notice), contain the tenant's request for a new tenancy, a schedule of the tenant's proposals for a new tenancy and other required matters, including notes that:
    - If the landlord wishes to ask the court to grant a new tenancy, it must do so by the start date specified in the tenant's section 26 request, unless the tenant has previously agreed to a later date or the tenant itself has applied to the court for a new tenancy. The landlord can accept the tenant's proposed terms, as set out in the section 26 request, or put forward its own terms.
    - The landlord can oppose the request for a new tenancy only on one or more of the grounds set out in section 30(1) of the 1954 Act (which are

summarised below) and, if the landlord wishes to oppose the request, then the landlord must notify the tenant of the relevant grounds *within two months* after receipt of the section 26 request, failing which the landlord will not be able to oppose the application and will have to grant a new tenancy (but is not bound by the tenant's proposed terms).

- Either party can ask the court to fix the rent that the tenant has to pay whilst negotiations for the new tenancy are continuing.
- The tenant cannot apply to the court for the new tenancy for two months following the date it served the s. 26 request, unless the landlord has previously given a counter-notice opposing the tenant's request.
- One of the parties must apply to the court before the tenant's proposed term start date, unless they have previously agreed in writing to an extension.

Next steps

In order to oppose the grant of a new lease, the landlord must serve a counter-notice as set out above.

If the landlord establishes any of the grounds for opposition, the court will make an order terminating the current tenancy and the date of termination of the tenancy will be three months after the proceedings are finally disposed of.

If the landlord does not succeed, the court will order a new tenancy and the court will settle the terms of the new lease, unless the parties agree these between themselves.

13.5.2   Acting for the tenant – tenant terminating a lease

If a tenant serves a section 26 request, then (subject to the statutory provisions for temporary continuation) the existing tenancy will terminate immediately before the commencement date specified in the request. However, where no section 26 request has been served and the tenant wishes to terminate the lease:

- Where the contractual term has not yet expired:
  - A tenant can simply vacate before the end of the contractual term of the lease (even though this can put the landlord in an uncertain position); or
  - Alternatively, a tenant can serve at least three months' written notice under Section 27 of the 1954 Act on the landlord to expire at the end of the contractual term.

- Where the contractual term has expired and the tenant remains in occupation ('holding over') by virtue of the 1954 Act:
  - The tenancy will not come to an end simply by the tenant subsequently ceasing to occupy.
  - The tenant has to give at least three months' written notice to the landlord to end the tenancy. That notice can expire on any day – not just a quarter day – and the rent is apportioned accordingly.

13.5.3 *Acting for the tenant – responding to landlord's s. 25 notice*

Where a tenant receives a section 25 notice (whether opposed or unopposed) and wants a new lease, it must ensure that before the date specified in the notice either a new lease is agreed, an extension is agreed with the landlord, or an application to court is made.

If a tenant receives a section 25 notice and wants to move out before the date specified in the notice, then it can either vacate before the contractual expiry date of the lease, or serve three months' written notice under section 27 of the 1954 Act.

Procedure under Landlord and Tenant Act 1954

Acting for landlord

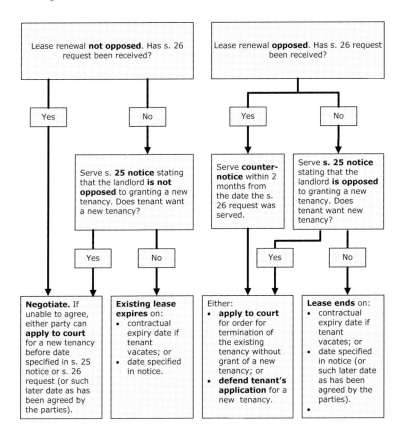

Acting for tenant

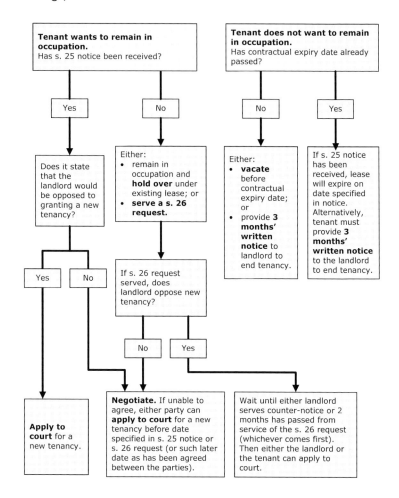

13.6 Who is the 'landlord' and who is the 'tenant'?

A section 25 notice must be given by the 'landlord' to the 'tenant', and a section 26 request must be made by the 'tenant' to the 'landlord'. Although in many cases the identity of the 'landlord' and the 'tenant' will be obvious, there are complicated rules about who this is for the purposes of the 1954 Act. Broadly speaking the tenant (and therefore the person entitled to a new lease) is the tenant who is in occupation of the premises. The landlord (the 1954 Act refers to the 'competent landlord') is the person who is entitled to possession of the premises for no less than 14 months after the expiry of the relevant lease. If therefore a tenant's immediate landlord's interest is pursuant to a lease which is due to come to an end shortly, it may be that for the purposes of the 1954 Act the 'landlord' is not the tenant's direct landlord, but is a superior landlord (even though they may not have a direct contractual relationship).

13.7 Group companies

The legislation now treats an individual, and a company that the individual controls, as one and the same, so:

- where premises are occupied by a company owned by an individual tenant, that tenant can claim it is in occupation (even though the company is a separate legal entity) and apply for renewal in its own name;

- where a landlord opposes renewal under section 30(1)(g) of the 1954 Act (the landlord intends to occupy the property for its own purposes), that landlord may now oppose renewal on the grounds of intended occupation by a company in which the landlord has a controlling interest; and

- intended occupation by a person with a controlling interest in a landlord company will suffice.

13.8 Grounds for a landlord to oppose renewal

There are seven grounds upon which the landlord can base an opposition to a new lease; those grounds are set out in the paragraphs of section 30(1) of the 1954 Act (and are listed below). The landlord can rely on any one or more of the grounds, provided that it has specified them in either its section 25 notice or in its counter notice to the tenant's section 26 request. If grounds (a), (b), (c) (which are all based on the tenant's default) or (e) are established, the court has a discretion whether to grant a new lease. However, if grounds (d), (f) or (g) are established, the court has no discretion and must refuse to grant a new tenancy. Certain grounds also entitle the tenant to receive compensation for not being awarded a new lease (see below).

The grounds upon which a landlord can seek to recover possession of the property or oppose a tenant's application for a renewal of its lease are set out below.

The table also shows whether the grounds are discretionary and whether the tenant may be entitled to compensation.

	Discretionary	Compensation
Default grounds		
(a) The tenant has been in breach of its repairing obligations under the lease.	√	✗
(b) The tenant has persistently delayed in paying rent.	√	✗

	Discretionary	Compensation
(c) Other substantial breaches of lease obligations by the tenant or other reasons connected with the use or management of the premises by the tenant.	√	✗
Non-fault grounds		
(d) The landlord can provide reasonably suitable alternative 'accommodation'.	✗	✗
(e) The current demise was created by a sub-letting of a larger premises and the landlord can let the larger premises (which will include the existing demised premises) at a higher rent than the aggregate rents under separate tenancies. (This ground is rarely used as it is difficult to establish the higher rental level for a letting as a whole).	√	√
(f) The landlord intends to demolish or reconstruct the property or carry out substantial works of construction and could not reasonably do so without obtaining possession.	✗	√
(g) On termination of the tenancy, the landlord intends to occupy the property for its own purposes. In order to rely upon this ground, the landlord must have owned the property for at least five years prior to the end of the term of the current lease. (There are also specific provisions which may apply where the landlord is a government department, local authority or certain other similar bodies.)	✗	√

The ground of opposition which is most frequently used is intended demolition or reconstruction. The landlord has to establish:

(i)   At the date of the court hearing, the necessary, firm and settled, intention to do the works at the end of the lease and that it has the ability to do the works – usually by having finance in place and the appropriate planning consent.

(ii)   That the works are material works of reconstruction/demolition.

(iii)   That vacant possession is required in order to do the works.

On this last point, the court will consider the extent of the rights reserved to the landlord in the lease to effect works and whether or not the tenant has actually to vacate in order for the works to be done. Even if the landlord is able to establish this ground, the court may order a new lease of the property upon completion of the works.

If the landlord successfully opposes the grant of a new lease on the basis of any one of the last three non-fault grounds outlined above, then the tenant will normally be entitled to compensation which will be calculated by reference to the rateable value of the property and the period of time for which the tenant has been in occupation. If the tenant (and any predecessor carrying out the same business) has occupied the property for more than 14 years then the compensation is (currently) two times the rateable value and if the tenant has occupied the property for less than 14 years then the compensation is (currently) set at the equivalent of the rateable value of the property.

Leases often contain a clause excluding the tenant's right to compensation – these clauses only work where the tenant (and any predecessor to its business) has been in occupation for less than five years prior to the end of the lease term.

In certain circumstances (broadly where the landlord is opposing renewal on 'non-fault' grounds), the tenant may also be able to apply for compensation for misrepresentation where, as a result of the misrepresentation:

- the landlord obtained an order for termination of the tenancy;

- the court was persuaded not to grant a new tenancy;

- the tenant vacated after withdrawing or not making
  an application.

13.9   The terms of the new lease

If a new lease is to be granted upon renewal then the
parties tend to agree the terms in line with those in the
old lease (with appropriate updating). If they are unable
to settle the new terms then the matter will be decided
upon by the court and the starting point for the court is
the terms of the old lease – the onus is on the party that
wants any changes to justify them. There are some basic
points which can be made:

- The tenant is only entitled to a new lease of the area
  which it occupied at the end of the old lease – it may
  have sublet the balance and not taken back
  occupation before the end of the term. However the
  landlord (in this situation) can require the tenant to
  take a lease of the whole of what was previously
  demised, rather than what the tenant still occupies.
  Secondly, if the landlord opposed on the grounds of
  redevelopment, and the tenant argued that the works
  could still be done while the tenant occupied part of
  the premises, then the tenant will have a new lease of
  that part.

- The court has no power to grant a lease outside the
  1954 Act.

- The maximum term that the court can order is 15
  years – the parties can always agree a longer term.

- The court can impose break provisions in the new
  lease.

- The rent will be at the then open market rent of the
  property, disregarding the tenant's occupation and the
  goodwill and improvements carried out within the
  last 21 years by the tenant or any predecessor

(including one under an earlier lease provided the landlord has never had possession of the property during that time).

- If the old lease contained an upwards only rent review, then the court is likely to order that for the new lease, but if there was no rent review in the old lease, then the court may order an upwards/downwards review clause in the new lease.

13.10 Interim rent

After the contractual term of the (old) lease expires and pending the grant of a new lease, there is an 'interim' period in which tenant continues to be liable for rent. The starting point is that the old lease rent continues to be payable. However, either party can apply for an 'interim rent' to be payable. Where there is no opposition to a new lease being granted, interim rent will usually (unless there is good reason otherwise) be the rent payable under the new tenancy.

Interim rent is payable from the earliest date that the tenancy could have been terminated by either the landlord's section 25 notice or the tenant's section 26 request and until the new lease commences.

The tenant should consider applying for an interim rent if the market rent is less than what it is paying under the old lease; the landlord should consider applying, if it believes that the rent is higher and it wants the tenant to start paying at that rate before the new lease is completed. Usually, the new lease rent will be backdated to the termination date, so it may not be a major point for either the landlord or the tenant.

13.11 Excluding a lease from the security of tenure provisions of the 1954 Act

While the 1954 Act prohibited the parties from simply contracting out of the security of tenure provisions outlined above, until 2004 it was possible to obtain a court order to that effect under a statutory procedure laid down in the 1954 Act.

Since 1 June 2004, amendments to the relevant provisions of the 1954 Act allow the security of tenure provisions to be specifically excluded from the lease without the need to make an application to court.

In order to do so, however, three requirements must be fulfilled:

- Service by the landlord on the tenant of a warning notice in prescribed form, which informs the tenant of the rights that it will be giving up by contracting out.

- Either:
  - where the landlord's notice is served at least 14 days prior to the earlier of the tenant entering into the tenancy or becoming contractually bound to do so, the making by the tenant of a declaration in prescribed form;

  or
  - where the landlord's notice is served less than 14 days prior to the earlier of the tenant entering into the tenancy or becoming contractually bound to do so, the making by the tenant of a statutory declaration in prescribed form.

  In the declaration or statutory declaration, the tenant acknowledges service of the landlord's notice and accepts the consequences of agreeing to contract out.

- The lease must include references to the service of the notice, to the making of the declaration or statutory declaration, and to the agreement between the parties to contract out.

The other crucial point to note here is that the notice and declaration/statutory declaration procedure must both be completed *before the tenant is contractually bound* to enter into the tenancy, which could be considerably earlier than the time of completion of the lease itself (which was the timing requirement for completing the old court-based contracting out procedure), particularly where there is a preceding agreement for lease.

Failure to comply with these statutory requirements is likely to render the contracting out ineffective, and thus expose the landlord to the risk of inadvertently granting a lease with the protection of the 1954 Act. Provided, however, that the statutory procedures are properly adhered to, the lease will not be protected and the tenant will have no right to renew its lease at the end of the lease term and will have no right to any compensation.

It is very common for leases to be 'contracted out' where they are for a short term. Landlords also often insist that any sublease of part is excluded from the security of tenure provisions, so the subtenant has no right to renew. This is (in part) to ensure that the landlord is able to regain control of the whole building at the end of the term or is only granting a lease of the whole building to one tenant upon renewal.

13.12 Points to consider

- A tenant with 1954 Act protection may 'hold-over' after the term of a lease comes to an end. If a landlord wants certainty it may serve a section 25 notice. A tenant may serve a section 26 request. A section 25 notice or a section 26 request must specify a date not less than six months and not more than twelve months in the future (and not before the contractual term date of the lease).

- A tenant cannot serve a section 26 request if the landlord has served a section 25 notice (and vice versa).

- If the tenant does not want to renew the lease, and no notices have been served, then the tenant can simply vacate the property on or before the end of the lease and the tenancy will expire at the end of the term. If it has done nothing, then in order to bring the lease to an end after the expiry of the contractual term, the tenant has to serve a 'section 27 notice', which has to provide for an end date which must be at least 3 months later.

- If it has done nothing, then in order to bring the lease to an end after the expiry of the contractual term, the tenant has to serve a 'section 27 notice', which has to provide for an end date which must be at least three months later.

- If rents have fallen, the tenant should seize the initiative so as to move onto the lower market rent as soon as possible – by terminating the old lease on the contractual term date and by making an application for interim rent at the earliest possible time. There is no incentive for the landlord to terminate in a falling market – unless it has a wider strategy, for instance, long term certainty of income.

- A landlord may oppose the grant of a new tenancy on one of the grounds in section 30(1).

- The terms of a new tenancy (if granted) will be on such terms as the court considers appropriate (save that the term cannot exceed 15 years) – the starting point for such terms is the terms of the expired lease.

- The parties may agree to the terms of a lease being excluded from the relevant provisions of the 1954 Act. To do so, a strict procedure must be followed, being a procedure completed prior to the tenant becoming contractually obliged to take the lease. The court has no power on a lease renewal to grant a 'contracted out' lease.

14 Termination for breach

14.1 Overview

Forfeiture is the procedure whereby if the lease contains a clause allowing the landlord to 'forfeit' (otherwise known as 're-entry') and the tenant is in breach of a term in the lease referred to in that clause, a landlord can terminate the term of the lease before its contractual end.

Where a lease is forfeited, the lease is brought to an end (subject to a tenant's right to apply for relief against forfeiture – see below). The landlord has no right to compensation for the loss of rent for the remainder of the term. However, it can claim against the tenant for any antecedent breaches (i.e. any breaches pre-dating the forfeiture).

The rules for forfeiture for non-payment of rent are different to those for breach of other covenants. Broadly, where there is a breach of covenant not relating to rent, the landlord has to serve formal notice (a 'section 146 notice') and comply with certain statutory procedures; where the breach relates to non-payment of rent the procedure is more straightforward. For this reason, many leases extend the definition of 'rent' to include service charges and often all other payments due under the lease – there is then no need to serve a section 146 notice if there are any arrears.

14.2　Re-entry and forfeiture

The landlord can only forfeit a lease if the lease specifically provides for this (and institutional leases invariably do so, usually for any breach of covenant).

If the landlord chooses to forfeit, it can do so either by 'peaceably' re-entering the property (which can include breaking the locks, as long as no one is resisting the re-entry) or by commencing court proceedings. A tenant may seek to ensure that peaceable re-entry does not occur by placing 24-hour security in the property (peaceable re-entry is normally carried out during the night or in the early morning).

The effects of forfeiture (peaceable re-entry in particular) can be extremely disruptive to a tenant's business, even if the tenant is subsequently able to regain possession.

14.3　Non-payment of rent

The terms of forfeiture clauses vary as to when a landlord can forfeit for non-payment of rent. Very often, the rent must be in arrears for 14 or 21 days before forfeiture can occur. The terms of the clause must be strictly adhered to. Depending on the wording of the forfeiture clause and the rent clauses, 'rent' can often be defined not only as yearly rent, but also as service charges and insurance monies.

In the case of non-payment of rent, there are no statutory restrictions on forfeiture – no notice need be served before forfeiture takes place.

14.4　Breaches other than non-payment of rent

Where a landlord wishes to forfeit for breaches other than non-payment of rent, it must serve formal notice on the tenant before forfeiting in accordance with section 146 of the *Law of Property Act* 1925 – such notices are time sensitive and the tenant should seek urgent professional advice as soon as a notice is received (or threatened). The notice has to provide details of the breach and require the tenant to remedy the breach (within a reasonable time) and to pay reasonable compensation to the landlord for the breach.

The landlord can go on to forfeit the lease only if the breach is not remedied within a reasonable time. As to what is a reasonable time, this will depend on how long it will take to remedy the breach, but often two to three weeks will be sufficient. Even if the breach is irremediable, the landlord must give a reasonable period – five days has been held to be reasonable in such circumstances.

14.5   Forfeiture and repairing covenants

Where the breach relates to the repairing covenant, the *Leasehold Property (Repairs) Act* 1938 will apply (whether the action relates to forfeiture or damages) to a lease which was granted for more than seven years and which still has more than three years left on the term. If seeking forfeiture or damages, the landlord has to comply with the 1938 Act by serving the section 146 notice and informing the tenant of its rights under the 1938 Act. The tenant then has 28 days within which to claim the benefit of the 1938 Act by serving a counter-notice. If such counter-notice is served, the landlord cannot take any further action without the consent of the court. That consent will only be granted if the landlord is able to establish one of the following grounds:

- the value of its interest has been substantially diminished by the breach or that it has to be remedied now to prevent a fall in value;

- the breach must be remedied to comply with legislation;

- where the tenant is not in full occupation, the breach must be remedied in the interests of the occupier;

- the breach can be remedied at a relatively small cost now in comparison with the likely costs later;

- there are special circumstances which make it equitable to grant consent.

The statutory protection afforded by the 1938 Act can be circumvented if the lease contains a 'Jervis v Harris' clause, which is discussed in Chapter 8.

14.6 Waiver

The landlord will not be able to forfeit a lease if it has waived the breach that it would be relying on as grounds for forfeiture. Waiver is, essentially, an action by the landlord, in circumstances where the landlord knew there was a breach of covenant, whereby the landlord treats the lease as continuing.

The landlord (or someone acting on behalf of the landlord) has to have knowledge of the breach; the most common form of waiver is demand or acceptance of rent after the landlord became aware of the breach. The courts take a very strict line on this point: accepting rent on a 'without prejudice' basis does not work; if the rent is paid in by direct debit, that will still be treated as waiver – even if the lease has a clause saying that acceptance of rent will not amount to waiver. Other examples of 'waiver' would be:

- discussing the surrender of the lease on an 'open' (i.e. not on a 'without prejudice' basis);

- distraining for rent (to be replaced by CRAR – see comments in Chapter 15, section 3);

- granting a licence to underlet or assign.

The effect of waiver will depend on the breach; where the breach has occurred ('a once and for all breach'), for instance, a breach of covenant against subletting, then, by waiving the covenant, the landlord cannot subsequently forfeit the lease for that breach – it may well have other remedies but it will not be able to forfeit; whereas, with a breach that continues ('a continuing breach'), such as a breach of a repairing covenant, the breach continues on each day, so waiver on one day will not prevent forfeiture on a later date.

14.7 Relief from forfeiture

There are a number of safeguards which give a tenant some protection against forfeiture; which of these safeguards will apply will depend upon the nature of the tenant's breach. The starting point is that if the landlord is in the process of forfeiting the lease then the tenant can usually (but not invariably) get relief from forfeiture by paying off the arrears or dealing with the breach relating to the forfeiture, provided that the tenant acts promptly.

Where the landlord has peaceably re-entered, the tenant can theoretically apply for relief at any time in the future. However, where forfeiture is by court proceedings, the period is six months from the possession order. In practice, the longer the tenant leaves it to apply for relief, the less likely the court is to grant relief.

There are different rules for relief for non-payment of rent and relief for breach of other covenants.

14.8 Relief for breach of covenant other than non-payment of rent

A tenant can apply for relief at any time when the landlord is in the process of forfeiting the lease;

depending on the type of action being taken, the tenant should apply for relief within a 'reasonable' time.

Generally, provided that the forfeiture process has not been completed, the court has a wide discretion to grant relief on such terms as to compensation, costs, claims and expenses as the court determines. In considering whether to grant relief the court will look at all the circumstances, including conduct and the losses that will be suffered by the tenant if relief is not granted. Where the breach is wilful and deliberate it is less likely that relief will be granted; where the breach is trivial relief will almost certainly be granted.

A subtenant has the right to apply to the court for relief from forfeiture – a mortgagee of the tenant has a similar right. The court has a wide discretion again as to the terms and the court will seek to ensure that the landlord is not prejudiced by the order, but here the court would grant relief by way of a vesting order, creating a new lease between the landlord and the subtenant.

14.9 Relief for non-payment of rent

As a general rule, if the tenant pays off all the arrears and costs at least five days before the hearing (where forfeiture is by court proceedings), then the action will automatically end and the lease will continue. If the matter goes to court and the court orders forfeiture, the tenant has a further four weeks (minimum) within which to make the required payments and if this is done then the lease continues.

14.10 Miscellaneous

If there is a guarantor under the lease, it is usually also provided that if the lease is forfeited the guarantor has to take a new lease from the landlord on substantially the same terms as the existing lease.

Forfeiture of a lease appears to be a drastic remedy to a tenant who is carrying on a business from premises and who may, possibly inadvertently, be in breach of the terms of the lease. However, considerable comfort can be taken from the fact that, in most circumstances, forfeiture is the last resort of the landlord, especially where the lease is at a full market rent as, if the tenant accepts the forfeiture it is released from any subsequent liability which would otherwise arise in respect of the lease but for the forfeiture. Forfeiture crystallises the tenant's liabilities under the lease at the date of forfeiture.

14.11　Points to consider

- Forfeiture is by no means the only course of action open to the landlord where there is non-payment of rent by the tenant – and there are a number of other remedies that should also be considered; see Chapter 15.
- If the landlord forfeits the lease, the lease will come to an end (subject to a tenant's application for relief) and the landlord will lose its income stream unless it is able to re-let.
- The landlord will become liable for the rates on the property from forfeiture onwards – and any empty rating relief may have been used up by the defaulting tenant.
- If the landlord wants to forfeit the lease, then it may want to cancel any direct debit/standing order (and not do any other waiver act) to prevent the tenant from arguing that the landlord has waived the breach by acceptance of rent.

15 Recovery of rent

15.1 Overview

If the tenant fails to pay its rent, the landlord has various options (as alternatives to forfeiture):

- the landlord can issue court proceedings for recovery of the rent against the tenant (or any guarantor, previous tenant or previous guarantor);

- the landlord may enter the property and seize goods on the property belonging to the tenant; this procedure is known as 'levying distress' or 'distraint';

- if there are subtenants then the landlord can serve notice requiring the subtenants to pay the subtenancy rent direct to the landlord – section 6 of the *Law of Distress Amendment Act* 1908;

- the landlord may be able to draw down from a rent deposit or rental guarantee – if there is one in place;

- the landlord can serve a statutory demand requiring payment of the rent and failure to comply will then enable the landlord to proceed with bankruptcy or liquidation proceedings against the tenant.

15.2 Recovery of arrears from former tenants/guarantors

In the case of 'other' (i.e. pre-1 January 1996) leases as defined in the *Landlord and Tenant (Covenants) Act*

1995, arrears may be recovered from the original tenant, whose liability continues throughout the term and from subsequent assignees (and its guarantors) under direct covenants given to the landlord.

'New' (i.e. post-31 December 1995) leases offer much more limited rights of recovery, since the original and each successive tenant (and any guarantor) is automatically released upon assignment. However, recovery from former tenants/guarantors will still be possible where its liability continues under an authorised guarantee agreement.

Arrears (whether in respect of an 'old' or 'new' lease) can only be recovered (under section 17(2) of the 1995 Act) from former tenants and their guarantors where the requisite statutory notice has been served within six months of the date when the amount claimed 'becomes due'. A Court of Appeal decision in 2007 had interpreted this to mean that in the case of an outstanding rent review any increased amount payable as a result of the review became due not upon determination of the review, but on the date liability accrued, meaning the relevant review date, even though the actual increase might not be known (and could not therefore be paid) until some time later.

The result of this was that in order to ensure full recovery of such sums, protective s.17(2)notices (specifying a 'nil' amount due now, but expressly subject to later increase) had to be served on all such former tenants/guarantors, both at the review date (or at the latest no more than six months thereafter) and on each subsequent rent payment date, until determination of the review, followed by service of a further s.17(4) notice within three months of the reviewed rent being determined.

On the case being appealed to the House of Lords [*Scottish & Newcastle plc v Raguz* [2008] UKHL 65], the court adopted a more common sense approach and held that the increased amount payable in respect of a reviewed rent only becomes due for this purpose once the new rent has been agreed or determined. It is now therefore the case that until such agreement or determination, the landlord's s.17(2) notices given on each payment date need only refer to the current (pre-review) rent; once the reviewed rent figure is known, that new amount should be specified in subsequent s.17(2) notices.

The other factor to be aware of is that under s.19 of the 1995 Act, a former tenant or guarantor making full payment in respect of a demand under a s.17 notice is entitled to be granted a statutory overriding lease of the premises on terms provided in s.19.

15.3 Levying distress

'Levying distress' or 'distraint' is the removal by a landlord of goods belonging to its tenant which are situated in the leased premises.

Although there are many rules concerning the way in which this remedy may be carried out, distraint can clearly have catastrophic consequences where the goods or equipment seized are essential for the tenant's business. As such, many commentators are of the view that distraint is a draconian remedy. Accordingly, the current distress regime will shortly be replaced by the new statutory commercial rent arrears recovery (CRAR) procedure for commercial leases, under the *Tribunals, Courts and Enforcement Act* 2007. When implemented, provisions in the 2007 Act will abolish the common law (and various statutory) remedies of distress, replacing them with the new statutory remedy of CRAR. While in practical terms CRAR will in some ways resemble distress, it will be narrower in its application, it will be subject to various conditions and restrictions and it will only be enforceable by an authorised court-certified 'enforcement agent' (or government officer acting in the course of his duty).

Provisions in a lease purporting to provide for seizure and/or sale of tenant's goods in order to recover rent or other sums under the lease will be void; however, while CRAR may not be modified by the terms of the lease, the parties can agree to include provisions preventing or restricting its exercise.

15.4 Law of Distress Amendment Act 1908: section 6

Whilst the remedy still exists (the 1908 Act will cease to have effect upon the introduction of the new CRAR procedure referred to above), the service of a notice on a subtenant under section 6 of the 1908 Act can be an effective remedy for a landlord if its tenant is not paying rent despite the fact that they have a subtenant. It then means that all future rents (i.e. rents that have not been paid when the notice is served) must be paid by the subtenant directly to the superior landlord until such time as the tenant's arrears are cleared.

This will often mean that such rents will not be paid until the next quarter's rent falls due from the subtenant. Once the arrears of rent referred to in the notice have been paid, if further rent is by then due, the landlord will need to serve a further section 6 notice to recover those rents from the subtenant.

15.5 Rent deposit

The use that a landlord may make of a rent deposit will depend on the terms of the rent deposit deed. The landlord must comply strictly with those terms.

A rent deposit may well provide sufficient monies to cover arrears. However, once the monies are used, there may be problems (from a practical point of view) in requiring the tenant to repay the relevant sums. For this reason, landlords often retain rent deposit monies until the end of the lease and use other remedies to recover rent during the term.

15.6 Tenant's insolvency

If the tenant becomes insolvent, there is little that the landlord can do other than to take such action as it can to minimise its loss. The issues surrounding the insolvency of a tenant are far too wide ranging to do them justice here but the basics can be very briefly summarised as follows (though as these summaries are subject to various technical qualifications, reference should always be made to a specialist guide should an insolvency issue arise).

Before taking any action to bring the lease to an end, the landlord should consider whether it is advantageous for the landlord to take back control of the property as by doing so it will resume liability for rates; it may therefore sometimes be better for a landlord to leave taking back control to a later date, and, in the meantime, consider various other options.

15.6.1 *What can the landlord do?*

Various options are summarised in the following table.

	Administration	Administrative receivership	Voluntary liquidation	Compulsory liquidation	Bankruptcy	Individual Voluntary Arrangement
Forfeiture by court proceedings	Not allowed, without consent of the administrator, unless the moratorium is lifted by the court.	Permitted	Yes, unless there has been a court determination to the contrary.	Leave of court required	Permitted	Not allowed without the consent of the court.
Forfeiture by peaceable re-entry	Not allowed, without the consent of the administrator, unless the moratorium is lifted by the court.	Permitted	Yes, unless there has been a court determination to the contrary.	Yes, leave of court probably not required – although some argue that it is an action or proceeding within s. 130 of the *Insolvency Act* 1986 – and therefore consent required.	Permitted	Not allowed without the consent of the court.

	Administration	Administrative receivership	Voluntary liquidation	Compulsory liquidation	Bankruptcy	Individual Voluntary Arrangement
Distress for rent	Not allowed, without the consent of the administrator, unless the moratorium is lifted by the court.	Can levy distress	Can levy distress but the liquidator can apply to restrain the distress.	No, but may proceed once the winding up order has been issued – with leave of court.	Yes, but only for the sums falling due within the last 6 months up to the order. Goods/receipts go to any preferential creditor in respect of distress levied less than 3 months before bankruptcy.	Not when the interim order is in place and court may restrain distress pending the outcome of an application for the interim order.
Disclaimer by office holder	Not possible	Not possible	Yes	Yes	Yes	Not possible

15.7 Points to consider

- Faced with non-payment of rent, the landlord has various remedies, summarised in this chapter and in Chapter 14. Nevertheless, before proceeding the landlord should take stock and consider whether it would be appropriate to sit down with the tenant and see if a payment plan can be agreed – for instance, it may work better for both parties if the rent is payable monthly in advance, rather than quarterly.

- When seeking to recover arrears of rent, insurance or service charge, always check that the sums have become due and whether and when interest can be charged on overdue sums and that the lease expressly provides for forfeiture; where appropriate make sure that notices are served on all previous tenants (under the lease) and any guarantors. In the case of companies, service should usually be on the relevant registered office.

- Conversely, when acting for a tenant, check that the relevant statutory procedures have been followed and that the notices have been served in accordance with the requirements in the lease – if any. If acting for a previous tenant or guarantor, check that any s.17 notices have been served in time.

- If there is a rent deposit agreement in place, make sure that the funds are where they should be and that interest has been properly accounted for; when acting for a tenant and a landlord assigns its reversion, check that the deposit monies have been moved to the new landlord; if acting for a landlord it may sometimes be preferable to delay seeking to forfeit the lease until the rent deposit has been used to meet any arrears.

- In an insolvency/default situation there are all sorts of issues which will need to be considered – take proper advice and consider the whole picture; you should have particular regard to the current market for the property and the client's main aims/long-term purposes!

16 Energy efficiency and certification

16.1 Overview

In Chapter 12, we looked at a range of statutory provisions affecting property occupiers and the impact of these on the landlord and tenant relationship and lease terms. In this Chapter, we consider in greater detail the recently-introduced energy performance and certification provisions which now apply to the substantial majority of commercially-let units and how these affect the respective rights and obligations of both landlord and tenant.

16.2 Energy Performance Certificates: regulations and requirements

The requirement for the provision of an Energy Performance Certificate ('EPC') is just one part of the government's policy to reduce carbon emissions from the built environment and its users, set within an overall general legislative agenda to address climate change.

The *Energy Performance of Buildings (Certificates and Inspections) (England and Wales) Regulations* 2007 (as subsequently amended) give effect to European Directive requirements for the introduction of mandatory energy-efficiency standards in both domestic and commercial, new and existing, buildings and for provision to be made for energy performance certification of buildings.

Following the initial introduction of certification requirements in residential sales during 2007, the Regulations subsequently extended the EPC requirements in phases to the construction, sale and letting of most commercial buildings during the course of 2008. The vast majority of commercial buildings are now caught by the Regulations, with the exception of those buildings where the useful floor area is below a (very low) specified threshold or in certain other specified circumstances.

An EPC informs the potential tenant or buyer about the energy performance of a building. It provides an energy rating for the building, based on the performance potential of the fabric of the building and its services (such as heating, ventilation and lighting). Standardised computer modelling produces a grading (based on CO_2 emissions per square metre of floor area) on a scale of A to G relating to the energy performance standards required by the *Building Regulations* 2000 (as subsequently amended).

The EPC is accompanied by a recommendation report, which suggests how the energy performance of the building could be improved, together with an indication of the payback period.

The Regulations also include requirements for air conditioning systems with a rated output of more than 12kW to be inspected at no more than five-yearly intervals by an energy assessor and for a written report to be produced assessing the energy efficiency, with advice and recommendations for possible improvements, replacement and alternative solutions.

16.3 EPC, buildings and let premises

For the purposes of the Regulations, a 'building' must have a roof and walls and have internal heating, mechanical ventilation or air conditioning. The Regulations apply to the whole of the building or to part(s) designed or altered for separate use – generally, an EPC 'should reflect the accommodation being sold or let' – i.e. the energy performance of the space sold or let.

Government guidance (CLG – *Improving the energy efficiency of our buildings: a guide to energy performance certificates for the construction, sale and let of non-dwellings* (2nd edition, July 2008)), on the scope and operation of the Regulations, acknowledges that use and occupancy patterns of commercial buildings can be complex and sets out explanations as to how the EPC requirements should be applied in a number of different situations, depending on the various occupancies of parts of buildings and the use of common and/or independent heating systems.

16.4 When is an EPC needed?

An EPC is required on every new letting of a commercial building which is subject to the Regulations and similarly upon the assignment of an existing lease of such building (which will be treated as a sale for these purposes).

The EPC must be provided free of charge by the landlord (or seller/assignor) to the prospective tenant (or buyer/assignee) as early as possible and at latest:

- upon the provision of any written information about the building requested by the prospective tenant or buyer; or

- on viewing; or

- in any event, prior to exchanging contracts for sale or letting.

An EPC is also needed upon completion of a newly constructed building or alteration to an existing building (so that it has greater or fewer parts designed or altered for separate use than it previously had before alteration), where the alterations include the provision or extension of fixed heating, hot water, air conditioning or mechanical ventilation.

16.5 When is an EPC not needed?

There are certain situations in which an EPC will not be required; these include:

- lease renewals or extensions;

- lease surrenders; and

- where the building is suitable for demolition and for redevelopment (e.g. planning consent obtained or applied for) and there are reasonable grounds to believe that the prospective tenant or buyer intends to demolish.

In addition, certain types of building are also excluded from the EPC requirements:

- buildings used solely or primarily as places of worship;

- temporary buildings with a planned use of less than two years;

- stand-alone buildings with a useful floor area of less than 50 m²; and

- low energy demand buildings such as a barn.

16.6 EPC costs and service charge

Whilst the Regulations require the EPC to be provided free of charge to prospective tenants or buyers, a landlord may organise an EPC for the whole building and may be able to recover the cost of producing a certificate, as a service charge cost. However, this will only be possible if the lease is very clearly drafted on the point: many will not specifically provide for such recovery and the standard 'sweeper' clause is unlikely to help. In addition, tenants with short term contracted out leases will argue that any such charge is unreasonable, in that they will obtain no practical benefit.

Similar points may be made in relation to air conditioning inspections; however, it may be easier here for the charge to form part of an 'annual inspection' and, if the service charge clause is appropriately worded, collect the charge under that head of expenditure.

Whether the recommendations produced at the same time will be covered is another matter – taken in isolation, they are likely to be viewed, for the most part, as improvements and not chargeable – save to the extent that they are subsequently picked up as part of the 'renewal' or 'repair' of the plant and equipment or the building itself.

16.7 EPC energy assessment and access to the premises

EPCs may only be issued by an accredited energy assessor. All energy assessors have to be members of an approved accreditation scheme, a number of which are now in place. There are three different categories of buildings and assessors have to be accredited to the applicable level of the building they are reviewing. Under the Regulations, the assessor owes the tenant/buyer a duty to carry out the energy assessment with reasonable care and skill, enforceable during the currency of the EPC.

Whether or not the lease specifically provides for such a right of access, the Regulations impose a specific duty on any relevant person to allow access to an energy assessor to carry out the assessment/inspection. The tenant is not therefore entitled to prevent the landlord's energy assessor having access to the property where the landlord is under a duty to provide an EPC (but this does not apply where the EPC is being obtained by the landlord voluntarily). What is unclear (and not provided for in the Regulations) is what happens if a tenant denies an assessor access, in breach of the Regulations.

16.8 Duration of the EPC

An EPC remains valid until the expiry of a period of ten years from when it is first made available, unless a subsequent EPC has been issued for the building.

Notwithstanding that the Regulations provide that a reference to a building includes part of a building, this does not mean that a new EPC for the building is required as a matter of course where a tenant obtains a separate EPC for a unit forming part of the building. The CLG guidance states that in such circumstances the previous EPC for the whole building remains valid, save in respect of transactions that relate soley to the part for which the subsequent EPC is obtained. From a practical point of view, however, it would be sensible for the landlord to obtain a new updated EPC for the building where works in the tenant's premises trigger the need for an EPC for that unit.

A new EPC will be required where there are works resulting in a material change to the unit – see further comments in section 16.4.

16.9 EPCs and negotiating lease terms generally

Suggestions as to how issues affecting EPCs might best be covered in commercial leases are many and varied. In our view, many of the changes put forward are not necessary and may well raise as many questions as answers. Common sense suggests that, at least in the short term, any drafting changes should be kept to a minimum.

The following are among the points which might be considered:

- Mutual rights for the provision of EPCs and related information and for the inspection of premises (with each party bearing its own costs).

- A bar on tenant's alterations which would have an adverse effect on the landlord's EPC.

- The tenant to pay landlord's costs for an updated EPC where required in relation to permitted tenant's alterations.

- The recovery of EPC costs through the service charge: this is likely to be contentious and resisted by tenants as a charge resulting from a dealing with the reversion; it may be better dealt with by way of a side agreement, if at all.

- Rent review assumptions and disregards: there is considerable uncertainty as to what may be achieved by drafting provisions for EPCs here which may only serve to complicate or confuse. The fact remains that an EPC is confirmation of the energy efficiency of a building – that is an innate characteristic of the building, which will be one of a number of factors impacting upon any assessment of rental value, regardless of whether an EPC is in place.

- A requirement for compliance with EPC recommendations is likely to be resisted by tenants, or at the very least qualified in relation to reasonableness and costs.

16.10 Display Energy Certificates

While this chapter focuses on EPCs, a further requirement in the Regulations for the provision of a

Display Energy Certificate (DEC) is also noteworthy, not least because of the possibility that this requirement, currently confined to 'public service' buildings, may well be subsequently extended to commercial buildings generally.

A DEC is required for any building with a total useful floor area of over 1,000 sq. m where the occupier is either a public authority (which includes central or local government, schools, the police and statutory and regulatory bodies) or an institution that provides public services to a large number of people and is visited by a large number of those people – for example, museums and public swimming pools.

The DEC has to be displayed prominently, in clear view of the public, and will provide information about the energy used in the building (which will be on a scale of A–G) and include the operational rating over the previous two years. Unlike an EPC, a DEC must be replaced annually and the recommendations which accompany it do not have to form part of the displayed certificate.

In contrast with EPCs, where an occupier is required to display a DEC in a building, the DEC will only remain valid for a period of 12 months, commencing on a date nominated by the energy assessor, which commencement date cannot be more than three months from the end of the 12-month period of energy consumption in the building upon which the operational rating for the DEC was based.

Good practice guidance published by the government (CLG – *Improving the energy efficiency of our buildings: a guide to display energy certificates and advisory reports for public buildings*, May 2008) describes the scope of and requirements for DECs and their application in practice. In order to comply with the duties imposed on an occupier of an affected building to display the DEC, the guidance recommends that the certificate should be no smaller than A3 size and should ideally be placed in the reception area (or entrance) or be clearly visible from it. The guidance also provides a series of practical examples for dealing with both single and shared occupation of relevant buildings.

16.11 Non-compliance and offences

Local authorities are responsible for enforcing the EPC requirements.

Failure to provide an EPC when required by the Regulations may result in service of a penalty charge notice, giving rise to liability to pay a specified penalty. The penalty for failing to make an EPC available to any prospective tenant or buyer when letting or selling non-dwellings is fixed, in most cases, at 12.5 per cent of the rateable value of the building (with a default penalty of £750 where the formula cannot be applied) and in any event cannot be less than £500 nor more than £5,000. (A formula is used because the costs of producing an EPC for non-dwellings may vary according to the size, complexity and use of the building.)

It is possible to raise a defence to a penalty charge notice where an EPC has been commissioned from an accredited energy assessor at least 14 days before it was required and where, despite all reasonable efforts, it has not been received at the relevant time.

The penalty for failure to display a DEC for public buildings is a fine of £500 and/or £1,000 for failing to have possession of a valid advisory report. Information must be available within seven days of the request being made.

16.12 Points to consider

- The duty to provide an EPC falls on the landlord (on a lease grant) or the seller (on an assignment).
- The EPC must be produced at the earliest opportunity and at the landlord's cost.
- Traditional service charge wording may not be wide enough to allow recovery of EPC costs from the tenant.
- Although EPCs have a ten-year lifespan, they may need earlier replacement in response to certain events, e.g. works to the tenant's premises.
- Specific EPC lease drafting changes should be kept to a minimum, at least in the short term, until market pratice settles down.

Green leases

17.1 Overview

The 'green lease' is a phrase which has in recent times become all too common. It is used to describe leases which incorporate new provisions and obligations which reflect an increasing concern about the effects of climate change. This concern has run in tandem with a raft of legislation which has pushed forward the concept of a green lease. For instance, the *Energy Performance of Buildings Directive*, which was introduced into the UK in 2006, has resulted in a change to the *Building Regulations*; the result of this legislation is that commercial buildings have to produce 27 per cent less carbon than before.

The government's introduction of EPCs is just one of the examples of policies which are being drawn up with the aim of promoting greater awareness of environmental issues; the government hope that, as a result of that awareness, owners/investors and occupiers of commercial buildings will put in place working policies which have the stated intent of reducing the effect that the occupancy of a building will have on the environment; some of those policies will be found in a 'green lease'.

The landlord/tenant company director will be mindful of the requirement in section 172 of the *Companies Act* 2006 for directors to have 'regard to the impact of the company's operations on the community and the environment'. They will also be aware of the cost savings that may be achievable, although this will need to be set against the cost of implementation of the policies promoted by a green lease.

Whether the green lease has detailed and onerous clauses or just some short 'policy statements', is another matter; some landlords are promoting leases with 'green' clauses, whereas others seem to be promoting a less prescriptive approach, with the parties agreeing to work towards the principles set out in a handbook.

Although it is clear that the 'direction of travel' is towards the imposition of more 'green' statutory targets and obligations (and thus the inclusion of more 'green' provisions in leases), we are still very much at the early stages of the evolution of the green lease and so in this chapter we have approached it by way of a review of some general principles which can then be applied in different ways, depending upon which approach is adopted, if at all.

17.2 The green building

Before considering the terms of a green lease, one has to place the lease in its context – the 'green building', for want of a better phrase.

The general principles of a green lease can be seen to fit easily with a new building, which has been designed (thanks, in part, to the *Building Regulations*) with these principles in mind and where, for instance, the occupier has required a BREEAM (Building Research Establishment Environmental Assessment Method) 'excellent' or even 'outstanding' rating. A new update to BREEAM came in to force on 1 August 2008; this update has included a new rank of 'outstanding' which applies to buildings which score more than 85 per cent; previously the top band was 'excellent' which applies to buildings which score 70 per cent. This change had been prompted, in part, because some buildings with an energy performance certificate rating of C achieve an 'excellent' rating – which is not what should be expected. In this example, a lease with 'green clauses' can be seen as no more than good practice – to ensure that, for example, the tenant:

- maintains the building's rating and energy certification;

- complies with various planning obligations, such as the establishment of a green travel plan;

- uses the air handling and conditioning plant, in line with its specification; and

- assists the landlord by providing it with certain types of information relating to building management and operation.

However, can the same be applied to a warehouse built, say, 40 years ago? Probably not, is the answer, but that still does not mean that some of the principles could not be considered and one or two could be applied, to a lesser degree. Some will view this as 'aspirational' and of little practical effect; however, by way of example, one building in Melbourne, Australia was refurbished according to the above principles in 2002 and the refurbishment costs were 5 per cent more than a more traditional scheme. However, the building has seen a 65 per cent reduction in energy consumption, a 90 per cent reduction in water consumption, an 80 per cent reduction in lighting consumption and an apparent 5–15 per cent increase in staff productivity.

The basic point is that 'green' principles and sustainability are now part of the market place and will apply to a greater or lesser extent, depending on the nature of the building and the policies of the parties concerned.

A green building will have some, if not all, of the following features:

- Materials: policies promoting the reuse of existing materials on site and requiring contractors to use materials from 'renewable' (i.e. commercially managed) and recycled resources and to adopt design principles which reduce the materials needed during construction; use of chemical free (or reduced chemical) cleaning and other products.

- Energy efficiency: promoting designs which optimise natural ventilation and lighting; hybrid passive mechanical ventilation, cooling and heating; reducing lighting and energy demands and using high efficiency artificial lighting; shading and low emission glazing; electricity from solar panels or other 'green' sources, where available; using open plan layouts.

- Water usage: collecting rainwater for use in open areas; efficient water supply and use and on site waste water treatment.

- Human environment: some of the above points should lead to improved internal air quality and better management of the internal temperature of the building; in addition, it could provide for, say, a landscaped roof garden and the use of the building could be linked to a green travel plan – with bicycle parking and security as well as showers, car share policies etc.

- Management: environmentally friendly management systems will promote the above matters and could help foster a 'community' spirit; they will also monitor and help fine tune the environmental performance of the building and its occupiers. Part of this management will be the requirement to enter into a 'green lease'.

17.3 The handbook

The 'green building' is likely to have prompted the production of a handbook for that particular property (which could form part of the health and safety file). Managing agents should ensure that this handbook is kept up to date and it can then be produced at the outset of lease negotiations – on the basis that the tenant will be providing some form of acknowledgement that it has seen the handbook and will comply with the relevant provisions.

The handbook could include the following information:

- The energy performance rating for the demise/building.

- Environmental management policies – targets for energy, water and waste reduction. These policies will depend on all sorts of factors, but examples of some of the 'headings' could be:
    - (i) energy reduction targets;
    - (ii) the operational range of the air conditioning system – e.g. it will not be on when the internal temperature is between 19–26°C;
    - (iii) policies/awareness: staff awareness campaigns – switch off campaigns – web site;
    - (iv) energy reduction targets;
    - (v) energy monitoring – half hour meter readings;
    - (vi) contractors to comply with the environmental policies;
    - (vii) management systems; and
    - (viii) collective waste re-cycling.
- Metering and monitoring of data.
- Performance details of air conditioning/heating systems.

- Environmental policies – such as a commitment to employ efficient management techniques – there should be one for the common parts and a basic framework for the areas to be let. (A good starting point would be The Carbon Trust's *Good Practice Guide 376: A strategic approach to energy and environmental management*, 2004.)

- Audits and reports.

- Waste re-cycling schemes – central collection – as well as waste disposal.

- Asbestos management file.

17.4 The green lease

A green lease will still contain all the elements you would expect to see in a standard 'institutional' lease, albeit there may be one or two qualifications.

What it will also contain are provisions clearly dividing up the responsibility for certain environmental matters, coupled with a framework within which the landlord and tenant can work together to achieve whatever targets they set themselves to reduce the impact that the occupancy of the building will have on the environment.

Some commentators are concerned that a lease with 'green lease provisions' will be unduly onerous and that this will have an adverse effect on rent review. It is a difficult concern to address simply but we would make the following general points:

- a lot will depend on the drafting and a green lease does not have to be onerous – it can suggest targets and help promote certain policies and co-ordinate certain actions – which in themselves may reduce costs;

- by following certain policies, the costs of heating and lighting may be reduced substantially – resulting in a reduction in the general service charge costs;

- by adopting certain policies construction costs can be reduced – e.g. lower energy needs would reduce the size of the mechanical and electrical systems;

- 'green design' appears to help increase productivity/attendance.

We would come back to the basic point which is that a green lease should provide a structure which the occupiers of the building can work around in order to reduce consumption and minimise the effect that that building and its occupancy has on the environment. It will not be a matter of one size fits all – some of the policies will be applicable to an occupier, others not. It is therefore important to ensure that the 'green' provisions are not too onerous and are flexible.

With this in mind, we would suggest that they are better placed in a handbook supplemental to a lease than put in as tenant covenants. This would allow for more flexibility – it is easier to update a handbook than a lease and, without a doubt, this is an area which will see substantial changes over a relatively short period of time. Whichever route the parties follow, the tenant will be concerned to ensure that failure to comply with the 'green' regulations will not result in forfeiture of the lease; this can be achieved by an express statement to that effect in the forfeiture clause. Nevertheless, the inclusion in a lease of 'green' provisions – even if they are not especially onerous and are set out in a supplemental handbook – will create a new range of rights and obligations and may therefore inevitably increase the scope for disagreement and dispute, particularly during the early years of the lease as landlords and tenants get to grips with the consequences of these new terms.

Landlords should devise frameworks which tenants have to fill out with their bespoke policies. For instance, the tenant could be obliged to draw up an energy

management policy and to provide a copy to the
landlord and that policy document could contain, for
instance:

- an energy conservation section containing the tenant's
proposals for minimising the consumption of energy;

- a waste reduction section containing the tenant's
proposals for reducing the quantity of waste
generated; and

- a sustainable transport section containing the tenant's
proposals for minimising the number of car journeys
by employees and visitors and in the delivery of
goods to or from the property.

Set out below are some further topics which
commentators have suggested should be covered – some
are more practical than others.

Clause	Commentary
AUDITS/POLICIES	
To provide full details of energy consumption and monitoring records and the tenant's environmental/waste minimisation policies.	Sub meters should be installed where possible to assess the overall energy performance of the buildings
Provisions setting energy efficiency targets with financial penalties if such targets are not met. (This would form part of an energy conservation plan – one part would be for the occupied units and the other for the common parts.)	The idea of penalties will not help promote the adoption of green lease policies and is highly contentious; the motivation should be lower energy bills
Landlord's right to inspect and test	In line with Regulations 8 and 9 of Directive 2009/91/EC on the energy performance of buildings, which are likely to be implemented within the next year

Clause	Commentary
Tenant to comply (and procure contractors and sub tenants comply) with the landlord's environmental policy	There will be one for the building and then one for the areas to be let; the second one will provide a basic framework and may go in to detail where the policies link in with the building, otherwise leaving the tenant to finalise one for the demise
Landlord to carry out a full environmental audit/survey every 3 years and provide that to the tenants or in a single let building the tenant covenants to carry this out and provide a copy to the landlord	If the landlord does this then it will seek to recover the cost via the service charge – one way or another the cost will fall on the tenants and it is therefore going to be difficult for many tenants to accept. On the plus side audits provide insights into how to reduce costs and can help establish future aims for an environmental policy.
Parties agree to set targets to reduce consumption and establish environmental policies	The reduction of energy consumption should result in cost savings, but there is likely to be a cost attached to such policies so this element may be difficult to follow through on – it might also be too vague to be enforceable. The idea of penalties will not help promote the adoption of green lease policies and is highly contentious; the motivation should be lower energy bills
SERVICE CHARGE	
Service charge to allow for regular consultations with and inspections by energy advisors and environmental consultants and provide for an annual audit of the building's performance levels	
The landlord to be able to adjust the service charge linked to consumption – to reflect individual tenant's initiatives in reducing energy consumption	This has the appearance of a penalty for non performance and will be resisted by most tenants even though it could be 'sold' on the basis that it is a reward for adopting good practice. It also introduces a conflict point – there are enough areas for disputes between landlord and tenants without the need for more. The fact of the matter is that if a tenant takes the initiative then its energy bills will be reduced through metering – assuming the unit is separately metered – without any action by the landlord.

Clause	Commentary
In the service charge improvements should be allowed as a cost where they improve the environmental performance of plant and equipment or have otherwise resulted in energy savings	
ALTERATIONS	
Alterations should not have an adverse impact on the energy performance/efficiency of a building (or the energy performance rating of the demise)	They will have to comply, in any event, with Approved Doc L2B. Sub-division should not interfere with HVAC systems (either by making it less efficient or consume more energy). See The Carbon Trust's *Good Practice Guide 376: A strategic approach to energy and environmental management*, 2004 – for further information on fit out specification clauses.
ASSIGNMENT	
As a pre condition to an assignment, the assignee has to sign up to the landlord's environmental policy	

17.5 Points to consider

- The concept of a green lease is not 'one size fits all'; it is very much a matter of ensuring that whatever 'green' obligations, targets, policies, enforcement procedures etc., the lease and any side document contain, they are relevant to the building (and its design) and 'proportionate'.

- The clauses adopted should be there to help reduce the carbon footprint of the building; they are likely to be (in part) aspirational – setting targets – and, further, they will have to be sufficiently flexible so as to apply equally to the existing tenant (and how it proposes to use the building) and a potential assignee or subtenant; as such, it will be difficult (especially in the current market) to link those clauses to a forfeiture clause in the lease.

- Following on from the last point, a framework with suggestions and targets and which provides the structure for the landlord and tenant to work together to reduce the carbon footprint (as well as a few simple requirements) is more likely to be acceptable than a prescriptive, rigid, vague and costly set of provisions.

- This is a rapidly evolving area; legislation is driving matters forward supported by a developing focus on corporate responsibility; in reviewing any green clause in a lease, step back from it and consider how it will work in, say, ten years time.

Miscellaneous

18

There are various matters which are beyond the scope of this guide, but we briefly mention a few below.

18.1 Rent deposits and bank guarantees

These will be required by landlords where they are not satisfied that the tenant's financial status is such that the tenant 'can stand on its own'; alternatively, the landlord may require a bank or parent company guarantee or guarantees from the directors.

Under a rent deposit, the tenant will deposit a sum of money which will represent the equivalent of a period of rent (and possibly service charge) payable under the lease (often six months or a year) plus the equivalent of VAT on that sum. Some other points to consider when negotiating the terms of a rent deposit are:

● Should the deposit be increased pro rata upon rent review – assuming the rent increases?

● Should interest accrue to the deposit account or should it be paid to the tenant at stated intervals?

● Should there be a release from the deposit if the tenant's accounts achieve a certain level, consistently, over a set period of time – a common test is that the audited accounts of the tenant over the last three consecutive financial years show a net profit (after tax) in excess of three times the total annual rent, insurance and service charge payable under the lease; another test is a 'net asset test', usually being a multiple of ten and often being a combination of the two.

- What happens if the landlord sells its interest? For instance, the deposit could be transferred to the new owner with a new rent deposit deed being completed, under which the outgoing landlord is released.

Personal guarantees follow fairly standard wording, but some only guarantee the payment of monies, sometimes being limited to just the principal rent, insurance and service charge due under the lease, and no more; in this they can mirror wording found in bank guarantees, which are linked to stated sums and would not be viewed as 'performance guarantees'. A full personal guarantee will go further and (in addition to paying all sums due) require the guarantor to comply with the tenant's covenants and, in some circumstances, if required by the landlord, to enter into a new lease.

Many guarantees also contain full indemnities, which extend the potential liability to more than just rents and other contractual payments under the lease – see section 18.2 for further explanation.

Bank guarantees are normally just for specified sums, capped at a maximum stated sum and in place for a set period of time. The bank will normally charge the tenant an arrangement fee for putting the guarantee in place (as well as any renewal) and will usually require some form of collateral from the tenant.

These are complicated documents and professional advice must be taken to ensure that, among other things, the rent deposit is protected if the landlord becomes insolvent or sells on its interest to a third party and is returned after a stated time, with interest credited to the tenant.

The Lease Code provides that tenants 'should be protected against the default or insolvency of the landlord' and that the conditions for releasing rent deposits and guarantees should be clearly stated.

18.2 Indemnities

Leases now often contain a wide ranging indemnity clause; these provide greater protection for the landlord than a simple claim for breach of contract/covenant.

An indemnity, when called upon, is a claim for a fixed amount and would be pursued as a debt claim; accordingly there is no need to prove loss itself, just that the event giving rise to the indemnity has occurred; there is no qualification to the claim, to the effect that the claim has to be 'reasonably foreseeable' (as would be the case for a damages claim); it would not be viewed as a 'penalty'; the limitation period for an indemnity starts from the date the claim arises and not when the breach occurred.

The proper place for an indemnity is where the wrongful act of the defendant (tenant) has exposed the claimant (landlord) to third party action; otherwise the landlord (as it is usually the tenant being asked to give the indemnities) should rely on a claim under breach of contract for damages.

The wording of the indemnity could well be wide enough (possibly inadvertently) to impose a potential liability on the tenant for pre-lease contamination – where possible, this should be excluded, when acting for a tenant (See Chapter 12 for further consideration of this point).

The effect of indemnities, if required, can be reduced by negotiating certain limitations, making the indemnity subject to conditions (to be complied with by the indemnified party) in favour of the party giving the indemnity (the indemnifier), which should include requirements as to:

- timely notification to the indemnifier of claims made (with full details);

- close consultation with the indemnifier in any negotiation on claims made or resultant actions or proceedings;

- indemnifier's consent to the settlement or compromise of any claim;

- indemnified party taking steps reasonably required by indemnifier with a view to settling claims without prejudicing or increasing indemnifier's liability;

- indemnified party mitigating its losses.

18.3   The covenant to use reasonable or best endeavours

Lawyers spend a lot of time arguing and writing about what this means and the courts spend an equal amount of time on the point. Without falling into the same trap:

- 'best endeavours' is more than 'reasonable endeavours';

- reasonable endeavours will normally mean taking a reasonable course of action – but not all the (reasonable) courses of action which may be available at the time;

- reasonable endeavours does not mean sacrificing ones own commercial interests;

- best endeavours will mean taking all the reasonable courses available at the time – this could mean that there is little practical difference between 'all reasonable' and 'best endeavours'.

It is unlikely there will ever be a clear ruling on this matter, as it will ultimately rest upon the relevant circumstances of each case [*Rhodia International Holding Ltd v Huntsman International Ltd* [2007] EWHC 292].

18.4 The landlord's covenant for quiet enjoyment

This misleadingly named covenant has very little to do with noise; it is more a covenant to the effect that the landlord will not interrupt the tenant's possession ('enjoyment') of the property. Under common law, there is an implied covenant in all leases, unless (which is almost invariably the case) there is an express covenant.

The basic effect of the covenant is twofold: (i) that the landlord is confirming that it has title to grant the lease at the time of the grant of the lease, (this is not the same as a covenant with full title guarantee and only gives some limited protection); and (ii) that the landlord will not do anything (substantial) to deprive the tenant of its ordinary and reasonable right of possession of the property. So what can amount to 'substantial' interference? The cases normally emphasise some element of physical interference; the following (on their particular facts) have been held to amount to breach of the covenant:

- failure to repair an adjacent culvert which subsequently (as a result of the lack of repair) let water damage the property;

- cutting off the gas supply;

- mining activities causing subsidence;

- regular excessive noise from an adjacent flat controlled by the landlord;

- scaffolding outside a shop obstructing the entrance – this will not always apply, especially where the landlord has reserved a right to put up scaffolding.

Special care should be taken where the landlord is, or may be, occupying adjacent premises which the landlord may wish to redevelop. In such circumstances, the landlord should ensure that it reserves sufficient rights to do so, to ensure that it will not breach the quiet enjoyment covenant in carrying out the required works.

Furthermore, the lease should be framed in such a way as to prevent rights of light being granted to the tenant at the outset or being subsequently acquired by the tenant. The lease should provide that any such rights that do arise are enjoyed expressly with and subject to the landlord's consent.

The landlord will not normally be liable for the acts of third parties or a superior landlord – unless the lease states otherwise. If a landlord is found liable it will be on the basis of a breach of covenant (contract) but as the breach may also involve various tortious activities which would enable the tenant to claim more by way of damages than for a simple breach of covenant. The tenant may also be able to obtain an injunction.

18.5 The landlord's covenant for non-derogation from grant

This is not usually referred to in the lease but is implied under common law. In effect it means that the landlord cannot grant a benefit on one hand and take it away with the other. To all intents and purposes there is little difference now between this covenant and the covenant for quiet enjoyment. The cases tend to involve situations where the landlord has retained adjacent land; the landlord has to do something on that land which renders the tenant's land substantially less fit for the purpose for which it was let; note that this is not the same as setting up a competing business, unless the landlord has entered into an express covenant to that effect.

Two old cases provide examples of where a breach has occurred:

- a wood drying shed required the free flow of air from adjacent premises and the landlord put up a building on adjacent land which interrupted the flow of air;

- an explosives store required a licence which was conditional upon there being no nearby buildings; the landlord constructed a building nearby which resulted in the loss of the licence.

18.6 Land Registry procedures

October 2003 heralded major changes in the law relating to title registration. Previously, leases of twenty-one years or more had to be registered at the Land Registry, but now this obligation applies to leases granted for a term of over seven years, and to leases with seven or more years to run when they change hands. (There are plans at some point in the future to reduce the qualifying period to three years.)

Apart from the relatively small additional expense of registration, there are other practical consequences:

- An accurate scale plan of the leased premises showing a north point must be provided. This may involve extra expense on the renewal of a lease of part of a building where the old lease had no plan or an inadequate plan, or on the assignment of such a lease.

- A registered lease is now a public document. Anyone can get a copy of it from the Land Registry. The landlord or tenant may apply to have sensitive parts of the lease excluded from the copy available to the public. The relevant provisions are complicated and do not guarantee confidentiality, as it is open to the Land Registry to take a different view on the merits of the application. (The position has been further complicated by the implementation on 1 January 2005 of certain provisions in the *Freedom of Information Act* 2000, which may also apply to requests for such information.)

A lease of less than seven years cannot be registered. But if it grants rights over other registered land which are not readily apparent on inspection there is a (fairly remote) danger that those rights can be lost if they are only periodically exercised, unless they are registered at the Land Registry.

Where the landlord's title is registered at the Land Registry, but where the lease itself is not registrable, an application should nevertheless be made to the Land Registry to note against the relevant titles any legal easements granted in or reserved by any such lease, since those easements cannot take effect at law until 'completed by registration' [s. 27 *Land Registration Act* 2002].

Another change put in place under the 2002 Act which affects all registered land, whether freehold or leasehold, was the abolition of land and charge certificates, as a prelude to fully paperless conveyancing.

The abolition of documents of title may make frauds easier. It is therefore all the more important to ensure that company numbers are registered as well as company names, and that the tenant keeps its registered address at the Land Registry up-to-date, so that any official notices reach it. A maximum of three addresses may be registered, one of which may be an e-mail address.

A further development in respect of leases and land registration was the introduction of a legal requirement for the inclusion of fourteen 'LR' standard clauses at the front of a 'prescribed clauses' lease, which (subject to certain exceptions) is essentially any registrable lease granted out of a registered estate on or after 19 June 2006. These act as a sort of extended 'particulars', providing a summary (in many cases by means of cross-reference to relevant clause or schedule numbers) of the essential ingredients of the lease, at least from a land registration point of view. They include information about the parties, title numbers, date, property, term, easements, covenants, etc., and it is from this information (and this information only) that the Land Registry will identify the relevant matters to be entered on the registers of title.

The important point to note is that any failure to comply with the required format and wording of these clauses or to complete the LR clauses properly and fully could result in the application for registration of the lease being rejected and/or may result in important rights and other matters not being entered as required in registers of title, affecting the validity or enforceability of such matters.

18.7 Tax

Taking a lease gives rise to various tax issues, some of which are very complicated and detailed advice should be taken at a very early stage to consider the impact of such taxes. The taxes which are most likely to be relevant are:

Stamp Duty Land Tax: This is now a substantial tax payable upon the grant of a lease. In some cases, the lease can be drafted to mitigate the liability.

VAT: In particular, it will be necessary to determine whether or not VAT will be charged on the rent and service charge and to ensure that the lease is structured so as to avoid, as far as possible, there being any irrecoverable VAT.

Capital Allowances: Clauses may be required in order to ensure that capital allowances are available to the party making capital payments or contributions.

18.8 Further reading and information

Service charges: RICS 2006 *Code of Practice on Service Charges in Commercial Property*:
www.servicechargecode.co.uk

The Lease Code: *The Code for Leasing Business Premises in England and Wales 2007*:
www.leasingbusinesspremises.co.uk

Dilapidations: *Property Litigation Association Protocol for Terminal Dilapidations Claims for Damages* which addresses some of the problems linked to dilapidations:
www.pla.org.uk

Advisers: For advice on property advisers/surveying firms: Royal Institution of Chartered Surveyors: contact centre: 020 7222 7000

Tax deduction: For information on the foreign landlords tax deduction scheme:
www.hmrc.gov.uk/cnr/nr_landlords.htm

The DDA: For information on the *Disability Discrimination Act* and the Code of Practice relating to the Act see the government's disabled people website pages at:
www.direct.gov.uk/en/DisabledPeople/RightsAndObligations/DisabilityRights/DG_4001068 or the Disability Rights Commission website at: www.drc.org

The CIS: For advice on the Construction Industry Scheme: www.hmrc.gov.uk/new-cis

Appendix A: Service Charge Code: drafting suggestions

1 DEFINITIONS AND INTERPRETATION

'"Interim Service Charge Sum" means a yearly sum assessed by the Landlord or the Landlord's Surveyor on account of the Service Charge for each Service Charge Accounting Period being a fair and reasonable estimate of the Service Charge payable by the Tenant in respect of that Service Charge Accounting Period

"Services" means the services to be provided by the Landlord for the benefit of the Building or some part or parts thereof as are set out in Schedule [ ]

"Service Charge" means the proportion or proportions of the Service Charge Expenditure attributable to the Property determined in accordance with the provisions of Schedule [ ]

"Service Charge Accounting Period" means [ ] in each year to (and including) [ ] in the following year or such other period of a year as shall be notified by the Landlord to the Tenant in writing

"Service Charge Certificate" means a certificate showing the Service Charge Expenditure and Service Charge for each Service Charge Accounting Period served pursuant to Schedule [ ]

"Service Charge Expenditure" means the reasonable costs properly incurred by the Landlord in any Service Charge Accounting Period in carrying out or procuring the carrying out of the Services and providing each item of the Services in accordance with the terms of this Lease.

> "Service Charges Code" means the Service Charges in
> Commercial Property – RICS Code of Practice (June
> 2006) published by RICS Books.'

Service Charge Code, paragraph 19:

'19. Where service charge payments are kept in a
separately identified account any interest earned can be
easily identified and, after any appropriate deductions
made (bank charges, tax, etc.), credited back to the
account.'

> "Service Charge Account" means a separate
> interest–bearing bank account maintained by the
> Landlord for the purpose of receiving and holding
> monies received from the Tenant on account of
> Service Charge

Service Charge Code, paragraphs 49 to 51:

'49. The owner will submit certified accounts to the
occupiers in a timely manner and in any event within
four months of the end of the service charge year.

50. The accounts will give an adequately detailed and
comprehensive summary of items of expenditure with full
explanations of any material variations (+ or −) against
the budget, and in a reasonably consistent format
year-on-year.

51. The budgets and accounts will be issued with a
report that provides the following minimum information:

(a) a reasonably comprehensive level of detail to enable
occupiers to compare expenditure against estimated
budget;

(b) explanations of significant individual costs and of
variances from the previous year's budget/accounts;

(c) comparison against the previous two years' actual
costs where appropriate;

(d)   information on core matters critical to that account
(e.g. levels of apportionment, contracts, report on
tendering, etc.);

(e)   the achieved and/or targeted measures of improved
management performance (e.g. success in delivering
improved quality services and greater value for
money);

(f)   separately identified on-site management team costs;

(g)   details of the results of the last previous and
forthcoming tendering exercise (occupiers will be
advised of the contractors who are providing the
services); and

(h)   a statement detailing how income generated from
operating the property (sometimes known as
'commercialisation' or 'mall income') is dealt with
and how shared services are charged, setting out
how they impact on the service charge and what
reimbursement has been made to the service charge
for these.'

"Certified Account" means [a] [an independently]
certified service charge account and report which
materially comply with the requirements of
[paragraphs 49–51 (inclusive)] of the Service Charges
Code.

2   LANDLORD'S COVENANTS

Service Charge Code, paragraphs 24 and 32:

'**24.** The aim is to achieve value for money and effective
service rather than lowest price.

32. The owner will procure quality service standards to
ensure that value for money is achieved at all times.'

> 2.1 Subject to the payment by the Tenant of the Annual Rent, the Insurance Rent, the Service Charge [(or where there shall be bona fide outstanding dispute in respect of the same any element of the demanded Service Charge admitted by the Tenant)] and VAT on such sums the Landlord shall [use its reasonable endeavours to] provide the Services:
> (a) in accordance with the principles of good estate management; and
> (b) in an economical and efficient manner to achieve value for money.

Service Charge Code, paragraph 23:

'**23.** The services provided will be beneficial and relevant to the needs of the property, its owner, its occupiers and their customers.'

> 2.2 In any event, the Services provided by the Landlord must be beneficial and relevant to the needs of the Building, and to the needs of the Landlord, the Tenant, and other occupiers of the Building.
> 2.3 The Landlord may from time to time withhold or make any addition, extension or variation to any of the Services where in its [absolute] [reasonable] discretion it deems it desirable to do so provided that in doing so the Landlord acts in accordance with the provisions of clauses 2.1 and 2.2.

3 SERVICE CHARGE: ASCERTAINMENT AND PAYMENT

Service Charge Code, paragraph 41:

'**41.** Apportionment of costs to each occupier will be fair and reasonable and applied consistently throughout the property having regard to the physical size, nature of use, and benefits to and use by the occupier(s).'

> 3.1 The Service Charge payable by the Tenant ... shall be ... a fair and reasonable proportion of the Service Charge Expenditure attributable to the Property from time to time as reasonably determined by the Landlord or the Landlord's Surveyor acting in accordance with the principles of good estate management and having regard to the physical size, nature of use and benefits to and use of the Property and other parts of the Building by the Tenant.

Service Charge Code, paragraph 64:

'64. Interest earned and late payment interest should be credited to the service charge account. Bank charges and account operating costs will be offset against the interest. Owners are required to perform their obligations under the terms of the lease and account to occupiers for any balancing charges due/owed at the end of the service charge period.'

> 3.2 All sums paid to the Landlord by the Tenant by way of Interim Service Charge Sum shall be paid into and held (until expended) by the Landlord in the Service Charge Account.
>
> 3.3 Interest earned on all monies held from time to time in the Service Charge Account will be credited to the Service Charge Account.
>
> 3.4 Bank charges and operating costs in connection with the Service Charge Account will be offset against interest earned.

Service Charge Code, paragraph 48:

'48. The owner will provide an estimate of likely service charge expenditure and appropriate explanatory commentary on it to the occupiers, together with their proportion of the costs, one month prior to the commencement of the service charge year.'

> 3.5 No later than one calendar month prior to the commencement of every Service Charge Accounting Period the Landlord shall serve or cause to be served on the Tenant written notice of the Interim Service Charge Sum for the relevant Service Charge Accounting Period (together with an appropriate explanatory commentary thereon) ... .

Service Charge Code, paragraph 49:

'**49.** The owner will submit certified accounts to the occupiers in a timely manner and in any event within four months of the end of the service charge year'.

> 3.6 As soon as practicable after the expiry of every Service Charge Accounting Period but in any event no later than four months after the end of the relevant Service Charge Accounting Period the Landlord shall serve or cause to be served on the Tenant a Service Charge Certificate and Certified Account for the relevant Service Charge Accounting Period.

Service Charge Code, paragraphs 52–54:

'**52.** Where the owner or manager has demonstrably complied with the provisions of the lease and this Code of Practice, the owner will allow occupiers a reasonable period (e.g. four months from issue) in which to raise enquiries in respect of the certified accounts. Owners will deal with reasonable enquiries promptly and efficiently and make all relevant paperwork available for inspection. Where copies of the supporting documentation concerning the certified accounts have been supplied, an appropriate fee will be charged.

53. If the account is certified by an auditor, such costs will be charged to the service charge account. (Owners will not use an external audit as a means of giving credibility to the charge at the occupiers' cost.)

54. If the occupier requests an independent audit, the owner will agree and the audit fee will be charged to the occupier.'

> 3.7 A Service Charge Certificate and Certified Account shall contain a detailed summary of the Service Charge Expenditure in respect of the Service Charge Accounting Period to which it relates together with the relevant calculations showing the Service Charge and the Landlord shall also supply to the Tenant copies of all receipts records and vouchers in relation to the provision of the Services (or make the same reasonably available for inspection).
>
> 3.8 Within four months from the date of service on it of the Service Charge Certificate and Certified Account the Tenant may:
>
> (a) raise reasonable enquiries [in writing] with the Landlord in respect of the Certified Account and the Landlord will deal with such enquiries promptly and efficiently and make all relevant documents available for inspection by the Tenant (the Tenant to pay the reasonable costs of the Landlord in respect of the supply of supporting documentation concerning the Certified Account); and/or
>
> (b) request an independent audit which the Landlord will supply (the Tenant to pay the audit fee).

Service Charge Code, paragraph 52 and section D8:

'52. Where the owner or manager has demonstrably complied with the provisions of the lease and this Code of Practice, the owner will allow occupiers a reasonable period (e.g. four months from issue) in which to raise enquiries in respect of the certified accounts. Owners will deal with reasonable enquiries promptly and efficiently and make all relevant paperwork available for inspection. Where copies of the supporting documentation concerning the certified accounts have been supplied, an appropriate fee will be charged.'

'D8 Dispute Resolution

RICS Dispute Resolution Service

1. Summary

In the light of an increasing culture change in the civil judicial system, which is encouraging people to resolve their disputes without the intervention of the courts, RICS intends that the Code provides access to alternative dispute resolution (ADR) for parties involved in disputes about service charge matters.'

> 3.9 Where the Landlord has served on the Tenant a Service Charge Certificate showing that the Service Charge for any Service Charge Accounting Period exceeds the Interim Service Charge Sum for that Service Charge Accounting Period the Tenant shall pay to the Landlord or as it shall direct a sum (the "Balancing Charge") equal to the amount by which the Service Charge exceeds the Interim Service Charge Sum, as follows:
>
> (a) Where the Tenant has raised reasonable enquiries with the Landlord in respect of the Certified Account, within ten Working Days of receipt by the Tenant of a reasonable response;
>
> (b) Where there is a dispute or difference between the Landlord and the Tenant in connection with [the Balancing Charge] [the Service Charge, the Service Charge Certificate or the Service Charge Expenditure or any other matter arising under this Schedule], within ten Working Days of such dispute or difference being settled or determined in accordance with the provisions of [Part 5 of this Schedule];
>
> (c) In any other case, within four months after such service.

Service Charge Code, paragraph 16:

'**16.** When significant variances (e.g. of more than 2% above RPI) in actual year-on-year costs against budget are likely, the owner will notify occupiers promptly, within the current service charge year. It is the manager's duty to identify quarterly whether there are unforeseen variances and notify accordingly. Best practice is to confirm the half yearly forecast on an un-audited basis'

> 3.10 The Landlord shall at the end of the sixth month of each Service Charge Accounting Period provide the Tenant with written confirmation of the half-yearly Service Charge Expenditure (as far as the same is then reasonably known to the Landlord) on an unaudited basis.
>
> 3.11 As soon as reasonably practicable after the Landlord becomes aware of the likelihood of significant variances in the cost of the Services which are in the Landlord's reasonable opinion likely to result in the Service Charge in respect of any Service Charge Accounting Period exceeding the Interim Service Charge Sum for such period by more than [RPI + 2%] the Landlord shall give written notice of this to the Tenant.

4 SERVICES: INCIDENTAL COSTS AND EXPENDITURE TO BE INCLUDED

Service Charge Code, 'Administration' section, page 12:

'Administration

Management fees

The fee for the management service is the reasonable price for the total cost of managing the provision of the services at the location. This total price will not be linked to a percentage of expenditure. Such linkage is no longer appropriate and a disincentive to the delivery of value for money. The total price for the management service will be a fixed fee for a reasonable period of time (e.g. three years) and may be subject to indexing which will constitute an important part of the regular tendering and benchmarking of the service in the market economy.'

> 4.1
>
> (a) The reasonable and proper fees (plus disbursements) of managing agents engaged by the Landlord in connection with the provision or carrying out of the Services in an amount which represents the reasonable price for the total cost of managing the provision of the Services at the Building.
>
> (b) The total amount of such fees (excluding disbursements) shall not exceed [ ] pounds (£[ ])] in respect of the [first] Service Charge Accounting Period (ending on [date]).]

5 RESOLUTION OF DISPUTES

Service Charge Code, paragraph 2 and section D8:

'2. Best practice requires occupiers to have the right to reasonably challenge the propriety of expenditure. Each party will bear their own costs unless agreed or determined otherwise. See section D8 *Dispute resolution*.'

'D8 Dispute resolution

RICS Dispute Resolution Service

1. Summary

In the light of an increasing culture change in the civil judicial system, which is encouraging people to resolve their disputes without the intervention of the courts, RICS intends that the Code provides access to alternative dispute resolution (ADR) for parties involved in disputes about service charge matters.

2. *Introduction*

...

Purpose of this section

This section provides information about the Royal Institution of Chartered Surveyors (RICS) Dispute Resolution Service. It also includes a proposal for a two stage dispute resolution process which includes consensual mediation and expert determination. One or both of these processes can be used to resolve issues and full blown disputes arising out of service charges. The objective of the process is to encourage agreement and avoid disputes escalating. Where disputes are inevitable, the process is designed to resolve them quickly, discreetly and effectively by an impartial expert's decision. The process avoids the need for court action.'

> 5.1 If any dispute or difference arises out of or in connection with the Service Charge, the Service Charge Certificate or the Service Charge Expenditure or any other matter arising under this Schedule, such dispute is to be resolved by using the alternative dispute resolution procedure provided by the RICS Dispute Resolution Service (as referred to in section D8 of the Service Charges Code) as follows:
>
> (a) In the first instance, the dispute or difference is to be subject to evaluative mediation (as referred to in section D8 of the Service Charges Code) by a mediator appropriately experienced in service charge issues.

(b) If either party fails or refuses to agree to or participate in the evaluative mediation referred to in paragraph (a) above, or if in any event the dispute or difference is not resolved to the satisfaction of both parties within [ninety] days after it has arisen, the dispute or difference shall be determined by an independent Surveyor acting as an expert and not as an arbitrator to be appointed by agreement between the Landlord and the Tenant or in default by the President for the time being of the Royal Institution of Chartered Surveyors (and references to the President shall include the duly appointed deputy of the President, or any person authorised by the President to make appointments on his behalf or other proper officer for the time being of the Royal Institution of Chartered Surveyors) on the application of either the Landlord or the Tenant.

5.2 In the absence of any agreement or determination to the contrary, the Landlord and the Tenant shall each bear their own costs in respect of the matters referred to in clause [5.1] above.

Appendix B: List of more common service charge items

This list is 'typical' but should not be considered to be definitive; each service charge regime should be drawn up to fit the relevant estate. An industrial estate should have a simpler service charge regime than a shopping centre. There may be particular issues on an estate which require extensive reworking of this list: for example, what if there are underground tunnels or a podium?

This list envisages services to a building within an estate.

The list may well need to be qualified and some of the services may be defined as being 'discretionary', with the landlord having the choice whether or not those services should be provided – the balance of the services being required, but probably subject to various qualifications, such as the landlord not being liable for an interruption in the services where it has used reasonable endeavours to resume the provision of the services.

Accommodation

To provide, maintain, repair, decorate and light any accommodation and facilities for staff and contractors (including an operating office, maintenance stores and a workshop) and an estate management office and security gatehouse.

Apparatus, plant machinery, etc.

To maintain and operate all smoke and/or fire alarms and ancillary apparatus and fire prevention and fire fighting equipment and apparatus and other safety equipment and any other apparatus plant machinery and equipment and the buildings housing them.

Boundary fences

To provide, maintain, repair, replace (where necessary) and treat the boundary fences gates and structures of the estate.

Building

To maintain, repair, amend, alter, rebuild, renew and reinstate and where appropriate clean, wash down paint and decorate the structure and all other parts of the building (but excluding any items or parts of any items the maintenance of which is the exclusive responsibility of the tenant or any other tenants in the building).

Car parks

To maintain, clean, repair and (where necessary) resurface the car parking areas on the estate and keep them marked out and clear from obstructions.

Contracts for services and maintenance

The reasonable and proper cost of any maintenance contracts or contracts for the carrying out of all or any of the estate services and other functions and duties.

Drainage

To maintain, repair, replace (where necessary) and clean storm and foul drainage systems.

Electricity, gas, etc.

The cost incurred by the landlord for the supply of electricity, gas, oil or other fuel for the provision of the estate services and for all purposes in connection with the common areas excluding items for which the tenant or any other tenants of the estate is or are liable to pay for.

Energy and supply services

To arrange the provision of water, gas, heating, cooling, air conditioning, ventilation, electricity and other energy and supply services.

Fees

The reasonable and proper fees and disbursements of:

- the accountant and any surveyor and any other individual firm or company employed or retained by the landlord for (or in connection with) such surveying or accounting functions or the management of the estate and the provision of the estate services;

- the managing agents for or in connection with:
  - the management of the estate;
  - the collection of sums due to the landlord from the tenants and occupiers of the estate;

- the performance of the estate services and any other duties in and about the estate or any part of it relating to (without limitation) the general management administration security maintenance protection and cleanliness of the estate;

- any party valuing the estate for the purposes of assessing the full cost of rebuilding and reinstatement;

- any party providing caretaking or security arrangements and services to the estate;

- any party employed or retained by the landlord to perform (or in connection with) any of the estate services or any of the functions or duties referred to in this paragraph.

The proper management charge of the landlord or a group company of the landlord for any of the estate services or the other functions and duties referred to above that shall be undertaken by the landlord and not by a third party.

Fixtures and fittings, etc.

To provide and maintain fixtures, fittings, furnishings, finishes, bins, receptacles, tools, appliances, materials, equipment and other things for the maintenance, appearance, upkeep or cleanliness of the common areas.

Interest

Any interest (at commercial rates) and fees in respect of money borrowed to finance the provision of the estate services.

Landscaping

To maintain hard and soft landscaping and planting within the common areas including foundations, sculptures, architectural, artistic or ornamental features or murals and to keep all such parts of the common areas as may from time to time be laid out as landscaping (including any lake, fountain or other water features) neat, clean, planted (where appropriate) properly tended, treated and free from weeds and the grass cut and repair pruning and replacement and replanting of plants and trees.

Lighting

To keep lit at appropriate times all roads, footpaths, vehicle parking areas, cycleways, footbridges, landscaped and water covered areas and appropriate parts of the common areas.

Nuisance

The reasonable and proper cost to the landlord of abating a nuisance in respect of the estate or any part of it insofar as the same is not the liability of any individual tenant.

Outgoings

All rates taxes assessments duties charges impositions and outgoings which are now or during the term shall be charged assessed or imposed on:

- the whole of the estate where there is no separate charge assessment or imposition on or in respect of an individual part;

- the whole of the estate common areas or any part of them.

Provision of signs and general amenities

To provide and maintain direction signs and notices, seats and other fixtures and amenities for the convenience of tenants and their visitors.

Regulations

The reasonable and proper costs charges and expenses of preparing and supplying to the tenants copies of any regulations made by the landlord relating to the estate.

Roads open

To keep open and unobstructed the access and circulation areas – the roadways, streets, plazas and other vehicular and pedestrian ways and similar areas comprised in the common areas and where appropriate to clear snow and ice from the common areas and to lay grit on those areas subject only to:

- any temporary closure from time to time; or

- closure at certain hours for reasons of security or operational purposes.

Security surveillance visitor control

To provide security services and personnel including closed circuit television and/or other plant and equipment.

Staff

The reasonable and proper cost of employing such staff as the landlord may in its reasonable discretion deem necessary for the performance of the estate services and the other functions and duties referred to in this schedule and all other incidental expenditure in relation to such employment including:

- insurance pension and welfare contributions;

- transport facilities and benefits in kind;

- the provision of uniforms and working clothing;

- the provision of vehicles or appliances, cleaning and other materials fixtures fittings and other equipment for the proper performance of their duties and storage for housing the same; and

- a notional rent (not exceeding the current market rent such rent to be determined by the landlord acting reasonably) for any suitable premises on the estate provided rent free for every such person's use occupancy or residence or for the purpose of estate management or for the purpose of storage.

Statutory requirements, etc.

The reasonable and proper cost of taking all steps deemed desirable or expedient by the landlord for complying with making representations against or otherwise contesting the incidence of the provisions of any statute by-law or notice concerning town planning public health highways streets drainage or other matters relating to or alleged to relate to the estate or any part of it for which any tenant is not directly and exclusively liable.

Transport services

To operate and maintain vehicles or other modes of transport, staff premises and equipment for a transport service or services within or for the benefit of the estate.

Vermin control

To provide adequate vermin and pest control for the estate.

Other services

To provide such other services for the benefit of the estate or the convenience of the users or occupiers thereof as the landlord may in accordance with the principles of good estate management reasonably consider desirable or appropriate.

Appendix C: Contamination issues

Imposing liability for historic contamination on tenant: landlord's issues

Positives +	Negatives –	Action
Bolsters 'clear lease' principle.	Tenant highly likely to resist, resulting in protracted negotiations to exclude or limit liability.	Ensure assumption (and extent) of liability by tenant is clearly documented in lease.
Reduces potential for arguments between parties as to who bears liability in particular instances of 'contamination'.	Even if agreed, may adversely impact on level of rent achievable on review.	Avoid any inadvertent warranties by the landlord: all information to be supplied by landlord 'for information only'; tenant to carry out its own surveys and inspections etc.
Encourages a more proactive approach by tenant in promptly managing problems arising.	Loss of direct control by landlord as to how remediation is effected.	Require remediation to standards set by landlord's consultants.
Shifts financial burden of any clean-up onto tenant.	Lower rent potential	State expressly that rent has been adjusted (downwards) to reflect assumption of liability by tenant.

Lease provisions: competing issues for landlord and tenant on contamination liability

Lease provision	Landlord	Tenant
Repair	Tenant's repair obligations to include remediation of all contamination where required.	Liability for historic contamination to be expressly excluded (or limited). Limit liability for 'new' contamination to that caused by and arising as a direct result of tenant's use and occupation.
Yielding up	Tenant to produce soil survey supported by consultant's warranty at termination of lease.	Exclude/limit liability consistent with repair obligation.
Statutory compliance	Tenant to comply with all remediation notices and take other required action. Tenant to maintain and hand over to landlord requisite registers, records, etc. e.g. asbestos.	Liability for historic contamination to be expressly excluded (or limited).
Nuisance	Tenant not to cause or permit a nuisance etc. to include contamination.	Liability for historic contamination to be expressly excluded (or limited). Limit to contamination caused by the tenant arising from tenant's use and occupation.
Indemnity	Tenant's indemnity to be widely drawn so as to encompass all liability for contamination/remediation.	Tenant's indemnity expressly to exclude historic contamination. Tenant to seek indemnity/warranty from landlord assuming liability for historic contamination.

Lease provision	Landlord	Tenant
Service charge	Include ability for landlord to recover costs incurred in remediation, audits, surveys and inspections.	Expressly exclude costs incurred in remediation, etc. Obligation for landlord to bear costs of monitoring and remediation.
Commercial confidentiality	Require tenant to submit 'edited' version of lease for registration to omit any commercially sensitive items in lease.	

Bibliography

Code for Leasing Business Premises in England and Wales 2007, The Joint Working Group on Commercial Leases, 2007. The code can be viewed at www.leasingbusinesspremises.co.uk

Code of Measuring Practice: A Guide for Property Professionals (6th edition), RICS Books, Coventry, 2007 (ISBN 978 1 84219 332 7)

A code of practice for commercial leases in England and Wales (2nd edition), Commercial Leases Working Group, 2002 (ISBN 1 84219 098 9). The code can be viewed at www.bpf.org.uk

Dilapidations (4th edition), RICS guidance note, RICS Books, Coventry, 2003 (ISBN 978 1 84219 075 3)

Dowding, N. and Reynolds, K., *Dilapidations: The Modern Law and Practice* (3rd edition), Sweet and Maxwell, Andover, 2005 (ISBN 978 0 42188 260 7)

Male, J. and Jefferies, T., *Case in Point: Rent Review*, RICS Books, Coventry, 2005 (ISBN 978 1 84219 225 2)

The Property Litigation Association's protocol on dilapidations can be found at www.pla.org.uk

Service Charges in Commercial Property, RICS Code of Practice, RICS Books, Coventry, 2006 (ISBN 10: 1 84219 300 7, ISBN 13: 978 1 84219 300 7)

The British Property Federation's guide to The Five Steps to improve energy efficiency and reduce CO_2 *emissions in rented office buildings* can be found at www.usablebuildings.co.uk

The British Property Federation/IPD Annual Lease Review for 2007 can be found at www.bpf.propertymall.com

BS EN ISO 14001:1996 *Environmental management systems. Specifications with guidance for use*, BSI, 1996 (ISBN 0 58026 708 3)

Office of National Statistics' publication: *Consumer Price Indices – A brief guide* (2004), can be found at www.statistics.gov.uk

CLG – *Improving the energy efficiency of our buildings: a guide to energy performance certificates for the construction, sale and let of non-dwellings* (2nd edition, July 2008) can be found at www.communities.gov.uk

CLG – *Improving the energy efficiency of our buildings: a guide to display energy certificates and advisory reports for public buildings* (May 2008) can be found at www.communities.gov.uk

The Carbon Trust's Good Practice Guide 376: *A strategic approach to energy and environmental management* (2004) can be found at www.carbontrust.co.uk

Index

serious irregularity, 43
use of arbitrator or
expert, 37–39
asbestos, 195–197
service charges, 78–79
assessors,
energy, access to premises
for
assessment/inspection
purposes, 245–246
assignments *see also*
transfers,
underleases, other
dealings
environmental policy,
257
green leases, 260
authorised guarantee
agreement (AGAs)
post-1995 leases,
164–166

bank guarantees, 262–264
bankruptcy *see* insolvency
best endeavours, 265–266
breaches of covenants *see*
forfeiture
break clauses
example, 16–17
preconditions and
material compliance,
17–19, 20
short leases, 14–15
time of the essence, 47

BREEAM (Building
Research
Establishment
Environmental
Assessment
Method), 81–82,
252
*British Property Federation
(BPF) IPD Annual
Lease Review* 2007
average lease term,
headlines, 14–15
*Building and Approved
Inspectors
(Amendment)
Regulations* 2006,
80–81
Building Research
Establishment
Environmental
Assessment Method
(BREEAM), 81–82,
252
business rates *see* rates

capital allowances, 11–13,
77 270–271
Capital Allowances Act
2001, 11–12
*Case in Point – Rent
Review* (RICS
Books, 2005), 26
change of use *see also* user
conservation areas, 192
listed buildings, 191
planning consent,
190–191

damages
  breach of repairing
    covenant, 119–121
  breach of statutory
    duties, consent to an
    assignment, etc., 167
decoration, 112–113
deductions from tax *see*
    tax deductions
Defective Premises Act
    1972, 202
  s. 4(4), 114
definitions
  associated company,
    178–180
  control, 178–180
  demise, 7–9
  dutyholder, 192
  insured risks, 91–92
  rent, 226
  repair obligations, 202
  service charge related
    terms, 273–275
  terrorist act, 96–98
demise, 6–7
  areas outside, description,
    11
  contaminated land,
    exclusion, 13
  definition
    fixtures and fittings,
      inclusion, 13, 124
    lease of part of
      building, 7–9
  floor area, 9
  repairing clause *see*
    repairs
demolition

listed buildings, 191
deposits *see* rent deposits
depreciation charges,
    65–66, 77
dilapidations, 25, 117–119
  limitation on damages,
    119–121
  *Property Litigation
    Association Protocol
    for Terminal
    Dilapidations Claims
    for Damages*, 271
  protocol at end of lease,
    122–123
  schedule, 126
*Dilapidations: The Modern
  Law and Practice*
  (3rd edition, 2004),
  120–121
disability discrimination,
    194–195, 203
*Disability Discrimination
  Act*, 1995 136
  service charges, 79–80
*Disability Discrimination
  Act* 2005 (DDA),
    136, 194–195, 271
  s. 21, 195
  s. 24, 195
discounts
  rent review, 35, 39–40
Display Energy Certificates
  (DEC), 247–249
distraint *see* levying distress
drafting a lease, 1–2

Health Act 2006, Pt. 1,
201
health and safety, 189–204
holding on trust, 177
hypothetical lease term,
40–41

improvements
compensation, statutory
provisions, 133–135
expenditure covered by
service charge, 62
*Income and Corporation
Taxes Act* 1988
s. 416, 178–180
indemnities, 264–265
indexed rent reviews,
49–50
indexed rents, 28
individual voluntary
arrangement *see*
insolvency
industrial property
empty rating relief, 24
inherent defects, 110–111,
125
insolvency
landlord, protection of
tenants
Lease Code, 264
tenant, recovery of rent,
237–239, 240
Insolvency Act 1986
s. 130, 238
institutional lease, 2–4
insurance
all risks, 94, 98

gaps in cover, 98, 102,
125
high risk items, 101, 104
'insured risks'
damage, reinstatement
by landlord, 109
definition, 91–92
landlord's insuring
responsibility
extending, to 125
interrelationship with
other lease terms,
100–101
Lease Code, 101–102
loss of rent, 94–95, 103
non-invalidation clause,
98–100
noted interests, 98–100
overview, 91
parties' mutual
responsibilities
reinstatement, 95–96
rent suspension, 93–95
plate glass, 92–93, 104
points to consider,
102–104
premiums
collection, 22
subrogation, 98–100
uninsured risks: flood
and terrorism,
96–98
usual risks, 91, 102
valuations, 62
internal management
charges, 62
interpreting a lease, 1–2

Jervis v Harris clauses
enforcing repair, 113–114

landlord, damage by
'insured risk', 109
*Re-insurance (Acts of
Terrorism) Act* 1993
s. 2, 97–98
renewal and termination
procedures, 207–208
acting for landlord –
landlord initiating
renewal, 208
next steps, 209
notice, 208–209
acting for landlord –
landlord opposing
renewal by
responding to
tenant's s. 26
request, 211
acting for landlord –
landlord opposing
renewal by service of
s. 25 notice, 209
next steps, 210
notice, 210–211
acting for tenant
response to landlord's s.
25 notice, 214–215
tenant terminating
lease, 213–214
acting for tenant – tenant
initiating renewal,
212
next steps, 213
notice, 212–213
Landlord and Tenant Act
1954
acting for landlord, 215
acting for tenant, 216

rent
arrears, recovery *see*
recovery of rent
days of grace, 25
definition, 226
interim, 222
non-payment, forfeiture,
227
payment, 21
recovery *see* recovery of
rent
retailers, monthly
payments, 21–22
review *see* rent review
set off, 22, 25
suspension, insurance
provisions, 93–95,
103
tax deduction, 23
value added tax, 21–22
VAT invoice, 25
rent deposits, 236,
262–264
rent review
additional rent, 39–40
arbitrator *see* arbitrators
assumptions, 32–34
balancing payments, 45
clause, 29–32, 54–55
discounts, 35, 39–40
disregards, 32–34
*Landlord and Tenant
Act* 1954, s. 34
34–35
expert *see* experts
fixed increases, 28
geared rent, 28
ground rent, 28

Service Charges in Commercial Property: A Guide to Good Practice (1996), 56
shopping centres
  open covenant 155–157
  service charges, 71–72
  'reasonable', 67
short term leases, 15
  service charges, 72–74
side agreements
  subleases, 174–175
silent lease, 2
sinking funds, 65–66, 76–77, 89
smoke free premises, 201
stamp duty land tax (SDLT), 15, 270
  effect of, on lease term, 15–16, 20
  rent review, 52–54
  service charges, 76
standard leases, 160–162
statutory provisions
  compliance, 189–204
subleases *see* transfers, underleases
surrender of lease
  inadvertent, 182–183
surveyors' fees, 25
sweeper clauses
  service charges, 60, 76, 89

tax deductions
  Non-Resident Landlords Scheme, 23, 271

rent, 23
service charges, 75–77
Telecommunications Act 1984
  Sch. 2, 202
telecommunications code, 202
tenants
  advice
    Lease Code, 18, 19
  insolvency, recovery of rent, 237–239, 240
  termination for breach *see* forfeiture
terrorism
  insurance, 96–98
Terrorism Act 2000
  s. 1, 97–98
third parties *see also* arbitrators; experts
  liability to, 201–202
Town and Country Planning Act 1990, 188, 191
Town and Country Planning (General Permitted Development) Order 1995
  Pt. 3, 142–146
Town and Country Planning (Use Classes) Order 1987
  lease drafting, 146–147
  planning consent, 142–146